Richard Harding Davis' Great War

Richard Harding Davis

Richard Harding Davis' Great War
The Last Campaigns of America's
First Outstanding War Correspondent

With the Allies

With the French in France and Salonika

Richard Harding Davis

Richard Harding Davis' Great War
The Last Campaigns of America's First Outstanding War Correspondent
With the Allies
With the French in France and Salonika
By Richard Harding Davis

First published under the titles

With the Allies
and
With the French in France and Salonika

Leonaur is an imprint of Oakpast Ltd
Copyright in this form © 2010 Oakpast Ltd

ISBN: 978-0-85706-296-3 (hardcover)
ISBN: 978-0-85706-295-6 (softcover)

http://www.leonaur.com

Publisher's Notes

In the interests of authenticity, the spellings, grammar and place names used have been retained from the original editions.

The opinions of the authors represent a view of events in which he was a participant related from his own perspective, as such the text is relevant as an historical document.

The views expressed in this book are not necessarily those of the publisher.

Contents

With the Allies	7
With the French in France and Salonika	131
Letters From the Front	274

H.M. ALBERT I., KING OF BELGIUM

With The Allies

Richard Harding Davis

Contents

Preface	15
The Germans In Brussels	17
"To Be Treated As A Spy"	30
The Burning of Louvain	52
Paris in War Time	60
The Battle of Soissons	65
The Bombardment of Rheims	72
The Spirit of the English	89
Our Diplomats in the War Zone	94
"Under Fire"	105
The Waste of War	115
War Correspondents	124

DEDICATED
WITHOUT PERMISSION
TO ALBERT,
KING OF THE BELGIUMS

Mr. Davis's passport on his last trip to Europe, 1915-1916

Preface

I have not seen the letter addressed by President Wilson to the American people calling upon them to preserve toward this war the mental attitude of neutrals. But I have seen the war. And I feel sure had President Wilson seen my war he would not have written his letter.

This is not a war against Germans, as we know Germans in America, where they are among our sanest, most industrious, and most responsible fellow countrymen. It is a war, as Winston Churchill has pointed out, against the military aristocracy of Germany, men who are six hundred years behind the times; who, to preserve their class against democracy, have perverted to the uses of warfare, to the destruction of life, every invention of modern times. These men are military mad. To our ideal of representative government their own idea is as far opposed as is martial law to the free speech of our town meetings.

One returning from the war is astonished to find how little of the true horror of it crosses the ocean. That this is so is due partly to the strict censorship that suppresses the details of the war, and partly to the fact that the mind is not accustomed to consider misery on a scale so gigantic. The loss of hundreds of thousands of lives, the wrecking of cities, and the laying waste of half of Europe cannot be brought home to people who learn of it only through newspapers and moving pictures and by sticking pins in a map. Were they nearer to it, near enough to see the women and children fleeing from the shells and to smell the dead on the battlefields, there would be no talk of neutrality.

Such lack of understanding our remoteness from the actual seat of war explains. But on the part of many Americans one finds another attitude of mind which is more difficult to explain. It is the cupidity that in the misfortunes of others sees only a chance for profit. In an offer made to its readers a prominent American magazine best expresses this attitude. It promises prizes for the essays on *What the war means to me.*

To the American women Miss Ida M. Tarbell writes:

This is her time to learn what her own country's industries can do, and to rally with all her influence to their support, urging them to make the things she wants, and pledging them her allegiance.

This appeal is used in a periodical with a circulation of over a million, as an advertisement for silk hose. I do not agree with Miss Tarbell that this is the time to rally to the support of home industries. I do not agree with the advertiser that when in Belgium several million women and children are homeless, starving, and naked that that is the time to buy his silk hose. To urge that charity begins at home is to repeat one of the most selfish axioms ever uttered, and in this war to urge civilized, thinking people to remain neutral is equally selfish.

Were the conflict in Europe a fair fight, the duty of every American would be to keep on the side-lines and preserve an open mind. But it is not a fair fight. To devastate a country you have sworn to protect, to drop bombs upon unfortified cities, to lay sunken mines, to levy blackmail by threatening hostages with death, to destroy cathedrals is not to fight fair.

That is the way Germany is fighting. She is defying the rules of war and the rules of humanity. And if public opinion is to help in preventing further outrages, and in hastening this unspeakable conflict to an end, it should be directed against the one who offends. If we are convinced that one opponent is fighting honestly and that his adversary is striking below the belt, then for us to maintain a neutral attitude of mind is unworthy and the attitude of a coward.

When a mad dog runs amuck in a village it is the duty of every farmer to get his gun and destroy it, not to lock himself indoors and toward the dog and the men who face him preserve a neutral mind.

Richard Harding Davis.

New York, Dec. 1st, 1914.

CHAPTER 1

The Germans In Brussels

When, on August 4, the *Lusitania*, with lights doused and airports sealed, slipped out of New York harbour the crime of the century was only a few days old. And for three days those on board the *Lusitania* of the march of the great events were ignorant. Whether or no between England and Germany the struggle for the supremacy of the sea had begun we could not learn.

But when, on the third day, we came on deck the news was written against the sky. Swinging from the funnels, sailors were painting out the scarlet-and-black colours of the Cunard line and substituting a mouse-like gray. Overnight we had passed into the hands of the admiralty, and the *Lusitania* had emerged a cruiser. That to possible German war-ships she might not disclose her position, she sent no wireless messages. But she could receive them; and at breakfast in the ship's newspaper appeared those she had overnight snatched from the air. Among them, without a scare-head, in the most modest of type, we read:

England and Germany have declared war.

Seldom has news so momentous been conveyed so simply or, by the Englishmen on board, more calmly accepted. For any exhibition they gave of excitement or concern, the news the radio brought them might have been the result of a by-election.

Later in the morning they gave us another exhibition of that repression of feeling, of that disdain of hysteria, that is a national characteristic, and is what Mr. Kipling meant when he wrote:

But oh, beware my country, when my country grows polite!

Word came that in the North Sea the English war-ships had destroyed the German fleet. To celebrate this battle which, were the news authentic, would rank with Trafalgar and might mean the end of the war, one of the ship's officers exploded a detonating bomb. Nothing else exploded. Whatever feelings of satisfaction our English cousins experienced they concealed.

Under like circumstances, on an American ship, we would have tied down the siren, sung the doxology, and broken everything on the bar. As it was, the Americans instinctively flocked to the smoking-room and drank to the British navy. While this ceremony was going forward, from the promenade-deck we heard tumultuous shouts and cheers. We believed that, relieved of our presence, our English friends had given way to rejoicings. But when we went on deck we found them deeply engaged in cricket. The cheers we had heard were over the retirement of a batsman who had just been given out, leg before wicket.

When we reached London we found no idle boasting, no vainglorious jingoism. The war that Germany had forced upon them the English accepted with a grim determination to see it through and, while they were about it, to make it final. They were going ahead with no false illusions. Fully did every one appreciate the enormous task, the personal loss that lay before him. But each, in his or her way, went into the fight determined to do his duty. There was no dismay, no hysteria, no "mafficking."

The secrecy maintained by the press and the people regarding anything concerning the war, the knowledge of which might embarrass the War Office, was one of the most admirable and remarkable conspiracies of silence that modern times have known. Officers of the same regiment even with each other would not discuss the orders they had received. In no single newspaper, with no matter how lurid a past record for sensationalism, was there a line to suggest that a British army had landed in France and that Great Britain was at war. Sooner than embarrass those who were conducting the fight, the individual English man and woman in silence suffered the most cruel anxiety of mind. Of that, on my return to London from Brussels, I was given an illustration. I had written to *The Daily Chronicle* telling where in Belgium I had seen a wrecked British airship, and beside it the grave of the aviator. I gave the information in order that the family of the dead officer might find the grave and bring the body home. The morning the letter was published an elderly gentleman, a retired officer of the navy, called at my rooms. His son, he said, was an aviator, and for a month of him no word had come. His mother was distressed. Could I describe the air-ship I had seen?

I was not keen to play the messenger of ill tidings, so I tried to gain time.

"What make of aeroplane does your son drive?" I asked.

As though preparing for a blow, the old gentleman drew himself up, and looked me steadily in the eyes.

"A Blériot monoplane," he said.

I was as relieved as though his boy were one of my own kinsmen.

"The air-ship I saw," I told him, "was an Avro biplane!"

Of the two I appeared much the more pleased.

The retired officer bowed.

"I thank you," he said. "It will be good news for his mother."

"But why didn't you go to the War Office?" I asked.

He reproved me firmly.

"They have asked us not to question them," he said, "and when they are working for all I have no right to embarrass them with my personal trouble."

As the chance of obtaining credentials with the British army appeared doubtful, I did not remain in London, but at once crossed to Belgium.

Before the Germans came, Brussels was an imitation Paris—especially along the inner boulevards she was Paris at her best. And her great parks, her lakes gay with pleasure-boats or choked with lily-pads, her haunted forests, where your taxicab would startle the wild deer, are the most beautiful I have ever seen in any city in the world. As, in the days of the Second Empire, Louis Napoleon bedecked Paris, so Leopold decorated Brussels. In her honour and to his own glory he gave her new parks, filled in her moats along her ancient fortifications, laid out boulevards shaded with trees, erected arches, monuments, museums. That these jewels he hung upon her neck were wrung from the slaves of the Congo does not make them the less beautiful. And before the Germans came the life of the people of Brussels was in keeping with the elegance, beauty, and joyousness of their surroundings.

At the Palace Hotel, which is the clearing-house for the social life of Brussels, we found everybody taking his ease at a little iron table on the sidewalk. It was night, but the city was as light as noonday—brilliant, elated, full of movement and colour. For Liége was still held by the Belgians, and they believed that all along the line they were holding back the German army. It was no wonder they were jubilant. They had a right to be proud. They had been making history. In order to give them time to mobilize, the Allies had asked them for two days to delay the German invader. They had held him back for fifteen. As David went against Goliath, they had repulsed the German. And as yet there had been no reprisals, no destruction of cities, no murdering of non-combatants; war still was something glad and glorious.

The signs of it were the Boy Scouts, everywhere helping every one, carrying messages, guiding strangers, directing traffic; and Red Cross nurses and aviators from England, smart Belgian officers exclaiming bitterly over the delay in sending them forward, and private automobiles upon the enamelled sides of which the transport officer with a piece of chalk had scratched, "For His Majesty," and piled the silk cushions high with ammunition. From table to table young girls passed jangling tiny tin milk-cans. They were supplicants, begging money for the wounded. There were so many of them and so often they made their rounds that, to protect you from themselves, if you subscribed a lump sum, you were exempt and were given a badge to prove you were immune.

Except for these signs of the times you would not have known Belgium was at war. The spirit of the people was undaunted. Into their daily lives the conflict had penetrated only like a burst of martial music. Rather than depressing, it inspired them. Wherever you ventured, you found them undismayed. And in those weeks during which events moved so swiftly that now they seem months in the past, we were as free as in our own "home town" to go where we chose.

For the war correspondent those were the happy days! Like everyone else, from the proudest nobleman to the boy in wooden shoes, we were given a *laissez-passer*, which gave us permission to go anywhere; this with a passport was our only credential. Proper credentials to accompany the army in the field had been formerly refused me by the war officers of England, France, and Belgium. So in Brussels each morning I chartered an automobile and without credentials joined the first army that happened to be passing. Sometimes you stumbled upon an *escarmouche*, sometimes you fled from one, sometimes you drew blank.

Over our early coffee we would study the morning papers and, as in the glad days of racing at home, from them try to dope out the winners. If we followed *La Dernière Heure* we would go to Namur; *L'Etoile* was strong for Tirlemont. Would we lose if we plunged on Wavre? Again, the favourite seemed to be Louvain. On a straight tip from the legation the English correspondents were going to motor to

Diest. From a Belgian officer we had been given inside information that the fight would be pulled off at Gembloux. And, unencumbered by even a sandwich, and too wise to carry a field-glass or a camera, each would depart upon his separate errand, at night returning to a perfectly served dinner and a luxurious bed. For the news-gatherers it was a game of chance. The wisest veterans would cast their nets south and see only harvesters in the fields, the amateurs would lose their way to the north and find themselves facing an army corps or running a gauntlet of shell-fire. It was like throwing a handful of coins on the table hoping that one might rest upon the winning number.

Over the map of Belgium we threw ourselves. Some days we landed on the right colour, on others we saw no more than we would see at state manoeuvres. Judging by his questions, the lay brother seems to think that the chief trouble of the war correspondent is dodging bullets. It is not. It consists in trying to bribe a station-master to carry you on a troop train, or in finding forage for your horse. What wars I have seen have taken place in spots isolated and inaccessible, far from the haunts of men. By day you followed the fight and tried to find the censor, and at night you sat on a cracker-box and by the light of a candle struggled to keep awake and to write deathless prose. In Belgium it was not like that.

The automobile which Gerald Morgan, of the *London Daily Telegraph*, and I shared was of surpassing beauty, speed, and comfort. It was as long as a Plant freight-car and as yellow; and from it flapped in the breeze more English, Belgian, French, and Russian flags than fly from the roof of the New York Hippodrome. Whenever we sighted an army we lashed the flags of its country to our headlights, and at sixty miles an hour bore down upon it.

The army always first arrested us, and then, on learning our nationality, asked if it were true that America had joined the Allies. After I had punched his ribs a sufficient number of times Morgan learned to reply without winking that it had. In those days the sun shone continuously; the roads, except where we ran on the blocks that made Belgium famous, were perfect; and overhead for miles noble trees met and embraced. The country was smiling and beautiful. In the fields the women (for the men were at the front) were gathering the crops, the stacks of golden grain stretched from village to village. The houses in these were white-washed and, the better to advertise chocolates, liqueurs, and automobile tires, were painted a cobalt blue; their roofs were of red tiles, and they sat in gardens of purple cabbages or gaudy hollyhocks.

In the orchards the pear-trees were bent with fruit. We never lacked for food; always, when we lost the trail and "checked," or burst a tire, there was an inn with fruit-trees trained to lie flat against the wall, or to spread over arbours and trellises. Beneath these, close by the roadside, we sat and drank red wine, and devoured omelettes and vast slabs of rye bread. At night we raced back to the city, through twelve miles of parks, to enamelled bathtubs, shaded electric light, and iced champagne; while before our table passed all the night life of a great city. And for suffering these hardships of war our papers paid us large sums.

On such a night as this, the night of August 18, strange folk in wooden shoes and carrying bundles, and who looked like emigrants from Ellis Island, appeared in front of the restaurant. Instantly they were swallowed up in a crowd and the dinner-parties, napkins in hand, flocked into the Place Rogier and increased the throng around them.

"The Germans!" those in the heart of the crowd called over their shoulders. "The Germans are at Louvain!"

That afternoon I had conscientiously cabled my paper that there were no Germans anywhere near Louvain. I had been west of Louvain, and the particular column of the French army to which I had attached myself certainly saw no Germans.

"They say," whispered those nearest the fugitives, "the German shells are falling in Louvain. Ten houses are on fire!" Ten houses! How monstrous it sounded! Ten houses of innocent country folk destroyed. In those days such a catastrophe was unbelievable. We smiled knowingly.

"Refugees always talk like that," we said wisely. "The Germans would not bombard an unfortified town. And, besides, there are no Germans south of Liége."

The morning following in my room I heard from the Place Rogier the warnings of many motor horns. At great speed innumerable automobiles were approaching, all coming from the west through the Boulevard du Regent, and without slackening speed passing northeast toward Ghent, Bruges, and the coast. The number increased and the warnings became insistent. At eight o'clock they had sent out a sharp request for right of way; at nine in number they had trebled, and the note of the sirens was raucous, harsh, and peremptory. At ten no longer were there disconnected warnings, but from the horns and sirens issued one long, continuous scream. It was like the steady roar of a gale in the rigging, and it spoke in abject panic.

The voices of the cars racing past were like the voices of human beings driven with fear. From the front of the hotel we watched them. There were taxicabs, racing cars, limousines. They were crowded with women and children of the rich, and of the nobility and gentry from the great *châteaux* far to the west. Those who occupied them were white-faced with the dust of the road, with weariness and fear. In cars magnificently upholstered, padded, and cushioned were piled trunks, handbags, dressing-cases. The women had dressed at a moment's warning, as though at a cry of fire. Many had travelled throughout the night, and in their arms the children, snatched from the pillows, were sleeping.

But more appealing were the peasants. We walked out along the inner *boulevards* to meet them, and found the side streets blocked with their carts. Into these they had thrown mattresses, or bundles of grain, and heaped upon them were families of three generations. Old men in blue smocks, white-haired and bent, old women in caps, the daughters dressed in their one best frock and hat, and clasping in their hands all that was left to them, all that they could stuff into a pillowcase or flour-sack. The tears rolled down their brown, tanned faces. To the people of Brussels who crowded around them they spoke in hushed, broken phrases. The terror of what they had escaped or of what they had seen was upon them. They had harnessed the plough-horse to the dray or market-wagon and to the invaders had left everything.

What, they asked, would befall the live stock they had abandoned, the ducks on the pond, the cattle in the field? Who would feed them and give them water? At the question the tears would break out afresh. Heartbroken, weary, hungry, they passed in an unending caravan. With them, all fleeing from the same foe, all moving in one direction, were family carriages, the servants on the box in disordered livery, as they had served dinner, or coatless, but still in the striped waistcoats and silver buttons of grooms or footmen, and bicyclers with bundles strapped to their shoulders, and men and women stumbling on foot, carrying their children. Above it all rose the breathless scream of the racing-cars, as they rocked and skidded, with brakes grinding and mufflers open; with their own terror creating and spreading terror.

Though eager in sympathy, the people of Brussels themselves were undisturbed. Many still sat at the little iron tables and smiled pityingly upon the strange figures of the peasants. They had had their trouble for nothing, they said. It was a false alarm. There were no Germans

Belgian refugees fleeing from Louvain to Brussels

nearer than Liége. And, besides, should the Germans come, the civil guard would meet them.

But, better informed than they, that morning the American minister, Brand Whitlock, and the Marquis Villalobar, the Spanish minister, had called upon the *burgomaster* and advised him not to defend the city. As Whitlock pointed out, with the force at his command, which was the citizen soldiery, he could delay the entrance of the Germans by only an hour, and in that hour many innocent lives would be wasted and monuments of great beauty, works of art that belong not alone to Brussels but to the world, would be destroyed. Burgomaster Max, who is a splendid and worthy representative of a long line of *burgomasters*, placing his hand upon his heart, said: "Honour requires it."

To show that in the protection of the Belgian Government he had full confidence, Mr. Whitlock had not as yet shown his colours. But that morning when he left the Hôtel de Ville he hung the American flag over his legation and over that of the British. Those of us who had elected to remain in Brussels moved our belongings to a hotel across the street from the legation. Not taking any chances, for my own use I reserved a green leather sofa in the legation itself.

Except that the *cafés* were empty of Belgian officers, and of English correspondents, whom, had they remained, the Germans would have arrested, there was not, up to late in the afternoon of the 19th of August, in the life and conduct of the citizens any perceptible change. They could not have shown a finer spirit. They did not know the city would not be defended; and yet with before them on the morrow the prospect of a battle which Burgomaster Max had announced would be contested to the very heart of the city, as usual the *cafés* blazed like open fireplaces and the people sat at the little iron tables. Even when, like great buzzards, two German aeroplanes sailed slowly across Brussels, casting shadows of events to come, the people regarded them only with curiosity. The next morning the shops were open, the streets were crowded. But overnight the soldier-king had sent word that Brussels must not oppose the invaders; and at the *gendarmerie* the civil guard, reluctantly and protesting, some even in tears, turned in their rifles and uniforms.

The change came at ten in the morning. It was as though a wand had waved and from a *fête*-day on the Continent we had been wafted to London on a rainy Sunday. The *boulevards* fell suddenly empty. There was not a house that was not closely shuttered. Along the route by which we now knew the Germans were advancing, it was as though the plague stalked. That no one should fire from a window, that to the conquerors no one should offer insult, Burgomaster Max sent out as special constables men he trusted. Their badge of authority was a walking-stick and a piece of paper fluttering from a buttonhole. These, the police, and the servants and caretakers of the houses that lined the boulevards alone were visible.

At eleven o'clock, unobserved but by this official audience, down the Boulevard Waterloo came the advance-guard of the German army. It consisted of three men, a captain and two privates on bicycles. Their rifles were slung across their shoulders, they rode unwarily, with as little concern as the members of a touring-club out for a holiday. Behind them, so close upon each other that to cross from one sidewalk to the other was not possible, came the *Uhlans*, infantry, and the guns. For two hours I watched them, and then, bored with the monotony of it, returned to the hotel. After an hour, from beneath my window, I still could hear them; another hour and another went by. They still were passing.

Boredom gave way to wonder. The thing fascinated you, against your will, dragged you back to the sidewalk and held you there open-eyed. No longer was it regiments of men marching, but something uncanny, inhuman, a force of nature like a landslide, a tidal wave, or lava sweeping down a mountain. It was not of this earth, but mysterious, ghostlike. It carried all the mystery and menace of a fog rolling toward you across the sea. The uniform aided this impression. In it each man moved under a cloak of invisibility. Only after the most numerous and severe tests at all distances, with all materials and combinations of colours that give forth no colour, could this gray have been discovered. That it was selected to clothe and disguise the German when he fights is typical of the General Staff, in striving for efficiency, to leave nothing to chance, to neglect no detail.

After you have seen this service uniform under conditions entirely opposite you are convinced that for the German soldier it is one of his strongest weapons. Even the most expert marksman cannot hit a target he cannot see. It is not the blue-gray of our Confederates, but a green-gray. It is the gray of the hour just before daybreak, the gray of unpolished steel, of mist among green trees.

I saw it first in the Grand Place in front of the Hôtel de Ville. It was impossible to tell if in that noble square there was a regiment or a brigade. You saw only a fog that melted into the stones, blended with the ancient house fronts, that shifted and drifted, but left you nothing at which to point.

Later, as the army passed under the trees of the Botanical Park, it merged and was lost against the green leaves. It is no exaggeration to say that at a few hundred yards you can see the horses on which the *Uhlans* ride but cannot see the men who ride them.

If I appear to overemphasize this disguising uniform it is because, of all the details of the German outfit, it appealed to me as one of the most remarkable. When I was near Namur with the rearguard of the French Dragoons and *Cuirassiers*, and they threw out pickets, we could distinguish them against the yellow wheat or green corse at half a mile, while these men passing in the street, when they have reached the next crossing, become merged into the gray of the paving-stones and the earth swallowed them. In comparison the yellow khaki of our own American army is about as invisible as the flag of Spain.

Major-General von Jarotsky, the German military governor of Brussels, had assured Burgomaster Max that the German army would not occupy the city but would pass through it. He told the truth. For three days and three nights it passed. In six campaigns I have followed other armies, but, excepting not even our own, the Japanese, or the British, I have not seen one so thoroughly equipped. I am not speaking of the fighting qualities of any army, only of the equipment and organization. The German army moved into Brussels as smoothly and as compactly as an Empire State express. There were no halts, no open places, no stragglers. For the gray automobiles and the gray motorcycles bearing messengers one side of the street always was kept clear; and so compact was the column, so rigid the vigilance of the file-closers, that at the rate of forty miles an hour a car could race the length of the column and need not for a single horse or man once swerve from its course.

All through the night, like the tumult of a river when it races between the cliffs of a canyon, in my sleep I could hear the steady roar of the passing army. And when early in the morning I went to the window the chain of steel was still unbroken. It was like the torrent that swept down the Connemaugh Valley and destroyed Johnstown. As a correspondent I have seen all the great armies and the military processions at the coronations in Russia, England, and Spain, and our own inaugural parades down Pennsylvania Avenue, but those armies and processions were made up of men. This was a machine, endless, tireless, with the delicate organization of a watch and the brute power of a steam roller. And for three days and three nights through Brussels it roared and rumbled, a cataract of molten lead.

The infantry marched singing, with their iron-shod boots beating out the time. They sang "Fatherland, My Fatherland." Between each line of song they took three steps. At times two thousand men were singing together in absolute rhythm and beat. It was like the blows from giant pile-drivers. When the melody gave way the silence was broken only by the stamp of iron-shod boots, and then again the song rose. When the singing ceased the bands played marches. They were followed by the rumble of the howitzers, the creaking of wheels and of chains clanking against the cobblestones, and the sharp, bell-like voices of the bugles.

More *Uhlans* followed, the hoofs of their magnificent horses ringing like thousands of steel hammers breaking stones in a road; and after them the giant siege-guns rumbling, growling, the *mitrailleuse* with drag-chains ringing, the field-pieces with creaking axles, complaining brakes, the grinding of the steel-rimmed wheels against the stones echoing and re-echoing from the house front. When at night for an instant the machine halted, the silence awoke you, as at sea you wake when the screw stops.

For three days and three nights the column of gray, with hundreds of thousands of bayonets and hundreds of thousands of lances, with gray transport wagons, gray ammunition carts, gray ambulances, gray cannon, like a river of steel, cut Brussels in two.

For three weeks the men had been on the march, and there was not a single straggler, not a strap out of place, not a pennant missing. Along the route, without for a minute halting the machine, the post-office carts fell out of the column, and as the men marched mounted postmen collected postcards and delivered letters. Also, as they marched, the cooks prepared soup, coffee, and tea, walking beside their stoves on wheels, tending the fires, distributing the smoking food. Seated in the motor-trucks cobblers mended boots and broken harness; farriers on tiny anvils beat out horseshoes. No officer followed a wrong turning, no officer asked his way. He followed the map strapped to his side and on which for his guidance in red ink his route was marked. At night he read this map by the light of an electric torch buckled to his chest.

To perfect this monstrous engine, with its pontoon bridges, its wireless, its hospitals, its aeroplanes that in rigid alignment sailed before it, its field telephones that, as it advanced, strung wires over which for miles the vanguard talked to the rear, all modern inventions had been prostituted. To feed it millions of men had been called from homes, offices, and workshops; to guide it, for years the minds of the high-born, with whom it is a religion and a disease, had been solely concerned.

It is, perhaps, the most efficient organization of modern times; and its purpose only is death. Those who cast it loose upon Europe are military-mad. And they are only a very small part of the German people. But to preserve their class they have in their own image created this terrible engine of destruction. For the present it is their servant. But, "though the mills of God grind slowly, yet they grind exceeding small." And, like Frankenstein's monster, this monster, to which they gave life, may turn and rend them.

Chapter 2

"To Be Treated As A Spy"

This story is a personal experience, but is told in spite of that fact and because it illustrates a side of war that is unfamiliar. It is unfamiliar for the reason that it is seamy and uninviting. With bayonet charges, bugle-calls, and aviators it has nothing in common.

Espionage is that kind of warfare of which, even when it succeeds, no country boasts. It is military service an officer may not refuse, but which few seek. Its reward is prompt promotion, and its punishment, in war time, is swift and without honour. This story is intended to show how an army in the field must be on its guard against even a supposed spy and how it treats him.

The war offices of France and Russia would not permit an American correspondent to accompany their armies; the English granted that privilege to but one correspondent, and that gentleman already had been chosen. So I was without credentials. To oblige Mr. Brand Whitlock, our minister to Belgium, the government there was willing to give me credentials, but on the day I was to receive them the government moved to Antwerp. Then the Germans entered Brussels, and, as no one could foresee that Belgium would heroically continue fighting, on the chance the Germans would besiege Paris, I planned to go to that city. To be bombarded you do not need credentials.

For three days a steel-gray column of Germans had been sweeping through Brussels, and to meet them, from the direction of Vincennes and Lille, the English and French had crossed the border. It was falsely reported that already the English had reached Hal, a town only eleven miles from Brussels, that the night before there had been a fight at Hal, and that close behind the English were the French.

With Gerald Morgan, of the *London Daily Telegraph*, with whom I had been in other wars, I planned to drive to Hal and from there on foot continue, if possible, into the arms of the French or English. We both were without credentials, but, once with the Allies, we believed we would not need them. It was the Germans we doubted. To satisfy them we had only a passport and a *laissez-passer* issued by General von Jarotsky, the new German military governor of Brussels, and his chief of staff, Lieutenant Geyer. Mine stated that I represented the Wheeler Syndicate of American newspapers, the *London Daily Chronicle*, and *Scribner's Magazine*, and that I could pass German military lines in Brussels and her environs. Morgan had a pass of the same sort. The question to be determined was: What were "environs" and how far do they extend? How far in safety would the word carry us forward?

On August 23 we set forth from Brussels in a taxicab to find out. At Hal, where we intended to abandon the cab and continue on foot, we found out. We were arrested by a smart and most intelligent-looking officer, who rode up to the side of the taxi and pointed an automatic at us. We were innocently seated in a public cab, in a street crowded with civilians and the passing column of soldiers, and why anyone should think he needed a gun only the German mind can explain. Later, I found that all German officers introduced themselves and made requests gun in hand. Whether it was because from every one they believed themselves in danger or because they simply did not know any better, I still am unable to decide. With no other army have I seen an officer threaten with a pistol an unarmed civilian. Were an American or English officer to act in such a fashion he might escape looking like a fool, he certainly would feel like one.

The four soldiers the officer told off to guard us climbed with alacrity into our cab and drove with us until the street grew too narrow both for their regiment and our taxi, when they chose the regiment and disappeared. We paid off the cabman and followed them. To reach the front there was no other way, and the very openness with which we trailed along beside their army, very much like small boys following a circus procession, seemed to us to show how innocent was our intent. The column stretched for fifty miles. Where it was going we did not know, but, we argued, if it kept on going and we kept on with it, eventually we must stumble upon a battle. The story that at Hal there had been a fight was evidently untrue; and the manner in which the column was advancing showed it was not expecting one. At noon it halted at Brierges, and Morgan decided Brierges was out of bounds and that the limits of our "environs" had been reached.

"If we go any farther," he argued, "the next officer who reads our papers will order us back to Brussels under arrest, and we will lose our *laissez-passer*. Along this road there is no chance of seeing anything. I prefer to keep my pass and use it in 'environs' where there is fighting."

So he returned to Brussels. I thought he was most wise, and I wanted to return with him. But I did not want to go back only because I knew it was the right thing to do, but to be ordered back so that I could explain to my newspapers that I returned because Colonel This or General That sent me back. It was a form of vanity for which I was properly punished. That Morgan was right was demonstrated as soon as he left me. I was seated against a tree by the side of the road eating a sandwich, an occupation which seems almost idyllic in its innocence but which could not deceive the Germans. In me they saw the hated *Spion*, and from behind me, across a ploughed field, four of them, each with an automatic, made me prisoner. One of them, who was an enthusiast, pushed his gun deep into my stomach. With the sandwich still in my hand, I held up my arms high and asked who spoke English. It turned out that the enthusiast spoke that language, and I suggested he did not need so many guns and that he could find my papers in my inside pocket.

With four automatics rubbing against my ribs, I would not have lowered my arms for all the papers in the Bank of England. They took me to a *café*, where their colonel had just finished lunch and was in a most genial humour. First he gave the enthusiast a drink as a reward for arresting me, and then, impartially, gave me one for being arrested. He wrote on my passport that I could go to Enghien, which was two miles distant. That pass enabled me to proceed unmolested for nearly two hundred yards. I was then again arrested and taken before another group of officers. This time they searched my knapsack and wanted to requisition my maps, but one of them pointed out they were only automobile maps and, as compared to their own, of no value. They permitted me to proceed to Enghien. I went to Enghien, intending to spend the night and on the morning continue. I could not see why I might not be able to go on indefinitely.

As yet no one who had held me up had suggested I should turn back, and as long as I was willing to be arrested it seemed as though I might accompany the German army even to the gates of Paris. But my reception in Enghien should have warned me to get back to Brussels. The Germans, thinking I was an English spy, scowled at me; and the Belgians, thinking the same thing, winked at me; and the landlord of the only hotel said I was "suspect" and would not give me a bed. But I sought out the *burgomaster*, a most charming man named Delano, and he wrote out a pass permitting me to sleep one night in Enghien.

"You really do not need this," he said; "as an American you are free to stay here as long as you wish." Then he, too, winked.

"But I *am* an American," I protested.

"But certainly," he said gravely, and again he winked. It was then I should have started back to Brussels. Instead, I sat on a moss-covered, arched stone bridge that binds the town together, and until night fell watched the gray tidal waves rush up and across it, stamping, tripping, stumbling, beating the broad, clean stones with thousands of iron heels, steel hoofs, steel chains, and steel-rimmed wheels. You hated it, and yet could not keep away. The Belgians of Enghien hated it, and *they* could not keep away. Like a great river in flood, bearing with it destruction and death, you feared and loathed it, and yet it fascinated you and pulled you to the brink. All through the night, as already for three nights and three days at Brussels, I had heard it; it rumbled and growled, rushing forward without pause or breath, with inhuman, pitiless persistence.

At daybreak I sat on the edge of the bed and wondered whether to go on or turn back. I still wanted someone in authority, higher than myself, to order me back. So, at six, riding for a fall, to find that one, I went, as I thought, along the road to Soignes. The gray tidal wave was still roaring past. It was pressing forward with greater speed, but in nothing else did it differ from the tidal wave that had swept through Brussels.

There was a group of officers seated by the road, and as I passed I wished them good morning and they said good morning in return. I had gone a hundred feet when one of them galloped after me and asked to look at my papers. With relief I gave them to him. I was sure now I would be told to return to Brussels. I calculated if at Hal I had luck in finding a taxicab, by lunch time I should be in the Palace Hotel.

"I think," said the officer, "you had better see our general. He is ahead of us."

I thought he meant a few hundred yards ahead, and to be ordered back by a general seemed more convincing than to be returned by a mere captain. So I started to walk on beside the mounted officers. This, as it seemed to presume equality with them, scandalized them greatly, and I was ordered into the ranks. But the one who had arrested me thought I was entitled to a higher rating and placed me with the colour-guard, who objected to my presence so violently that a long discussion followed, which ended with my being ranked below a second lieutenant and above a sergeant. Between one of each of these I was definitely placed, and for five hours I remained definitely placed. We advanced with a rush that showed me I had surprised a surprise movement. The fact was of interest not because I had discovered one of their secrets, but because to keep up with the column I was forced for five hours to move at what was a steady trot. It was not so fast as the running step of the Italian *bersagliere*, but as fast as our "double-quick."

The men did not bend the knees, but, keeping the legs straight, shot them forward with a quick, sliding movement, like men skating or skiing. The toe of one boot seemed always tripping on the heel of the other. As the road was paved with roughly hewn blocks of Belgian granite this kind of going was very strenuous, and had I not been in good shape I could not have kept up. As it was, at the end of the five hours I had lost fifteen pounds, which did not help me, as during the same time the knapsack had taken on a hundred. For two days the men in the ranks had been rushed forward at this unnatural gait and were moving like automatons.

Many of them fell by the wayside, but they were not permitted to lie there. Instead of summoning the ambulance, they were lifted to their feet and flung back into the ranks. Many of them were moving in their sleep, in that partly comatose state in which you have seen men during the last hours of a six days' walking match. Their rules, so the sergeant said, were to halt every hour and then for ten minutes rest. But that rule is probably only for route marching.

On account of the speed with which the surprise movement was made our halts were more frequent, and so exhausted were the men that when these "thank you, ma'ams" arrived, instead of standing at ease and adjusting their accoutrements, as though they had been struck with a club they dropped to the stones. Some in an instant were asleep. I do not mean that some sat down; I mean that the whole column lay flat in the road. The officers also, those that were not mounted, would tumble on the grass or into the wheat-field and lie on their backs, their arms flung out like dead men. To the fact that they were lying on their field-glasses, holsters, swords, and water-bottles they appeared indifferent.

At the rate the column moved it would have covered thirty miles each day. It was these forced marches that later brought Von Kluck's army to the right wing of the Allies before the army of the crown prince was prepared to attack, and which at Sezanne led to his repulse and to the failure of his advance upon Paris.

While we were pushing forward we passed a wrecked British airship, around which were gathered a group of staff-officers. My papers were given to one of them, but our column did not halt and I was not allowed to speak. A few minutes later they passed in their automobiles on their way to the front; and my papers went with them. Already I was miles beyond the environs, and with each step away from Brussels my pass was becoming less of a safeguard than a menace. For it showed what restrictions General Jarotsky had placed on my movements, and my presence so far out of bounds proved I had disregarded them. But still I did not suppose that in returning to Brussels there would be any difficulty.

I was chiefly concerned with the thought that the length of the return march was rapidly increasing and with the fact that one of my shoes, a faithful friend in other campaigns, had turned traitor and was cutting my foot in half. I had started with the column at seven o'clock, and at noon an automobile, with flags flying and the black eagle of the staff enamelled on the door, came speeding back from the front. In it was a very blond and distinguished-looking officer of high rank and many decorations. He used a single eye-glass, and his politeness and his English were faultless. He invited me to accompany him to the general staff.

That was the first intimation I had that I was in danger. I saw they were giving me far too much attention. I began instantly to work to set myself free, and there was not a minute for the next twenty-four hours that I was not working. Before I stepped into the car I had decided upon my line of defence. I would pretend to be entirely unconscious that I had in any way laid myself open to suspicion; that I had erred through pure stupidity and that I was where I was solely because I was a damn fool. I began to act like a damn fool. Effusively I expressed my regret at putting the General Staff to inconvenience.

"It was really too stupid of me," I said. "I cannot forgive myself. I should not have come so far without asking Jarotsky for proper papers. I am extremely sorry I have given you this trouble. I would like to see the general and assure him I will return at once to Brussels."

I ignored the fact that I was being taken to the general at the rate of sixty miles an hour. The blond officer smiled uneasily and with his single glass studied the sky. When we reached the staff he escaped from me with the alacrity of one released from a disagreeable and humiliating duty. The staff were at luncheon, seated in their luxurious motor-cars or on the grass by the side of the road. On the other side of the road the column of dust-covered gray ghosts were being rushed past us. The staff, in dress uniforms, flowing cloaks, and gloves, belonged to a different race. They knew that. Among themselves they were like priests breathing incense. Whenever one of them spoke to another they saluted, their heels clicked, their bodies bent at the belt line.

One of them came to where, in the middle of the road, I was stranded and trying not to feel as lonely as I looked. He was much younger than myself and dark and handsome. His face was smooth-shaven, his figure tall, lithe, and alert. He wore a uniform of light blue and silver that clung to him and high boots of patent leather. His waist was like a girl's, and, as though to show how supple he was, he kept continually bowing and shrugging his shoulders and in elegant protest gesticulating with his gloved hands. He should have been a moving-picture actor. He reminded me of Anthony Hope's fascinating but wicked Rupert of Hentzau. He certainly was wicked, and I got to hate him as I never imagined it possible to hate anybody. He had been told off to dispose of my case, and he delighted in it. He enjoyed it as a cat enjoys playing with a mouse. As actors say, he saw himself in the part. He "ate" it.

"You are an English officer out of uniform," he began. "You have been taken inside our lines." He pointed his forefinger at my stomach and wiggled his thumb. "And you know what *that* means!"

I saw playing the damn fool with him would be waste of time.

"I followed your army," I told him, "because it's my business to follow armies and because yours is the best-looking army I ever saw." He made me one of his mocking bows.

"We thank you," he said, grinning. "But you have seen too much."

"I haven't seen anything," I said, "that everybody in Brussels hasn't seen for three days."

He shook his head reproachfully and with a gesture signified the group of officers.

"You have seen enough in this road," he said, "to justify us in shooting you now."

The sense of drama told him it was a good exit line, and he returned to the group of officers. I now saw what had happened. At

Enghien I had taken the wrong road. I remembered that, to confuse the Germans, the names on the sign-post at the edge of the town had been painted out, and that instead of taking the road to Soignes I was on the road to Ath. What I had seen, therefore, was an army corps making a turning movement intended to catch the English on their right and double them up upon their centre. The success of this manoeuvre depended upon the speed with which it was executed and upon its being a complete surprise.

As later in the day I learned, the Germans thought I was an English officer who had followed them from Brussels and who was trying to slip past them and warn his countrymen. What Rupert of Hentzau meant by what I had seen on the road was that, having seen the Count de Schwerin, who commanded the Seventh Division, on the road to Ath, I must necessarily know that the army corps to which he was attached had separated from the main army of Von Kluck, and that, in going so far south at such speed, it was bent upon an attack on the English flank. All of which at the time I did not know and did not *want* to know. All I wanted was to prove I was not an English officer, but an American correspondent who by accident had stumbled upon their secret. To convince them of that, strangely enough, was difficult.

When Rupert of Hentzau returned the other officers were with him, and, fortunately for me, they spoke or understood English. For the rest of the day what followed was like a legal argument. It was as cold-blooded as a game of bridge. Rupert of Hentzau wanted an English spy shot for his supper; just as he might have desired a grilled bone. He showed no personal animus, and, I must say for him, that he conducted the case for the prosecution without heat or anger. He mocked me, grilled and taunted me, but he was always charmingly polite.

As Whitman said, "I want Becker," so Rupert said, *"Fe, fo, fi, fum, I want the blood of an Englishman."* He was determined to get it. I was even more interested that he should not. The points he made against me were that my German pass was signed neither by General Jarotsky nor by Lieutenant Geyer, but only stamped, and that any rubber stamp could be forged; that my American passport had not been issued at Washington, but in London, where an Englishman might have imposed upon our embassy; and that in the photograph pasted on the passport I was wearing the uniform of a British officer.

I explained that the photograph was taken eight years ago, and that the uniform was one I had seen on the west coast of Africa, worn by the West African Field Force. Because it was unlike any known military uniform, and as cool and comfortable as a golf jacket, I had had it copied. But since that time it had been adopted by the English Brigade of Guards and the Territorials. I knew it sounded like fiction; but it was quite true.

Rupert of Hentzau smiled delightedly.

"Do you expect us to believe that?" he protested.

"Listen," I said. "If you could invent an explanation for that uniform as quickly as I told you that one, standing in a road with eight officers trying to shoot you, you would be the greatest general in Germany."

That made the others laugh; and Rupert retorted: "Very well, then, we will concede that the entire British army has changed its uniform to suit your photograph. But if you are *not* an officer, why, in the photograph, are you wearing war ribbons?"

I said the war ribbons were in my favour, and I pointed out that no officer of any one country could have been in the different campaigns for which the ribbons were issued.

"They prove," I argued, "that I am a correspondent, for only a correspondent could have been in wars in which his own country was not engaged."

I thought I had scored; but Rupert instantly turned my own witness against me.

"Or a military *attaché*," he said. At that they all smiled and nodded knowingly.

He followed this up by saying, accusingly, that the hat and clothes I was then wearing were English. The clothes were English, but I knew he did not know that, and was only guessing; and there were no marks on them. About my hat I was not certain. It was a felt Alpine hat, and whether I had bought it in London or New York I could not remember. Whether it was evidence for or against I could not be sure. So I took it off and began to fan myself with it, hoping to get a look at the name of the maker. But with the eyes of the young prosecuting attorney fixed upon me, I did not dare take a chance. Then, to aid me, a German aeroplane passed overhead, and those who were giving me the third degree looked up. I stopped fanning myself and cast a swift glance inside the hat. To my intense satisfaction I read, stamped on the leather lining: "Knox, New York."

I put the hat back on my head and a few minutes later pulled it off and said: "Now, for instance, my hat. If I were an Englishman would I cross the ocean to New York to buy a hat?"

The passport and photograph which though endorsed by Mr. Whitlock and Mr. Gibson, led to the arrest of Mr. Davis

It was all like that. They would move away and whisper together, and I would try to guess what questions they were preparing. I had to arrange my defence without knowing in what way they would try to trip me, and I had to think faster than I ever have thought before. I had no more time to be scared, or to regret my past sins, than has a man in a quicksand. So far as I could make out, they were divided in opinion concerning me. Rupert of Hentzau, who was the adjutant or the chief of staff, had only one simple thought, which was to shoot me. Others considered me a damn fool; I could hear them laughing and saying: "*Er ist ein dummer Mensch.*"

And others thought that whether I was a fool or not, or an American or an Englishman, was not the question; I had seen too much and should be put away. I felt if, instead of having Rupert act as my interpreter, I could personally speak to the general I might talk my way out of it, but Rupert assured me that to set me free the Count de Schwerin lacked authority, and that my papers, which were all against me, must be submitted to the general of the army corps, and we would not reach him until midnight.

"And *then!*—" he would exclaim, and he would repeat his pantomime of pointing his forefinger at my stomach and wiggling his thumb. He was very popular with me.

Meanwhile they were taking me farther away from Brussels and the "environs."

"When you picked me up," I said, "I was inside the environs, but by the time I reach 'the' general he will see only that I am fifty miles beyond where I am permitted to be. And who is going to tell him it was *you* brought me there? *You* won't!"

Rupert of Hentzau only smiled like the cat that has just swallowed the canary.

He put me in another automobile and they whisked me off, always going farther from Brussels, to Ath and then to Ligne, a little town five miles south. Here they stopped at a house the staff occupied, and, leading me to the second floor, put me in an empty room that seemed built for their purpose. It had a stone floor and whitewashed walls and a window so high that even when standing you could see only the roof of another house and a weather-vane. They threw two bundles of wheat on the floor and put a sentry at the door with orders to keep it open. He was a wild man, and thought I was, and every time I moved his automatic moved with me. It was as though he were following me with a spotlight.

My foot was badly cut across the instep and I was altogether forlorn and disreputable. So, in order to look less like a tramp when I met the general, I bound up the foot, and, always with one eye on the sentry, and moving very slowly, shaved and put on dry things. From the interest the sentry showed it seemed evident he never had taken a bath himself, nor had seen anyone else take one, and he was not quite easy in his mind that he ought to allow it. He seemed to consider it a kind of suicide. I kept on thinking out plans, and when an officer appeared I had one to submit. I offered to give the money I had with me to anyone who would motor back to Brussels and take a note to the American minister, Brand Whitlock. My proposition was that if in five hours, or by seven o'clock, he did not arrive in his automobile and assure them that what I said about myself was true, they need not wait until midnight, but could shoot me then.

"If I am willing to take such a chance," I pointed out, "I must be a friend of Mr. Whitlock. If he repudiates me, it will be evident I have deceived you, and you will be perfectly justified in carrying out your plan." I had a note to Whitlock already written. It was composed entirely with the idea that they would read it, and it was much more intimate than my very brief acquaintance with that gentleman justified. But from what I have seen and heard of the ex-mayor of Toledo I felt he would stand for it.

The note read:

Dear Brand:
I am detained in a house with a garden where the railroad passes through the village of Ligne. Please come quick, or send someone in the legation automobile.
                                                    Richard.

The officer to whom I gave this was Major Alfred Wurth, a reservist from Bernburg, on the Saale River. I liked him from the first because after we had exchanged a few words he exclaimed incredulously: "What nonsense! Anyone could tell by your accent that you are an American." He explained that, when at the university, in the same pension with him were three Americans.

"The staff are making a mistake," he said earnestly. "They will regret it."

I told him that I not only did not want them to regret it, but I did not want them to make it, and I begged him to assure the staff that I was an American. I suggested also that he tell them, if anything happened to me there were other Americans who would at once declare war on Germany. The number of these other Americans I overestimated by about ninety millions, but it was no time to consider details.

He asked if the staff might read the letter to the American minister, and, though I hated to deceive him, I pretended to consider this.

"I don't remember just what I wrote," I said, and, to make sure they *would* read it, I tore open the envelope and pretended to reread the letter.

"I will see what I can do," said Major Wurth; "meanwhile, do not be discouraged. Maybe it will come out all right for you."

After he left me the Belgian gentleman who owned the house and his cook brought me some food. She was the only member of his household who had not deserted him, and together they were serving the staff-officers, he acting as butler, waiter, and valet. The cook was an old peasant woman with a ruffled white cap, and when she left, in spite of the sentry, she patted me encouragingly on the shoulder. The owner of the house was more discreet, and contented himself with winking at me and whispering: "*Ça va mal pour vous en bas!*" As they both knew what was being said of me downstairs, their visit did not especially enliven me. Major Wurth returned and said the staff could not spare any one to go to Brussels, but that my note had been forwarded to "the" general.

That was as much as I had hoped for. It was intended only as a "stay of proceedings." But the manner of the major was not reassuring. He kept telling me that he thought they would set me free, but even as he spoke tears would come to his eyes and roll slowly down his cheeks. It was most disconcerting. After a while it grew dark and he brought me a candle and left me, taking with him, much to my relief, the sentry and his automatic. This gave me since my arrest my first moment alone, and, to find anything that might further incriminate or help me, I used it in going rapidly through my knapsack and pockets. My notebook was entirely favourable. In it there was no word that any German could censor.

My only other paper was a letter, of which all day I had been conscious. It was one of introduction from Colonel Theodore Roosevelt to President Poincaré, and whether the Germans would consider it a clean bill of health or a death-warrant I could not make up my mind. Half a dozen times I had been on the point of saying: "Here is a letter from the man your Kaiser delighted to honour, the only civilian who ever reviewed the German army, a former President of the United

States."

But I could hear Rupert of Hentzau replying: "Yes, and it is recommending you to our enemy, the President of France!"

I knew that Colonel Roosevelt would have written a letter to the German Emperor as impartially as to M. Poincaré, but I knew also that Rupert of Hentzau would not believe that. So I decided to keep the letter back until the last moment. If it was going to help me, it still would be effective; if it went against me, I would be just as dead. I began to think out other plans. Plans of escape were foolish. I could have crawled out of the window to the rain gutter, but before I had reached the rooftree I would have been shot. And bribing the sentry, even were he willing to be insulted, would not have taken me farther than the stairs, where there were other sentries. I was more safe inside the house than out. They still had my passport and *laissez-passer*, and without a pass one could not walk a hundred yards.

As the staff had but one plan, and no time in which to think of a better one, the obligation to invent a substitute plan lay upon me. The plan I thought out and which later I outlined to Major Wurth was this: Instead of putting me away at midnight, they would give me a pass back to Brussels. The pass would state that I was a suspected spy and that if before midnight of the 26th of August I were found off the direct road to Brussels, or if by that hour I had not reported to the military governor of Brussels, any one could shoot me on sight. As I have stated, without showing a pass no one could move a hundred yards, and every time I showed my pass to a German it would tell him I was a suspected spy, and if I were not making my way in the right direction he had his orders. With such a pass I was as much a prisoner as in the room at Ligne, and if I tried to evade its conditions I was as good as dead.

The advantages of my plan, as I urged them upon Major Wurth, were that it prevented the General Staff from shooting an innocent man, which would have greatly distressed them, and were he not innocent would still enable them, after a reprieve of two days, to shoot him. The distance to Brussels was about fifty miles, which, as it was impossible for a civilian to hire a bicycle, motorcar, or cart, I must cover on foot, making twenty-five miles a day. Major Wurth heartily approved of my substitute plan, and added that he thought if any motor-trucks or ambulances were returning empty to Brussels, I should be permitted to ride in one of them. He left me, and I never saw him again. It was then about eight o'clock, and as the time passed and he did not return and midnight grew nearer, I began to feel very lonely. Except for the Roosevelt letter, I had played my last card.

As it grew later I persuaded myself they did not mean to act until morning, and I stretched out on the straw and tried to sleep. At midnight I was startled by the light of an electric torch. It was strapped to the chest of an officer, who ordered me to get up and come with him. He spoke only German, and he seemed very angry. The owner of the house and the old cook had shown him to my room, but they stood in the shadow without speaking. Nor, fearing I might compromise them—for I could not see why, except for one purpose, they were taking me out into the night—did I speak to them. We got into another motorcar and in silence drove north from Ligne down a country road to a great *château* that stood in a magnificent park.

Something had gone wrong with the lights of the *château*, and its hall was lit only by candles that showed soldiers sleeping like dead men on bundles of wheat and others leaping up and down the marble stairs. They put me in a huge armchair of silk and gilt, with two of the gray ghosts to guard me, and from the hall, when the doors of the drawing-room opened, I could see a long table on which were candles in silver candlesticks or set on plates, and many maps and half-empty bottles of champagne. Around the table, standing or seated, and leaning across the maps, were staff-officers in brilliant uniforms.

They were much older men and of higher rank than any I had yet seen. They were eating, drinking, gesticulating. In spite of the tumult, some, in utter weariness, were asleep. It was like a picture of 1870 by Détaille or De Neuville. Apparently, at last I had reached the headquarters of the mysterious general. I had arrived at what, for a suspected spy, was an inopportune moment. The Germans themselves had been surprised, or somewhere south of us had met with a reverse, and the air was vibrating with excitement and something very like panic. Outside, at great speed and with sirens shrieking, automobiles were arriving, and I could hear the officers shouting: "*Die Englischen kommen!*"

To make their reports they flung themselves up the steps, the electric torches, like bull's-eye lanterns, burning holes in the night. Seeing a civilian under guard, they would stare and ask questions. Even when they came close, owing to the light in my eyes, I could not see them. Sometimes, in a half circle, there would be six or eight of the electric torches blinding me, and from behind them voices barking at me with strange, guttural noises. Much they said I could not understand, much

I did not want to understand, but they made it quite clear it was no fit place for an Englishman.

When the door from the drawing-room opened and Rupert of Hentzau appeared, I was almost glad to see him.

Whenever he spoke to me he always began or ended his sentence with "*Mr. Davis.*" He gave it an emphasis and meaning which was intended to show that he knew it was *not* my name. I would not have thought it possible to put so much insolence into two innocent words. It was as though he said: "Mr. Davis, *alias* Jimmy Valentine." He certainly would have made a great actor.

"*Mr. Davis,*" he said, "you are free."

He did not look as disappointed as I knew he would feel if I were free, so I waited for what was to follow.

"You are free," he said, "under certain conditions." The conditions seemed to cheer him. He recited the conditions. They were those I had outlined to Major Wurth. But I am sure Rupert of Hentzau did not guess that. Apparently, he believed Major Wurth had thought of them, and I did not undeceive him. For the substitute plan I was not inclined to rob that officer of any credit. I felt then, and I feel now, that but for him and his interceding for me I would have been left in the road. Rupert of Hentzau gave me the pass. It said I must return to Brussels by way of Ath, Enghien, Hal, and that I must report to the military governor on the 26th or "be treated as a spy"—"*so wird er als Spion behandelt.*" The pass, literally translated, reads:

> The American reporter Davis must at once return to Brussels *via* Ath, Enghien, Hal, and report to the government at the latest on August 26th. If he is met on any other road, or after the 26th of August, he will be handled as a spy. Automobiles returning to Brussels, if they can unite it with their duty, can carry him.
>
> Chief of General Staff.
>
> Von Gregor, Lieutenant-Colonel.

Fearing my military education was not sufficient to enable me to appreciate this, for the last time Rupert stuck his forefinger in my stomach and repeated cheerfully: "And you know what *that* means. And you will start," he added, with a most charming smile, "in three hours."

He was determined to have his grilled bone.

"At three in the morning!" I cried. "You might as well take me out

MR. DAVIS'S TICKET OF LEAVE.

REVERSE SIDE OF TICKET OF LEAVE.
THE INK WRITING (LOWER HALF) IS THE VISÉ STATING HE IS "NOT AT ALL" TO BE TREATED AS A SPY.

and shoot me now!"

"You will start in three hours," he repeated.

"A man wandering around at that hour," I protested, "wouldn't live five minutes. It can't be done. *You* couldn't do it." He continued to grin. I knew perfectly well the general had given no such order, and that it was a cat-and-mouse act of Rupert's own invention, and he knew I knew it. But he repeated: "You will start in three hours, Mr. *Davis*."

I said: "I am going to write about this, and I would like you to read what I write. What is your name?"

He said: "I am the Baron von"—it sounded like "Hossfer"—and, in any case, to that name, care of General de Schwerin of the Seventh Division, I shall mail this book. I hope the Allies do not kill Rupert of Hentzau before he reads it! After that! He would have made a great actor.

They put me in the automobile and drove me back to Ligne and the *impromptu* cell. But now it did not seem like a cell. Since I had last occupied it my chances had so improved that returning to the candle on the floor and the bundles of wheat was like coming home. Though I did not believe Rupert had any authority to order me into the night at the darkest hour of the twenty-four, I was taking no chances. My nerve was not in a sufficiently robust state for me to disobey any German. So, lest I should oversleep, until three o'clock I paced the cell, and then, with all the terrors of a burglar, tiptoed down the stairs. There was no light, and the house was wrapped in silence.

Earlier there had been everywhere sentries, and, not daring to breathe, I waited for one of them to challenge, but, except for the creaking of the stairs and of my ankle-bones, which seemed to explode like firecrackers, there was not a sound. I was afraid, and wished myself safely back in my cell, but I was more afraid of Rupert, and I kept on feeling my way until I had reached the garden. There some one spoke to me in French, and I found my host.

"The animals have gone," he said; "all of them. I will give you a bed now, and when it is light you shall have breakfast." I told him my orders were to leave his house at three.

"But it is murder!" he said. With these cheering words in my ears, I thanked him, and he bid me *bonne chance*.

In my left hand I placed the pass, folded so that the red seal of the General Staff would show, and a match-box. In the other hand I held ready a couple of matches. Each time a sentry challenged I struck the matches on the box and held them in front of the red seal. The instant the matches flashed it was a hundred to one that the man would shoot, but I could not speak German, and there was no other way to make him understand. They were either too surprised or too sleepy to fire, for each of them let me pass. But after I had made a mark of myself three times I lost my nerve and sought cover behind a haystack. I lay there until there was light enough to distinguish trees and telegraph-poles, and then walked on to Ath.

After that, when they stopped me, if they could not read, the red seal satisfied them; if they were officers and could read, they cursed me with strange, unclean oaths, and ordered me, in the German equivalent, to beat it. It was a delightful walk. I had had no sleep the night before and had eaten nothing, and, though I had cut away most of my shoe, I could hardly touch my foot to the road. Whenever in the villages I tried to bribe any one to carry my knapsack or to give me food, the peasants ran from me. They thought I was a German and talked Flemish, not French. I was more afraid of them and their shotguns than of the Germans, and I never entered a village unless German soldiers were entering or leaving it. And the Germans gave me no reason to feel free from care. Every time they read my pass they were inclined to try me all over again, and twice searched my knapsack.

After that happened the second time I guessed my letter to the President of France might prove a menace, and, tearing it into little pieces, dropped it over a bridge, and with regret watched that historical document from the ex-President of one republic to the President of another float down the Sambre toward the sea. By noon I decided I would not be able to make the distance. For twenty-four hours I had been without sleep or food, and I had been put through an unceasing third degree, and I was nearly out. Added to that, the chance of my losing the road was excellent; and if I lost the road the first German who read my pass was ordered by it to shoot me. So I decided to give myself up to the occupants of the next German car going toward Brussels and ask them to carry me there under arrest.

I waited until an automobile approached, and then stood in front of it and held up my pass and pointed to the red seal. The car stopped, and the soldiers in front and the officer in the rear seat gazed at me in indignant amazement. The officer was a general, old and kindly looking, and, by the grace of Heaven, as slow-witted as he was kind. He spoke no English, and his French was as bad as mine, and in consequence he had no idea of what I was saying except that I had orders from the General Staff to proceed at once to Brussels. I made a mystery of the pass, saying it was very confidential, but the red seal satisfied him. He bade me courteously to take the seat at his side, and with intense satisfaction I heard him command his orderly to get down and fetch my knapsack. The general was going, he said, only so far as Hal, but that far he would carry me. Hal was the last town named in my pass, and from Brussels only eleven miles distant. According to the schedule I had laid out for myself, I had not hoped to reach it by walking until the next day, but at the rate the car had approached I saw I would be there within two hours.

My feelings when I sank back upon the cushions of that car and stretched out my weary legs and the wind whistled around us are too sacred for cold print. It was a situation I would not have used in fiction. I was a condemned spy, with the hand of every German properly against me, and yet under the protection of a German general, and in luxurious ease, I was escaping from them at forty miles an hour. I had but one regret. I wanted Rupert of Hentzau to see me. At Hal my luck still held. The steps of the Hôtel de Ville were crowded with generals. I thought never in the world could there be so many generals, so many flowing cloaks and spiked helmets. I was afraid of them. I was afraid that when my general abandoned me the others might not prove so slow-witted or so kind. My general also seemed to regard them with disfavour. He exclaimed impatiently. Apparently, to force his way through them, to cool his heels in an anteroom, did not appeal. It was long past his luncheon hour and the restaurant of the Palace Hotel called him. He gave a sharp order to the chauffeur.

"I go on to Brussels," he said. "Desire you to accompany me?" I did not know how to ask him in French not to make me laugh. I saw the great Palace of Justice that towers above the city with the same emotions that one beholds the Statue of Liberty, but not until we had reached the inner boulevards did I feel safe. There I bade my friend a grateful but hasty *adieu*, and in a taxicab, unwashed and unbrushed, I drove straight to the American legation. To Mr. Whitlock I told this story, and with one hand that gentleman reached for his hat and with the other for his stick. In the automobile of the legation we raced to the Hôtel de Ville. There Mr. Whitlock, as the moving-picture people say, "registered" indignation. Mr. Davis was present, he made it understood, not as a ticket-of-leave man, and because he had been ordered to report, but in spite of that fact. He was there as the friend of the American minister, and the word "*Spion*" must be removed from his papers.

And so, on the pass that Rupert gave me, below where he had written that I was to be treated as a spy, they wrote I was "not at all," "*gar nicht*," to be treated as a spy, and that I was well known to the American minister, and to that they affixed the official seal.[1]

That ended it, leaving me with one valuable possession. It is this: should anyone suggest that I *am* a spy, or that I am *not* a friend of Brand Whitlock, I have the testimony of the Imperial German Government to the contrary.

---

1. Literal translation of *visé* on the pass:

                                                 Brussels, August 25th, 1914.

Herr Davis was on the 25th of August at the headquarters of the German Government accompanied by the American minister and is not at all to be treated as a spy. He is highly recommended by the American minister and is well known in America.

                                                          Albert Bovey,
                               Translator to Major-General Jarotsky,

CHAPTER 3

The Burning of Louvain

After the Germans occupied Brussels they closed the road to Aix-la-Chapelle. A week later, to carry their wounded and prisoners, they reopened it. But for eight days Brussels was isolated. The mail-trains and the telegraph office were in the hands of the invaders. They accepted our cables, censored them, and three days later told us, if we still wished, we could forward them. But only from Holland. By this they accomplished three things: they learned what we were writing about them, for three days prevented any news from leaving the city, and offered us an inducement to visit Holland, so getting rid of us.

The despatches of those diplomats who still remained in Brussels were treated in the same manner. With the most cheerful complacency the military authorities blue-pencilled their despatches to their governments. When the diplomats learned of this, with their code cables they sent open cables stating that their confidential despatches were being censored and delayed. They still were delayed. To get any message out of Brussels it was necessary to use an automobile, and nearly every automobile had taken itself off to Antwerp. If a motor-car appeared it was at once commandeered. This was true also of horses and bicycles. All over Brussels you saw delivery wagons, private carriages, market carts with the shafts empty and the horse and harness gone. After three days a German soldier who did not own a bicycle was poor indeed.

Requisitions were given for these machines, stating they would be returned after the war, by which time they will be ready for the scrapheap. Any one on a bicycle outside the city was arrested, so the only way to get messages through was by going on foot to Ostend or Holland, or by an automobile for which the German authorities had given a special pass. As no one knew when one of these automobiles might start, we carried always with us our cables and letters, and intrusted them to any stranger who was trying to run the lines.

No one wished to carry our despatches, as he feared they might contain something unfavourable to the Germans, which, if he were arrested and the cables read, might bring him into greater trouble. Money for himself was no inducement. But I found if I gave money for the Red Cross no one would refuse it, or to carry the messages.

Three out of four times the stranger would be arrested and ordered back to Brussels, and our despatches, with their news value departed, would be returned.

An account of the Germans entering Brussels I sent by an English boy named Dalton, who, after being turned back three times, got through by night, and when he arrived in England his adventures were published in all the London papers. They were so thrilling that they made my story, for which he had taken the trip, extremely tame reading.

Hugh Gibson, secretary of the American legation, was the first person in an official position to visit Antwerp after the Belgian Government moved to that city, and, even with his passes and flag flying from his automobile, he reached Antwerp and returned to Brussels only after many delays and adventures. Not knowing the Belgians were advancing from the north, Gibson and his American flag were several times under fire, and on the days he chose for his excursion his route led him past burning towns and dead and wounded and between the lines of both forces actively engaged.

He was carrying despatches from Brand Whitlock to Secretary Bryan. During the night he rested at Antwerp the first Zeppelin airship to visit that city passed over it, dropping one bomb at the end of the block in which Gibson was sleeping. He was awakened by the explosion and heard all of those that followed.

The next morning he was requested to accompany a committee appointed by the Belgian Government to report upon the outrage, and he visited a house that had been wrecked, and saw what was left of the bodies of those killed. People who were in the streets when the air-ship passed said it moved without any sound, as though the motor had been shut off and it was being propelled by momentum.

One bomb fell so near the palace where the Belgian Queen was sleeping as to destroy the glass in the windows and scar the walls. The bombs were large, containing smaller bombs of the size of shrapnel. Like shrapnel, on impact they scattered bullets over a radius of forty yards. One man, who from a window in the eighth story of a hotel watched the air-ship pass, stated that before each bomb fell he saw electric torches signal from the roofs, as though giving directions as to where the bombs should strike.

After my arrest by the Germans, I found my usefulness in Brussels as a correspondent was gone, and I returned to London, and from there rejoined the Allies in Paris.

I left Brussels on August 27th with Gerald Morgan and Will Irwin, of *Collier's*, on a train carrying English prisoners and German wounded. In times of peace the trip to the German border lasts three hours, but in making it we were twenty-six hours, and by order of the authorities we were forbidden to leave the train.

Carriages with cushions naturally were reserved for the wounded, so we slept on wooden benches and on the floor. It was not possible to obtain food, and water was as scarce. At Graesbeek, ten miles from Brussels, we first saw houses on fire. They continued with us to Liége.

Village after village had been completely wrecked. In his march to the sea Sherman lived on the country. He did not destroy it, and as against the burning of Columbia must be placed to the discredit of the Germans the wiping out of an entire countryside.

For many miles we saw procession after procession of peasants fleeing from one burning village, which had been their home, to other villages, to find only blackened walls and smouldering ashes. In no part of northern Europe is there a countryside fairer than that between Aix-la-Chapelle and Brussels, but the Germans had made of it a graveyard. It looked as though a cyclone had uprooted its houses, gardens, and orchards and a prairie fire had followed.

At seven o'clock in the evening we arrived at what for six hundred years had been the city of Louvain. The Germans were burning it, and to hide their work kept us locked in the railroad carriages. But the story was written against the sky, was told to us by German soldiers incoherent with excesses; and we could read it in the faces of women and children being led to concentration camps and of citizens on their way to be shot.

The day before the Germans had sentenced Louvain to become a wilderness, and with German system and love of thoroughness they left Louvain an empty, blackened shell. The reason for this appeal to the torch and the execution of non-combatants, as given to Mr. Whitlock and myself on the morning I left Brussels by General von Lutwitz, the military governor, was this: The day before, while the German military commander of the troops in Louvain was at the Hôtel de Ville talking to the *burgomaster*, a son of the *burgomaster*, with an automatic pistol, shot the chief of staff and German staff surgeons.

Lutwitz claimed this was the signal for the civil guard, in civilian clothes on the roofs, to fire upon the German soldiers in the open square below. He said also the Belgians had quick-firing guns, brought from Antwerp. As for a week the Germans had occupied Louvain and closely guarded all approaches, the story that there was any gun-running is absurd.

"Fifty Germans were killed and wounded," said Lutwitz, "and for that Louvain must be wiped out—so!" In pantomime with his fist he swept the papers across his table.

"The Hôtel de Ville," he added, "was a beautiful building; it is a pity it must be destroyed."

Were he telling us his soldiers had destroyed a kitchen-garden, his tone could not have expressed less regret.

Ten days before I had been in Louvain, when it was occupied by Belgian troops and King Albert and his staff. The city dates from the eleventh century, and the population was forty-two thousand. The citizens were brewers, lace-makers, and manufacturers of ornaments for churches. The university once was the most celebrated in European cities and was the headquarters of the Jesuits.

In the Louvain College many priests now in America have been educated, and ten days before, over the great yellow walls of the college, I had seen hanging two American flags. I had found the city clean, sleepy, and pretty, with narrow, twisting streets and smart shops and *cafés*. Set in flower gardens were the houses, with red roofs, green shutters, and white walls.

Over those that faced south had been trained pear-trees, their branches, heavy with fruit, spread out against the walls like branches of candelabra. The town hall was an example of Gothic architecture, in detail and design more celebrated even than the town hall of Bruges or Brussels. It was five hundred years old, and lately had been repaired with taste and at great cost.

Opposite was the Church of St. Pierre, dating from the fifteenth century, a very noble building, with many chapels filled with carvings of the time of the Renaissance in wood, stone, and iron. In the university were one hundred and fifty thousand volumes.

Near it was the bronze statue of Father Damien, priest of the leper colony in the South Pacific, of whom Robert Louis Stevenson wrote.

On the night of the 27th these buildings were empty, exploded cartridges. Statues, pictures, carvings, parchments, archives—all these were gone.

No one defends the sniper. But because ignorant Mexicans, when their city was invaded, fired upon our sailors, we did not destroy Vera Cruz. Even had we bombarded Vera Cruz, money could have restored that city. Money can never restore Louvain. Great architects and artists, dead these six hundred years, made it beautiful, and their handiwork belonged to the world. With torch and dynamite the Germans turned those masterpieces into ashes, and all the Kaiser's horses and all his men cannot bring them back again.

When our troop train reached Louvain, the entire heart of the city was destroyed, and the fire had reached the Boulevard Tirlemont, which faces the railroad station. The night was windless, and the sparks rose in steady, leisurely pillars, falling back into the furnace from which they sprang. In their work the soldiers were moving from the heart of the city to the outskirts, street by street, from house to house.

In each building they began at the first floor and, when that was burning steadily, passed to the one next. There were no exceptions—whether it was a store, chapel, or private residence, it was destroyed. The occupants had been warned to go, and in each deserted shop or house the furniture was piled, the torch was stuck under it, and into the air went the savings of years, souvenirs of children, of parents, heirlooms that had passed from generation to generation.

The people had time only to fill a pillowcase and fly. Some were not so fortunate, and by thousands, like flocks of sheep, they were rounded up and marched through the night to concentration camps. We were not allowed to speak to any citizen of Louvain, but the Germans crowded the windows of the train, boastful, gloating, eager to interpret.

In the two hours during which the train circled the burning city war was before us in its most hateful aspect.

In other wars I have watched men on one hilltop, without haste, without heat, fire at men on another hill, and in consequence on both sides good men were wasted. But in those fights there were no women or children, and the shells struck only vacant stretches of veldt or uninhabited mountain sides.

At Louvain it was war upon the defenceless, war upon churches,

Louvain after the bombardment

colleges, shops of milliners and lace-makers; war brought to the bedside and the fireside; against women harvesting in the fields, against children in wooden shoes at play in the streets.

At Louvain that night the Germans were like men after an orgy.

There were fifty English prisoners, erect and soldierly. In the ocean of gray the little patch of khaki looked pitifully lonely, but they regarded the men who had outnumbered but not defeated them with calm, uncurious eyes. In one way I was glad to see them there. Later they will bear witness. They will tell how the enemy makes a wilderness and calls it war. It was a most weird picture. On the high ground rose the broken spires of the Church of St. Pierre and the Hôtel de Ville, and descending like steps were row beneath row of houses, roofless, with windows like blind eyes. The fire had reached the last row of houses, those on the Boulevard de Jodigne. Some of these were already cold, but others sent up steady, straight columns of flame. In others at the third and fourth stories the window curtains still hung, flowers still filled the window-boxes, while on the first floor the torch had just passed and the flames were leaping. Fire had destroyed the electric plant, but at times the flames made the station so light that you could see the second-hand of your watch, and again all was darkness, lit only by candles.

You could tell when an officer passed by the electric torch he carried strapped to his chest. In the darkness the gray uniforms filled the station with an army of ghosts. You distinguished men only when pipes hanging from their teeth glowed red or their bayonets flashed.

Outside the station in the public square the people of Louvain passed in an unending procession, women bareheaded, weeping, men carrying the children asleep on their shoulders, all hemmed in by the shadowy army of gray wolves. Once they were halted, and among them were marched a line of men. These were on their way to be shot. And, better to point the moral, an officer halted both processions and, climbing to a cart, explained why the men were to die. He warned others not to bring down upon themselves a like vengeance.

As those being led to spend the night in the fields looked across to those marked for death they saw old friends, neighbours of long standing, men of their own household. The officer bellowing at them from the cart was illuminated by the headlights of an automobile. He looked like an actor held in a spotlight on a darkened stage.

It was all like a scene upon the stage, unreal, inhuman. You felt it could not be true. You felt that the curtain of fire, purring and crackling and sending up hot sparks to meet the kind, calm stars, was only a painted backdrop; that the reports of rifles from the dark ruins came from blank cartridges, and that these trembling shopkeepers and peasants ringed in bayonets would not in a few minutes really die, but that they themselves and their homes would be restored to their wives and children.

You felt it was only a nightmare, cruel and uncivilized. And then you remembered that the German Emperor has told us what it is. It is his Holy War.

CHAPTER 4

Paris in War Time

Those who, when the Germans approached, fled from Paris, described it as a city doomed, as a waste place, desolate as a graveyard. Those who run away always are alarmists. They are on the defensive. They must explain why they ran away.

Early in September Paris was like a summer hotel out of season. The owners had temporarily closed it; the windows were barred, the furniture and paintings draped in linen, a caretaker and a night-watchman were in possession.

It is an old saying that all good Americans go to Paris when they die. Most of them take no chances and prefer to visit it while they are alive. Before this war, if the visitor was disappointed, it was the fault of the visitor, not of Paris. She was all things to all men. To some she offered triumphal arches, statues, paintings; to others by day racing, and by night Maxims and the Rat Mort. Some loved her for the bookstalls along the Seine and ateliers of the Latin Quarter; some for her parks, forests, gardens, and boulevards; some because of the Luxembourg; some only as a place where everybody was smiling, happy, and polite, where they were never bored, where they were always young, where the lights never went out and there was no early call. Should they today revisit her they would find her grown grave and decorous, and going to bed at sundown, but still smiling bravely, still polite.

You cannot wipe out Paris by removing two million people and closing Cartier's and the Café de Paris. There still remains some hundred miles of boulevards, the Seine and her bridges, the Arc de Triomphe, with the sun setting behind it, and the Gardens of the Tuilleries. You cannot send them to the store-house or wrap them in linen. And the spirit of the people of Paris you cannot crush nor stampede.

Between Paris in peace and Paris today the most striking difference is lack of population. Idle rich, the employees of the government, and tourists of all countries are missing. They leave a great emptiness. When you walk the streets you feel either that you are up very early, before any one is awake, or that you are in a boom town from which the boom has departed.

On almost every one of the noted shops "*Fermé*" is written, or it has been turned over to the use of the Red Cross. Of the smaller shops those that remain open are chiefly bakeshops and chemists, but no man need go naked or hungry; in every block he will find at least one place where he can be clothed and fed. But the theatres are all closed. No one is in a mood to laugh, and certainly no one wishes to consider anything more serious than the present crisis. So there are no revues, operas, or comedies.

The thing you missed perhaps most were the children in the Avenue des Champs Elysées. For generations over that part of the public garden the children have held sway. They knew it belonged to them, and into the gravel walks drove their tin spades with the same sense of ownership as at Deauville they dig up the shore. Their straw hats and bare legs, their Normandy nurses, with enormous head-dresses, blue for a boy and pink for a girl, were, of the sights of Paris, one of the most familiar. And when the children vanished they left a dreary wilderness. You could look for a mile, from the Place de la Concorde to the Arc de Triomphe, and not see a child. The stalls, where they bought hoops and skipping-ropes, the flying wooden horses, Punch-and-Judy shows, booths where with milk they refreshed themselves and with bonbons made themselves ill, all were deserted and boarded up.

The closing down of the majority of the shops and hotels was not due to a desire on the part of those employed in them to avoid the Germans, but to get at the Germans.

On shop after shop are signs reading: "The proprietor and staff are with the colours," or "The personnel of this establishment is mobilized," or "Monsieur ——— informs his clients that he is with his regiment."

In the absence of men at the front, Frenchwomen, at all times capable and excellent managers, have surpassed themselves. In my hotel there were employed seven women and one man. In another hotel I visited the entire staff was composed of women.

An American banker offered his twenty-two polo ponies to the government. They were refused as not heavy enough. He did not know that, and supposed he had lost them. Later he learned from the

French colonial troops leaving Paris for the front

wife of his trainer, a Frenchwoman, that those employed in his stables at Versailles who had not gone to the front at the approach of the Germans had fled, and that for three weeks his string of twenty-two horses had been fed, groomed, and exercised by the trainer's wife and her two little girls.

To an American it was very gratifying to hear the praise of the French and English for the American ambulance at Neuilly. It is the outgrowth of the American hospital, and at the start of this war was organized by Mrs. Herrick, wife of our ambassador, and other ladies of the American colony in Paris, and the American doctors. They took over the Lycée Pasteur, an enormous school at Neuilly, that had just been finished and never occupied, and converted it into what is a most splendidly equipped hospital. In walking over the building you find it hard to believe that it was intended for any other than its present use. The operating rooms, kitchens, wards, rooms for operating by Roentgen rays, and even a chapel have been installed.

The organization and system are of the highest order. Everyone in it is American. The doctors are the best in Paris. The nurses and orderlies are both especially trained for the work and volunteers. The spirit of helpfulness and unselfishness is everywhere apparent. Certain members of the American colony, who never in their lives thought of any one save themselves, and of how to escape boredom, are toiling like chambermaids and hall porters, performing most disagreeable tasks, not for a few hours a week, but unceasingly, day after day. No task is too heavy for them or too squalid. They help all alike—Germans, English, major-generals, and black *Turcos*.

There are three hundred patients. The staff of the hospital numbers one hundred and fifty. It is composed of the best-known American doctors in Paris and a few from New York. Among the volunteer nurses and attendants are wives of bankers in Paris, American girls who have married French titles, and girls who since the war came have lost employment as teachers of languages, stenographers, and governesses. The men are members of the Jockey Club, art students, medical students, clerks, and *boulevardiers*. They are all working together in most admirable harmony and under an organization that in its efficiency far surpasses that of any other hospital in Paris. Later it is going to split the American colony in twain. If you did not work in the American ambulance you won't belong.

Attached to the hospital is a squadron of automobile ambulances, ten of which were presented by the Ford Company and ten purchased. Their chassis have been covered with khaki hoods and fitted to carry two wounded men and attendants. On their runs they are accompanied by automobiles with medical supplies, tires, and gasoline. The ambulances scout at the rear of the battle line and carry back those which the field-hospitals cannot handle.

One day I watched the orderlies who accompany these ambulances handling about forty English wounded, transferring them from the automobiles to the reception hall, and the smartness and intelligence with which the members of each crew worked together was like that of a champion polo team. The editor of a London paper, who was in Paris investigating English hospital conditions, witnessed the same performance, and told me that in handling the wounded it surpassed in efficiency anything he had seen.

CHAPTER 5

The Battle of Soissons

The struggle for the possession of Soissons lasted two days. The second day's battle, which I witnessed, ended with the city in the possession of the French. It was part of the seven days' of continuous fighting that began on September 6th at Meaux. Then the German left wing, consisting of the army of General von Kluck, was at Claye, within fifteen miles of Paris. But the French and English, instead of meeting the advance with a defence, themselves attacked. Steadily, at the rate of ten miles a day, they drove the Germans back across the Aisne and the Marne, and so saved the city.

When this retrograde movement of the Germans began, those who could not see the nature of the fighting believed that the German line of communication, the one from Aix-la-Chapelle through Belgium, had proved too long, and that the left wing was voluntarily withdrawing to meet the new line of communication through Luxembourg. But the fields of battle beyond Meaux, through which it was necessary to pass to reach the fight at Soissons, showed no evidence of leisurely withdrawal. On both sides there were evidences of the most desperate fighting and of artillery fire that was widespread and desolating. That of the Germans, intended to destroy the road from Meaux and to cover their retreat, showed marksmanship so accurate and execution so terrible as, while it lasted, to render pursuit impossible.

The battlefield stretched from the hills three miles north of Meaux for four miles along the road and a mile to either side. The road is lined with poplars three feet across and as high as a five-storey building. For the four miles the road was piled with branches of these trees. The trees themselves were split as by lightning, or torn in half, as with your hands you could tear apart a loaf of bread. Through some, solid shell had passed, leaving clean holes. Others looked as though drunken woodsmen with axes from roots to topmost branches had slashed them in crazy fury. Some shells had broken the trunks in half as a hurricane snaps a mast.

That no human being could survive such a bombardment were many gruesome proofs. In one place for a mile the road was lined with those wicker baskets in which the Germans carry their ammunition. These were filled with shells, unexploded, and behind the trenches were hundreds more of these baskets, some for the shells of the siege-guns, as large as lobster-pots or umbrella-stands, and others, each with three compartments, for shrapnel. In gutters along the road and in the wheat-fields these brass shells flashed in the sunshine like tiny mirrors.

The four miles of countryside over which for four days both armies had ploughed the earth with these shells was the picture of complete desolation. The rout of the German army was marked by knapsacks, uniforms, and accoutrements scattered over the fields on either hand as far as you could see. Red Cross flags hanging from bushes showed where there had been dressing stations. Under them were bloodstains, bandages and clothing, and boots piled in heaps as high as a man's chest, and the bodies of those German soldiers that the first aid had failed to save.

After death the body is mercifully robbed of its human aspect. You are spared the thought that what is lying in the trenches among the shattered trees and in the wheat-fields staring up at the sky was once a man. It appears to be only a bundle of clothes, a scarecrow that has tumbled among the grain it once protected. But it gives a terrible meaning to the word "missing." When you read in the reports from the War Office that five thousand are "missing," you like to think of them safely cared for in a hospital or dragging out the period of the war as prisoners. But the real missing are the unidentified dead. In time some peasant will bury them, but he will not understand the purpose of the medal each wears around his neck. And so, with the dead man will be buried his name and the number of his regiment. No one will know where he fell or where he lies. Someone will always hope that he will return. For, among the dead his name did not appear. He was reported "missing."

The utter wastefulness of war was seldom more clearly shown. Carcasses of horses lined the road. Some few of these had been killed by shell-fire. Others, worn out and emaciated, and bearing the brand of the German army, had been mercifully destroyed; but the greater number of them were the farm horses of peasants, still wearing their head-stalls or the harness of the plough. That they might not aid the enemy as remounts, the Germans in their retreat had shot them. I saw four and five together in the yards of stables, the bullet-hole of an automatic in the head of each. Others lay beside the market cart, others by the canal, where they had sought water.

Less pitiful, but still evidencing the wastefulness of war, were the motor-trucks, and automobiles that in the flight had been abandoned. For twenty miles these automobiles were scattered along the road. There were so many one stopped counting them. Added to their loss were two shattered German airships. One I saw twenty-six kilometres outside of Meaux and one at Bouneville. As they fell they had buried their motors deep in the soft earth and their wings were twisted wrecks of silk and steel.

All the fields through which the army passed had become waste land. Shells had re-ploughed them. Horses and men had camped in them. The haystacks, gathered by the sweat of the brow and patiently set in trim rows were trampled in the mud and scattered to the winds. All the smaller villages through which I passed were empty of people, and since the day before, when the Germans occupied them, none of the inhabitants had returned. These villages were just as the Germans had left them. The streets were piled with grain on which the soldiers had slept, and on the sidewalks in front of the better class of houses tables around which the officers had eaten still remained, the bottles half empty, the food half eaten.

In a *château* beyond Neufchelles the doors and windows were open and lace curtains were blowing in the breeze. From the garden you could see paintings on the walls, books on the tables. Outside, on the lawn, surrounded by old and charming gardens, apparently the general and his staff had prepared to dine. The table was set for a dozen, and on it were candles in silver sticks, many bottles of red and white wine, champagne, liqueurs, and coffee-cups of the finest china. From their banquet some alarm had summoned the officers. The place was as they had left it, the coffee untasted, the candles burned to the candlesticks, and red stains on the cloth where the burgundy had spilled. In the bright sunlight, and surrounded by flowers, the deserted table and the silent, stately château seemed like the sleeping palace of the fairy-tale.

Though the humour of troops retreating is an ugly one, I saw no outrages such as I saw in Belgium. Except in the villages of Neufchelles and Varreddes, there was no sign of looting or wanton destruction. But in those two villages the interior of every home and shop was completely wrecked. In the other villages the destruction was such as is permitted by the usages of war, such as the blowing up of bridges, the burning of the railroad station, and the cutting of telegraph-wires.

Not until Bouneville, thirty kilometres beyond Meaux, did I catch up with the Allies. There I met some English Tommies who were trying to find their column. They had no knowledge of the French language, or where they were, or where their regiment was, but were quite confident of finding it, and were as cheerful as at manoeuvres. Outside of Chaudun the road was blocked with *tirailleurs*, Algerians in light-blue *Zouave* uniforms, and native *Turcos* from Morocco in khaki, with khaki turbans. They shivered in the autumn sunshine, and were wrapped in burnooses of black and white. They were making a turning movement to attack the German right, and were being hurried forward. They had just driven the German rearguard out of Chaudun, and said that the fighting was still going on at Soissons. But the only sign I saw of it were two *Turcos* who had followed the Germans too far. They lay sprawling in the road, and had so lately fallen that their rifles still lay under them. Three miles farther I came upon the advance line of the French army, and for the remainder of the day watched a most remarkable artillery duel, which ended with Soissons in the hands of the Allies.

Soissons is a pretty town of four thousand inhabitants. It is chiefly known for its haricot beans, and since the Romans held it under Caesar it has been besieged many times. Until today the Germans had held it for two weeks. In 1870 they bombarded it for four days, and there is, or was, in Soissons, in the Place de la République, a monument to those citizens of Soissons whom after that siege the Germans shot. The town lies in the valley of the River Aisne, which is formed by two long ridges running south and north.

The Germans occupied the hills to the south, but when attacked offered only slight resistance and withdrew to the hills opposite. In Soissons they left a rearguard to protect their supplies, who were destroying all bridges leading into the town. At the time I arrived a force of *Turcos* had been ordered forward to clean Soissons of the Germans, and the French artillery was endeavouring to disclose their positions on the hills. The loss of the bridges did not embarrass the black men. In rowboats they crossed to Soissons and were warmly greeted. Sois-

French infantry advancing through the vineyards of the Aisne valley

sons was drawing no colour-line. The *Turcos* were followed by engineers, who endeavoured to repair one bridge and in consequence were heavily shelled with shrapnel, while, with the intent to destroy the road and retard the French advance, the hills where the French had halted were being pounded by German siege-guns.

This was at a point four kilometres from Chaudun, between the villages of Breuil and Courtelles. From this height you could see almost to Compiègne, and thirty miles in front in the direction of Saint-Quentin. It was a panorama of wooded hills, gray villages in fields of yellow grain, miles of poplars marking the roads, and below us the flashing waters of the Aisne and the canal, with at our feet the steeples of the cathedral of Soissons and the gate to the old abbey of Thomas à Becket. Across these steeples the shells sang, and on both sides of the Aisne Valley the artillery was engaged. The wind was blowing forty knots, which prevented the use of the French aeroplanes, but it cleared the air, and, helped by brilliant sunshine, it was possible to follow the smoke of the battle for fifteen miles. The wind was blowing toward our right, where we were told were the English, and though as their shrapnel burst we could see the flash of guns and rings of smoke, the report of the guns did not reach us. It gave the curious impression of a bombardment conducted in utter silence.

From our left the wind carried the sounds clearly. The jar and roar of the cannon were insistent, and on both sides of the valley the hill-tops were wrapped with white clouds. Back of us in the wheat-fields shells were setting fire to the giant haystacks and piles of grain, which in the clear sunshine burned a blatant red. At times shells would strike in the villages of Breuil and Vauxbain, and houses would burst into flames, the gale fanning the fire to great height and hiding the village in smoke. Some three hundred yards ahead of us the shells of German siege-guns were trying to destroy the road, which the poplars clearly betrayed. But their practice was at fault, and the shells fell only on either side. When they struck they burst with a roar, casting up black fumes and digging a grave twenty yards in circumference.

But the French soldiers disregarded them entirely. In the trenches which the Germans had made and abandoned they hid from the wind and slept peacefully. Others slept in the lee of the haystacks, their red breeches and blue coats making wonderful splashes of colour against the yellow grain. For seven days these same men had been fighting without pause, and battles bore them.

Late in the afternoon, all along the fifteen miles of battle, firing ceased, for the Germans were falling back, and once more Soissons, freed of them as fifteen hundred years ago she had freed herself of the Romans, held out her arms to the Allies.

Chapter 6

The Bombardment of Rheims

In several ways the city of Rheims is celebrated. Some know her only through her cathedral, where were crowned all but six of the kings of France, and where the stained-glass windows, with those in the cathedrals of Chartres and Burgos, Spain, are the most beautiful in all the world. Children know Rheims through the wicked magpie which the archbishop excommunicated, and to their elders, if they are rich, Rheims is the place from which comes all their champagne.

On September 4th the Germans entered Rheims, and occupied it until the 12th, when they retreated across the Vesle to the hills north of the city.

On the 18th the French forces, having entered Rheims, the Germans bombarded the city with field-guns and howitzers.

Rheims is fifty-six miles from Paris, but, though I started at an early hour, so many bridges had been destroyed that I did not reach the city until three o'clock in the afternoon. At that hour the French artillery, to the east at Nogent and immediately outside the northern edge of the town, were firing on the German positions, and the Germans were replying, their shells falling in the heart of the city.

The proportion of those that struck the cathedral or houses within a hundred yards of it to those falling on other buildings was about six to one. So what damage the cathedral suffered was from blows delivered not by accident but with intent. As the priests put it, firing on the church was "*exprès*."

The cathedral dominates not only the city but the countryside. It rises from the plain as Gibraltar rises from the sea, as the pyramids rise from the desert. And at a distance of six miles, as you approach from Paris along the valley of the Marne, it has more the appearance of a fortress than a church. But when you stand in the square beneath and look up, it is entirely ecclesiastic, of noble and magnificent proportions, in design inspired, much too sublime for the kings it has crowned, and almost worthy of the king in whose honour, seven hundred years ago, it was reared. It has been called "perhaps the most beautiful structure produced in the Middle Ages." On the west façade, rising tier upon tier, are five hundred and sixty statues and carvings. The statues are of angels, martyrs, patriarchs, apostles, the vices and virtues, the Virgin and Child. In the centre of these is the famous rose window; on either side giant towers.

At my feet down the steps leading to the three portals were pools of blood. There was a priest in the square, a young man with white hair and with a face as strong as one of those of the saints carved in stone, and as gentle. He was *curé doyen* of the Church of St. Jacques, M. Chanoine Frezet, and he explained the pools of blood. After the Germans retreated, the priests had carried the German wounded up the steps into the nave of the cathedral and for them had spread straw upon the stone flagging.

The *curé* guided me to the side door, unlocked it, and led the way into the cathedral. It is built in the form of a crucifix, and so vast is the edifice that many chapels are lost in it, and the lower half is in a shadow. But from high above the stained windows of the thirteenth century, or what was left of them, was cast a glow so gorgeous, so wonderful, so pure that it seemed to come direct from the other world.

From north and south the windows shed a radiance of deep blue, like the blue of the sky by moonlight on the coldest night of winter, and from the west the great rose window glowed with the warmth and beauty of a thousand rubies. Beneath it, bathed in crimson light, where for generations French men and women have knelt in prayer, where Joan of Arc helped place the crown on Charles VII, was piled three feet of dirty straw, and on the straw were gray-coated Germans, covered with the mud of the fields, caked with blood, white and haggard from the loss of it, from the lack of sleep, rest, and food. The entire west end of the cathedral looked like a stable, and in the blue and purple rays from the gorgeous windows the wounded were as unreal as ghosts. Already two of them had passed into the world of ghosts. They had not died from their wounds, but from a shell sent by their own people.

It had come screaming into this backwater of war, and, tearing out leaded window-panes as you would destroy cobwebs, had burst among those who already had paid the penalty. And so two of them, done with pack-drill, goose-step, half rations and forced marches, lay under the straw the priests had heaped upon them. The toes of their boots were pointed grotesquely upward. Their gray hands were clasped rigidly as though in prayer.

Half hidden in the straw, the others were as silent and almost as still. Since they had been dropped upon the stone floor they had not moved, but lay in twisted, unnatural attitudes. Only their eyes showed that they lived. These were turned beseechingly upon the French Red Cross doctors, kneeling waist-high in the straw and unreeling long white bandages. The wounded watched them drawing slowly nearer, until they came, fighting off death, clinging to life as shipwrecked sailors cling to a raft and watch the boats pulling toward them.

A young German officer, his smart cavalry cloak torn and slashed, and filthy with dried mud and blood and with his eyes in bandages, groped toward a pail of water, feeling his way with his foot, his arms outstretched, clutching the air. To guide him a priest took his arm, and the officer turned and stumbled against him. Thinking the priest was one of his own men, he swore at him, and then, to learn if he wore shoulder-straps, ran his fingers over the priest's shoulders, and, finding a silk cassock, said quickly in French: "Pardon me, my father; I am blind."

As the young *curé* guided me through the wrecked cathedral his indignation and his fear of being unjust waged a fine battle. "Every summer," he said, "thousands of your fellow countrymen visit the cathedral. They come again and again. They love these beautiful windows. They will not permit them to be destroyed. Will you tell them what you saw?"

It is no pleasure to tell what I saw. Shells had torn out some of the windows, the entire sash, glass, and stone frame—all was gone; only a jagged hole was left. On the floor lay broken carvings, pieces of stone from flying buttresses outside that had been hurled through the embrasures, tangled masses of leaden window-sashes, like twisted coils of barbed wire, and great brass candelabra. The steel ropes that supported them had been shot away, and they had plunged to the flagging below, carrying with them their scarlet silk tassels heavy with the dust of centuries. And everywhere was broken glass. Not one of the famous blue windows was intact. None had been totally destroyed, but each had been shattered, and through the apertures the sun blazed blatantly.

We walked upon glass more precious than precious stones. It was beyond price. No one can replace it. Seven hundred years ago the

THE MIDDLE PORTAL IN WEST FAÇADE,
SHOWING EFFECTS OF THE FIRE

secret of the glass died. Diamonds can be bought anywhere, pearls can be matched, but not the stained glass of Rheims. And under our feet, with straw and caked blood, it lay crushed into tiny fragments. When you held a piece of it between your eye and the sun it glowed with a light that never was on land or sea.

War is only waste. The German Emperor thinks it is thousands of men in flashing breastplates at manoeuvres, galloping past him, shouting *"Hoch der Kaiser!"* Until this year that is all of war he has ever seen.

I have seen a lot of it, and real war is his high-born officer with his eyes shot out, his peasant soldiers with their toes sticking stiffly through the straw, and the windows of Rheims, that for centuries with their beauty glorified the Lord, swept into a dust heap.

Outside the cathedral I found the bombardment of the city was still going forward and that the French batteries to the north and east were answering gun for gun. How people will act under unusual conditions no one can guess. Many of the citizens of Rheims were abandoning their homes and running through the streets leading west, trembling, weeping, incoherent with terror, carrying nothing with them. Others were continuing the routine of life with anxious faces but making no other sign. The great majority had moved to the west of the city to the Paris gate, and for miles lined the road, but had taken little or nothing with them, apparently intending to return at nightfall. They were all of the poorer class. The houses of the rich were closed, as were all the shops, except a few *cafés* and those that offered for sale bread, meat, and medicine.

During the morning the bombardment destroyed many houses. One to each block was the average, except around the cathedral, where two hotels that face it and the Palace of Justice had been pounded but not destroyed. Other shops and residences facing the cathedral had been ripped open from roof to cellar. In one a fire was burning briskly, and firemen were playing on it with hose. I was their only audience. A sight that at other times would have collected half of Rheims and blocked traffic, in the excitement of the bombardment failed to attract. The Germans were using howitzers. Where shells hit in the street they tore up the Belgian blocks for a radius of five yards, and made a hole as though a water-main had burst. When they hit a house, that house had to be rebuilt. Before they struck it was possible to follow the direction of the shells by the sound. It was like the jangling of many telegraph-wires.

A hundred yards north of the cathedral I saw a house hit at the third story. The roof was of gray slate, high and sloping, with tall chimneys. When the shell exploded the roof and chimneys disappeared. You did not see them sink and tumble; they merely vanished. They had been a part of the sky-line of Rheims; then a shell removed them and another roof fifteen feet lower down became the sky-line.

I walked to the edge of the city, to the northeast, but at the outskirts all the streets were barricaded with carts and paving-stones, and when I wanted to pass forward to the French batteries the officers in charge of the barricades refused permission. At this end of the town, held in reserve in case of a German advance, the streets were packed with infantry. The men were going from shop to shop trying to find one the Germans had not emptied. Tobacco was what they sought.

They told me they had been all the way to Belgium and back, but I never have seen men more fit. Where Germans are haggard and show need of food and sleep, the French were hard and moved quickly and were smiling.

One reason for this is that even if the commissariat is slow they are fed by their own people, and when in Belgium by the Allies. But when the Germans pass the people hide everything eatable and bolt the doors. And so, when the German supply wagons fail to come up the men starve.

I went in search of the American consul, William Bardel. Everybody seemed to know him, and all men spoke well of him. They liked him because he stuck to his post, but the mayor had sent for him, and I could find neither him nor the mayor.

When I left the cathedral I had told my chauffeur to wait near by it, not believing the Germans would continue to make it their point of attack. He waited until two houses within a hundred yards of him were knocked down, and then went away from there, leaving word with the sentry that I could find him outside the gate to Paris. When I found him he was well outside and refused to return, saying he would sleep in his car.

On the way back I met a steady stream of women and old men fleeing before the shells. Their state was very pitiful. Some of them seemed quite dazed with fear and ran, dodging, from one sidewalk to the other, and as shells burst above them prayed aloud and crossed themselves. Others were busy behind the counters of their shops serving customers, and others stood in doorways holding in their hands their knitting. Frenchwomen of a certain class always knit. If they were waiting to be electrocuted they would continue knitting.

The bombardment had grown sharper and the rumble of guns was uninterrupted, growling like thunder after a summer storm or as the shells passed shrieking and then bursting with jarring detonations. Underfoot the pavements were inch-deep with fallen glass, and as you walked it tinkled musically. With inborn sense of order, some of the housewives abandoned their knitting and calmly swept up the glass into neat piles. Habit is often so much stronger than fear. So is curiosity. All the boys and many young men and maidens were in the middle of the street watching to see where the shells struck and on the lookout for aeroplanes. When about five o'clock one sailed over the city, no one knew whether it was German or French, but everyone followed it, apparently intending if it launched a bomb to be in at the death.

I found all the hotels closed and on their doors I pounded in vain, and was planning to go back to my car when I stumbled upon the Hôtel du Nord. It was open and the proprietress, who was knitting, told me the *table-d'hôte* dinner was ready. Not wishing to miss dinner, I halted an aged citizen who was fleeing from the city and asked him to carry a note to the American consul inviting him to dine. But the aged man said the consulate was close to where the shells were falling and that to approach it was as much as his life was worth. I asked him how much his life was worth in money, and he said two *francs*.

He did not find the consul, and I shared the *table d'hôte* with three tearful old French ladies, each of whom had husband or son at the front. That would seem to have been enough without being shelled at home. It is a commonplace, but it is nevertheless true that in war it is the women who suffer. The proprietress walked around the table, still knitting, and told us tales of German officers who until the day before had occupied her hotel, and her anecdotes were not intended to make German officers popular.

The bombardment ceased at eight o'clock, but at four the next morning it woke me, and as I departed for Paris salvoes of French artillery were returning the German fire.

Before leaving I revisited the cathedral to see if during the night it had been further mutilated. Around it shells were still falling, and the square in front was deserted. In the rain the roofless houses, shattered windows, and broken carvings that littered the street presented a picture of melancholy and useless desolation. Around three sides of the square not a building was intact. But facing the wreckage the

THE CHAPEL OF THE CATHEDRAL AND ROBING-ROOM OF THE KINGS. ON THE RIGHT IS THE PALACE OF THE ARCHBISHOP, COMPLETELY GUTTED. STRETCHING BEYOND THE CHAPEL, THE CITY FOR ONE SQUARE HALF MILE WAS DESTROYED. THE PHOTOGRAPH WAS TAKEN BY E. ASHMEAD-BATLETT, FROM THE TOWER OF THE CATHEDRAL. THE LEDGE OF THE TOWER SHOWS IN THE FOREGROUND.

bronze statue of Joan of Arc sat on her bronze charger, uninjured and untouched. In her right hand, lifted high above her as though defying the German shells, someone overnight had lashed the flag of France.

The next morning the newspapers announced that the cathedral was in flames, and I returned to Rheims. The papers also gave the two official excuses offered by the Germans for the destruction of the church. One was that the French batteries were so placed that in replying to them it was impossible to avoid shelling the city.

I know where the French batteries were, and if the German guns aimed at them by error missed them and hit the cathedral, the German marksmanship is deteriorating. To find the range the artillery sends what in the American army are called brace shots—one aimed at a point beyond the mark and one short of it. From the explosions of these two shells the gunner is able to determine how far he is off the target and accordingly regulates his sights. Not more, at the most, than three of these experimental brace shots should be necessary, and, as one of each brace is purposely aimed to fall short of the target, only three German shells, or, as there were two French positions, six German shells should have fallen beyond the batteries and into the city. *And yet for four days the city was bombarded!*

To make sure, I asked French, English, and American army officers what margin of error they thought excusable after the range was determined. They all agreed that after his range was found an artillery officer who missed it by from fifty to one hundred yards ought to be court-martialled. The Germans "missed" by one mile.

The other excuse given by the Germans for the destruction of the cathedral was that the towers had been used by the French for military purposes. On arriving at Rheims the question I first asked was whether this was true. The Abbé Chinot, *curé* of the chapel of the cathedral, assured me most solemnly and earnestly it was not. The French and the German staffs, he said, had mutually agreed that on the towers of the cathedral no quick-firing guns should be placed, and by both sides this agreement was observed. After entering Rheims the French, to protect the innocent citizens against bombs dropped by German airships, for two nights placed a search-light on the towers, but, fearing this might be considered a breach of agreement as to the *mitrailleuses*, the Abbé Chinot ordered the search-light withdrawn.

Five days later, during which time the towers were not occupied and the cathedral had been converted into a hospital for the German wounded and Red Cross flags were hanging from both towers, the

Germans opened fire upon it. Had it been the search-light to which the Germans objected, they would have fired upon it when it was in evidence, not five days after it had disappeared.

When, with the Abbé Chinot, I spent the day in what is left of the cathedral, the Germans still were shelling it. Two shells fell within twenty-five yards of us. It was at that time that the photographs that illustrate this chapter were taken.

The fire started in this way. For some months the northeast tower of the cathedral had been under repair and surrounded by scaffolding. On September 19th a shell set fire to the outer roof of the cathedral, which is of lead and oak. The fire spread to the scaffolding and from the scaffolding to the wooden beams of the portals, hundreds of years old. The Abbé Chinot, young, alert, and daring, ran out upon the scaffolding and tried to cut the cords that bound it.

In other parts of the city the fire department was engaged with fire lit by the bombardment, and unaided, the flames gained upon him. Seeing this, he called for volunteers, and, under the direction of the Archbishop of Rheims, they carried on stretchers from the burning building the wounded Germans. The rescuing parties were not a minute too soon. Already from the roofs molten lead, as deadly as bullets, was falling among the wounded. The blazing doors had turned the straw on which they lay into a prairie fire.

Splashed by the molten lead and threatened by falling timbers, the priests, at the risk of their lives and limbs, carried out the wounded Germans, sixty in all.

But, after bearing them to safety, their charges were confronted with a new danger. Inflamed by the sight of their own dead, four hundred citizens having been killed by the bombardment, and by the loss of their cathedral, the people of Rheims who were gathered about the burning building called for the lives of the German prisoners. "They are barbarians," they cried. "Kill them!" Archbishop Landreaux and Abbé Chinot placed themselves in front of the wounded.

"Before you kill them," they cried, "you must first kill us."

This is not highly coloured fiction, but fact. It is more than fact. It is history, for the picture of the venerable archbishop, with his cathedral blazing behind him, facing a mob of his own people in defence of their enemies, will always live in the annals of this war and in the annals of the church.

There were other features of this fire and bombardment which the Catholic Church will not allow to be forgotten. The leaden roofs were

ABBÉ CHINOT AND FRENCH OFFICER
STANDING ON STONE ROOF OF CATHEDRAL.
THE OUTER ROOF OF LEAD AND OAK THAT WAS DESTROYED BY
SHELLS AND FIRE RESTED ON THE ARCHES AND ROSE TO THE PEAK
SHOWN IN THE BACKGROUND.

destroyed, the oak timbers that for several hundred years had supported them were destroyed, stone statues and flying buttresses weighing many tons were smashed into atoms, but not a single crucifix was touched, not one waxen or wooden image of the Virgin disturbed, not one painting of the Holy Family marred.

I saw the Gobelin tapestries, more precious than spun gold, intact, while sparks fell about them, and lying beneath them were iron bolts twisted by fire, broken rooftrees and beams still smouldering.

But the special Providence that saved the altars was not omnipotent. The windows that were the glory of the cathedral were wrecked. Through some the shells had passed, others the explosions had blown into tiny fragments. Where, on my first visit, I saw in the stained glass gaping holes, now the whole window had been torn from the walls. Statues of saints and crusader and cherubim lay in mangled fragments. The great bells, each of which is as large as the Liberty Bell in Philadelphia, that for hundreds of years for Rheims have sounded the angelus, were torn from their oak girders and melted into black masses of silver and copper, without shape and without sound. Never have I looked upon a picture of such pathos, of such wanton and wicked destruction.

The towers still stand, the walls still stand, for beneath the roofs of lead the roof of stone remained, but what is intact is a pitiful, distorted mass where once were exquisite and noble features. It is like the face of a beautiful saint scarred with vitriol.

Two days before, when I walked through the cathedral, the scene was the same as when kings were crowned. You stood where Joan of Arc received the homage of France. When I returned I walked upon charred ashes, broken stone, and shattered glass. Where once the light was dim and holy, now through great breaches in the walls rain splashed. The spirit of the place was gone.

Outside the cathedral, in the direction from which the shells came, for three city blocks every house was destroyed. The palace of the archbishop was gutted, the chapel and the robing-room of the kings were cellars filled with rubbish. Of them only crumbling walls remain. And on the south and west the *façades* of the cathedral and flying buttresses and statues of kings, angels, and saints were mangled and shapeless.

I walked over the district that had been destroyed by these accidental shots, and it stretched from the northeastern outskirts of Rheims in a straight line to the cathedral. Shells that fell short of the cathedral

Left portal, looking out from nave of cathedral. The statues surrounding this door were not placed in the niches they occupied, but were a part of the stone arch. Only one other such door exists.

for a quarter of a mile destroyed entirely three city blocks. The heart of this district is the Place Godinot. In every direction at a distance of a mile from the Place Godinot I passed houses wrecked by shells—south at the Paris gate, north at the railroad station.

There is no part of Rheims that these shells the Germans claim were aimed at French batteries did not hit. If Rheims accepts the German excuse she might suggest to them that the next time they bombard, if they aim at the city they may hit the batteries.

The Germans claim also that the damage done was from fires, not shells. But that is not the case; destruction by fire was slight. Houses wrecked by shells where there was no fire outnumbered those that were burned ten to one. In no house was there probably any other fire than that in the kitchen stove, and that had been smothered by falling masonry and tiles.

Outside the wrecked area were many shops belonging to American firms, but each of them had escaped injury. They were filled with American typewriters, sewing-machines, and cameras. A number of *cafés* bearing the sign "American Bar" testified to the nationality and tastes of many tourists.

I found our consul, William Bardel, at the consulate. He is a fine type of the German-American citizen, and, since the war began, with his wife and son has held the fort and tactfully looked after the interests of both Americans and Germans. On both sides of him shells had damaged the houses immediately adjoining. The one across the street had been destroyed and two neighbours killed.

The street in front of the consulate is a mass of fallen stone, and the morning I called on Mr. Bardel a shell had hit his neighbour's chestnut-tree, filled his garden with chestnut burrs, and blown out the glass of his windows. He was patching the holes with brown wrapping-paper, but was chiefly concerned because in his own garden the dahlias were broken. During the first part of the bombardment, when firing became too hot for him, he had retreated with his family to the corner of the street, where are the cellars of the Roderers, the champagne people. There are worse places in which to hide in than a champagne cellar.

Mr. Bardel has lived six years in Rheims and estimated the damage done to property by shells at thirty millions of dollars, and said that unless the seat of military operations was removed the champagne crop for this year would be entirely wasted. It promised to be an especially good year. The seasons were propitious, being dry when sun was needed and wet when rain was needed, but unless the grapes were gathered by the end of September the crops would be lost.

Of interest to Broadway is the fact that in Rheims, or rather in her cellars, are stored nearly fifty million bottles of champagne belonging to six of the best-known houses. Should shells reach these bottles, the high price of living in the lobster palaces will be proportionately increased.

Except for Red Cross volunteers seeking among the ruins for wounded, I found that part of the city that had suffered completely deserted. Shells still were falling and houses as yet intact, and those partly destroyed were empty. You saw pitiful attempts to save the pieces. In places, as though evictions were going forward, chairs, pictures, cooking-pans, bedding were piled in heaps. There was none to guard them; certainly there was no one so unfeeling as to disturb them.

I saw neither looting nor any effort to guard against it. In their common danger and horror the citizens of Rheims of all classes seemed drawn closely together. The manner of all was subdued and gentle, like those who stand at an open grave.

The shells played the most inconceivable pranks. In some streets the houses and shops along one side were entirely wiped out and on the other untouched. In the Rue du Cardinal du Lorraine every house was gone. Where they once stood were cellars filled with powdered stone. Tall chimneys that one would have thought a strong wind might dislodge were holding themselves erect, while the surrounding walls, three feet thick, had been crumpled into rubbish.

In some houses a shell had removed one room only, and as neatly as though it were the work of masons and carpenters. It was as though the shell had a grievance against the lodger in that particular room. The waste was appalling.

Among the ruins I saw good paintings in rags and in gardens statues covered with the moss of centuries smashed. In many places, still on the pedestal, you would see a headless Venus, or a flying Mercury chopped off at the waist.

Long streamers of ivy that during a century had crept higher and higher up the wall of some noble mansion, until they were part of it, still clung to it, although it was divided into a thousand fragments. Of one house all that was left standing was a slice of the front wall just wide enough to bear a sign reading: "This house is for sale; elegantly furnished." Nothing else of that house remained.

In some streets of the destroyed area I met not one living person.

The sculptor's studio on top of the south tower. Reading from right to left: French aviators, Abbé Chinot, Gerald Morgan, E. Ashmead-Batlett, Richard harding Davis. At the time Captain Granville Fotescue made this photograph the cathedral was being shelled.

The noise made by my feet kicking the broken glass was the only sound. The silence, the gaping holes in the sidewalk, the ghastly tributes to the power of the shells, and the complete desolation, made more desolate by the bright sunshine, gave you a curious feeling that the end of the world had come and you were the only survivor.

This impression was aided by the sight of many rare and valuable articles with no one guarding them. They were things of price that one may not carry into the next world but which in this are kept under lock and key.

In the Rue de l'Université, at my leisure, I could have ransacked shop after shop or from the shattered drawing-rooms filled my pockets. Shopkeepers had gone without waiting to lock their doors, and in houses the fronts of which were down you could see that, in order to save their lives, the inmates had fled at a moment's warning.

In one street a high wall extended an entire block, but in the centre a howitzer shell had made a breach as large as a barn door. Through this I had a view of an old and beautiful garden, on which oasis nothing had been disturbed. Hanging from the walls, on diamond-shaped lattices, roses were still in bloom, and along the gravel walks flowers of every colour raised their petals to the sunshine. On the terrace was spread a tea-service of silver and on the grass were children's toys—hoops, tennis-balls, and flat on its back, staring up wide-eyed at the shells, a large, fashionably dressed doll.

In another house everything was destroyed except the mantel over the fireplace in the drawing-room. On this stood a *terra-cotta* statuette of Harlequin. It is one you have often seen. The legs are wide apart, the arms folded, the head thrown back in an ecstasy of laughter. It looked exactly as though it were laughing at the wreckage with which it was surrounded. No one could have placed it where it was after the house fell, for the approach to it was still on fire. Of all the fantastic tricks played by the bursting shells it was the most curious.

CHAPTER 7

The Spirit of the English

When I left England for home I had just returned from France and had motored many miles in both countries. Everywhere in this greatest crisis of the century I found the people of England showing the most undaunted and splendid spirit. To their common enemy they are presenting an unbroken front. The civilian is playing his part just as loyally as the soldier, the women as bravely as the men.

They appreciate that not only their own existence is threatened, but the future peace and welfare of the world require that the military party of Germany must be wiped out. That is their burden, and with the heroic Belgians to inspire them, without a whimper or a whine of self-pity, they are bearing their burden.

Everyone in England is making sacrifices great and small. As long ago as the middle of September it was so cold along the Aisne that I have seen the French, sooner than move away from the open fires they had made, risk the falling shells. Since then it has grown much colder, and Kitchener issued an invitation to the English people to send in what blankets they could spare for the army in the field and in reserve. The idea was to dye the blankets khaki and then turn them over to the supply department. In one week, so eagerly did the people respond to this appeal, Kitchener had to publish a card stating that no more blankets were needed. He had received over half a million.

The reply to Kitchener's appeal for recruits was as prompt and generous. The men came so rapidly that the standard for enlistment was raised. That is, I believe, in the history of warfare without precedent. Nations often have lowered their requirements for enlistment, but after war was once well under way to make recruiting more difficult is new. The sacrifices are made by every class.

There is no business enterprise of any sort that has not shown itself unselfish. This is true of the greengrocery, the bank, the department store, the Cotton Exchange. Each of these has sent employees to the front, and while they are away is paying their wages and, on the chance of their return, holding their places open. Men who are not accepted as recruits are enrolled as special constables. They are those who could not, without facing ruin, neglect their business. They have signed on as policemen, and each night for four hours patrol the posts of the regular bobbies who have gone to the front.

The ingenuity shown in finding ways in which to help the army is equalled only by the enthusiasm with which these suggestions are met. Just before his death at the front, Lord Roberts called upon all racing-men, yachtsmen, and big-game shots to send him, for the use of the officers in the field, their field-glasses. The response was amazingly generous.

Other people gave their pens. The men whose names are best known to you in British literature are at the service of the government and at this moment are writing exclusively for the Foreign Office. They are engaged in answering the special pleading of the Germans and in writing monographs, appeals for recruits, explanations of why England is at war. They do not sign what they write. They are, of course, not paid for what they write. They have their reward in knowing that to direct public opinion fairly will be as effective in bringing this war to a close as is sticking bayonets into *Uhlans*.

The stage, as well as literature, has found many ways in which it can serve the army. One theatre is giving all the money taken in at the door to the Red Cross; all of them admit men in uniform free, or at half price, and a long list of actors have gone to the front. Among them are several who are well known in America. Robert Lorraine has received an officer's commission in the Royal Flying Corps, and Guy Standing in the navy. The former is reported among the wounded. Gerald du Maurier has organized a reserve battalion of actors, artists, and musicians.

There is not a day passes that the most prominent members of the theatrical world are not giving their services free to benefit performances in aid of Belgian refugees, Red Cross societies, or to some one of the funds under royal patronage. Whether their talent is to act or dance, they are using it to help along the army. Seymour Hicks and Edward Knoblauch in one week wrote a play called *England Expects*, which was an appeal in dramatic form for recruits, and each night the play was produced recruits crowded over the footlights.

The old sergeants are needed to drill the new material and cannot be spared for recruiting. And so members of Parliament and members of the cabinet travel all over the United Kingdom—and certainly these days it is united—on that service. Even the prime minister and the first lord of the admiralty, Winston Churchill, work overtime in addressing public meetings and making stirring appeals to the young men. And wherever you go you see the young men by the thousands marching, drilling, going through setting-up exercises. The public parks, golf-links, even private parks like Bedford Square, are filled with them, and in Green Park, facing the long beds of geraniums, are lines of cavalry horses and the khaki tents of the troopers.

Everyone is helping. Each day the King and Queen and Princess Mary review troops or visit the wounded in some hospital; and the day before sailing, while passing Buckingham Palace, I watched the young Prince of Wales change the guard. In a businesslike manner he was listening to the sentries repeat their orders; and in turn a young sergeant, also in a most businesslike manner, was in whispers coaching the boy officer in the proper manner to guard the home of his royal parents. Since then the young prince has gone to the front and is fighting for his country. And the King is in France with his soldiers.

As the song says, *all the heroes do not go to war*, and the warriors at the front are not the only ones this war has turned out-of-doors. The number of Englishwomen who have left their homes that the Red Cross may have the use of them for the wounded would fill a long roll of honour. Some give an entire house, like Mrs. Waldorf Astor, who has loaned to the wounded Cliveden, one of the best-known and most beautiful places on the Thames. Others can give only a room. But all over England the convalescents have been billeted in private houses and made nobly welcome.

Even the children of England are helping. The Boy Scouts, one of the most remarkable developments of this decade, has in this war scored a triumph of organization. This is equally true of the Boy Scouts in Belgium and France. In England military duties of the most serious nature have been intrusted to them. On the east coast they have taken the place of the coast guards, and all over England they are patrolling railroad junctions, guarding bridges, and carrying despatches. Even if the young men who are now drilling in the parks and the Boy Scouts never reach Berlin nor cross the Channel, the training and sense of responsibility that they are now enjoying are all for their future good.

They are coming out of this war better men, not because they

Wounded British marines leaving the trenches before Antwerp

have been taught the manual of arms, but in spite of that fact. What they have learned is much more than that. Each of them has, for an ideal, whether you call it a flag, or a king, or a geographical position on the map, offered his life, and for that ideal has trained his body and sacrificed his pleasures, and each of them is the better for it. And when peace comes his country will be the richer and the more powerful.

Chapter 8

Our Diplomats in the War Zone

When the war broke loose those persons in Europe it concerned the least were the most upset about it. They were our fellow countrymen. Even today, above the roar of shells, the crash of falling walls, forts, forests, cathedrals, above the scream of shrapnel, the sobs of widows and orphans, the cries of the wounded and dying, all over Europe, you still can hear the shrieks of the Americans calling for their lost suitcases.

For some of the American women caught by the war on the wrong side of the Atlantic the situation was serious and distressing. There were thousands of them travelling alone, chaperoned only by a man from Cook's or a letter of credit. For years they had been saving to make this trip, and had allowed themselves only sufficient money after the trip was completed to pay the ship's stewards. Suddenly they found themselves facing the difficulties of existence in a foreign land without money, friends, or credit. During the first days of mobilization they could not realize on their checks or letters. American bank-notes and Bank of England notes were refused. Save gold, nothing was of value, and everyone who possessed a gold piece, especially if he happened to be a banker, was clinging to it with the desperation of a dope fiend clutching his last pill of cocaine. We can imagine what it was like in Europe when we recall the conditions at home.

In New York, when I started for the seat of war, three banks in which for years I had kept a modest balance refused me a hundred dollars in gold, or a check, or a letter of credit. They simply put up the shutters and crawled under the bed. So in Europe, where there actually was war, the women tourists, with nothing but a worthless letter of credit between them and sleeping in a park, had every reason to be panic-stricken. But to explain the hysteria of the hundred thousand other Americans is difficult—so difficult that while they live they will still be explaining. The worst that could have happened to them was temporary discomfort offset by adventures. Of those they experienced they have not yet ceased boasting.

On August 5th, one day after England declared war, the American Government announced that it would send the *Tennessee* with a cargo of gold. In Rome and in Paris Thomas Nelson Page and Myron T. Herrick were assisting every American who applied to them, and committees of Americans to care for their fellow countrymen had been organized. All that was asked of the stranded Americans was to keep cool and, like true sports, suffer inconvenience. Around them were the French and English, facing the greatest tragedy of centuries, and meeting it calmly and with noble self-sacrifice. The men were marching to meet death, and in the streets, shops, and fields the women were taking up the burden the men had dropped.

And in the Rue Scribe and in Cockspur Street thousands of Americans were struggling in panic-stricken groups, bewailing the loss of a hatbox, and protesting at having to return home second-class. Their suffering was something terrible. In London, in the Ritz and Carlton restaurants, American refugees, loaded down with fat pearls and seated at tables loaded with fat food, besought your pity. The imperial suite, which on the fast German liner was always reserved for them, "except when Prince Henry was using it," was no longer available, and they were subjected to the indignity of returning home on a nine-day boat and in the captain's cabin. It made their blue blood boil; and the thought that their emigrant ancestors had come over in the steerage did not help a bit.

The experiences of Judge Richard William Irwin, of the Superior Court of Massachusetts, and his party, as related in the *Paris Herald*, were heartrending. On leaving Switzerland for France they were forced to carry their own luggage, all the porters apparently having selfishly marched off to die for their country, and the train was not lighted, nor did any one collect their tickets. "We have them yet!" says Judge Irwin. He makes no complaint, he does not write to the Public Service Commission about it, but he states the fact. No one came to collect his ticket, and he has it yet. Something should be done. Merely because France is at war Judge Irwin should not be condemned to go through life clinging to a first-class ticket.

In another interview Judge George A. Carpenter, of the United States Court of Chicago, takes a more cheerful view. "I can't see anything for Americans to get hysterical about," he says. "They seem to think their little delays and difficulties are more important than all the troubles of Europe. For my part, I should think these people would be glad to settle down in Paris." A wise judge!

For the hysterical Americans it was fortunate that in the embassies and consulates of the United States there were fellow country-men who would not allow a war to rattle them. When the representatives of other countries fled our people not only stayed on the job but held down the jobs of those who were forced to move away. At no time in many years have our diplomats and consuls appeared to such advantage. They deserve so much credit that the administration will undoubtedly try to borrow it. Mr. Bryan will point with pride and say: "These men who bore themselves so well were my appointments."

Some of them were. But back of them, and coaching them, were first and second secretaries and consuls-general and consuls who had been long in the service and who knew the language, the short cuts, and what ropes to pull. And they had also the assistance of every lost and strayed, past and present American diplomat who, when the war broke, was caught off his base. These were commandeered and put to work, and volunteers of the American colonies were made honorary *attachés*, and without pay toiled like fifteen-dollar-a-week bookkeepers.

In our embassy in Paris one of these latter had just finished struggling with two American women. One would not go home by way of England because she would not leave her Pomeranian in quarantine, and the other because she could not carry with her twenty-two trunks. They demanded to be sent back from Havre on a battle-ship. The volunteer diplomat bowed. "Then I must refer you to our naval *attaché*, on the first floor," he said. "Any tickets for battle-ships must come through him."

I suggested he was having a hard time.

"If we remained in Paris," he said, "we all had to help. It was a choice between volunteering to aid Mr. Herrick at the embassy or Mrs. Herrick at the American Ambulance Hospital and tending wounded *Turcos*. But between soothing terrified Americans and washing niggers, I'm sorry now I didn't choose the hospital."

In Paris there were two embassies running overtime; that means from early morning until after midnight, and each with a staff enlarged to six times the usual number. At the residence of Mr. Herrick, in the *Rue François Ier*, there was an *impromptu* staff composed chiefly

Mr. Herrick   Mr. Poincaré
The United States ambassador, Myron T. Herrick, and President Poincaré leaving the American Ambulance Hospital in Paris.

of young American bankers, lawyers, and business men. They were men who inherited, or who earned, incomes of from twenty thousand to fifty thousand a year, and all day, and every day, without pay, and certainly without thanks, they assisted their bewildered, penniless, and homesick fellow countrymen. Below them in the cellar was stored part of the two million five hundred thousand dollars voted by Congress to assist the stranded Americans. It was guarded by quick-firing guns, loaned by the French War Office, and by six petty officers from the *Tennessee*. With one of them I had been a shipmate when the *Utah* sailed from Vera Cruz. I congratulated him on being in Paris.

"They say Paris is some city," he assented, "but all I've seen of it is this courtyard. Don't tell anybody, but, on the level, I'd rather be back in Vera Cruz!"

The work of distributing the money was carried on in the chancelleries of the embassy in the Rue de Chaillot. It was entirely in the hands of American army and navy officers, twenty of whom came over on the warship with Assistant Secretary of War Breckinridge. Major Spencer Cosby, the military *attaché* of the embassy, was treasurer of the fund, and every application for aid that had not already been investigated by the civilian committee appointed by the ambassador was decided upon by the officers. Mr. Herrick found them invaluable. He was earnest in their praise. They all wanted to see the fighting; but in other ways they served their country.

As a kind of "king's messenger" they were sent to our other embassies, to the French Government at Bordeaux, and in command of expeditions to round up and convoy back to Paris stranded Americans in Germany and Switzerland. Their training, their habit of command and of thinking for others, their military titles helped them to success. By the French they were given a free road, and they were not only of great assistance to others, but what they saw of the war and of the French army will be of lasting benefit to themselves. Among them were officers of every branch of the army and navy and of the marine and aviation corps. Their reports to the War Department, if ever they are made public, will be mighty interesting reading.

The regular staff of the embassy was occupied not only with Americans but with English, Germans, and Austrians. These latter stood in a long line outside the embassy, herded by *gendarmes*. That line never seemed to grow less. Myron T. Herrick, our ambassador, was at the embassy from early in the morning until midnight. He was always smiling, helpful, tactful, optimistic. Before the war came he was already popular, and the manner in which he met the dark days, when the Germans were within fifteen miles of Paris, made him thousands of friends. He never asked any of his staff to work harder than he worked himself, and he never knocked off and called it a day's job before they did. Nothing seemed to worry or daunt him; neither the departure of the other diplomats, when the government moved to Bordeaux and he was left alone, nor the advancing Germans and threatened siege of Paris, nor even falling bombs.

Herrick was as democratic as he was efficient. For his exclusive use there was a magnificent audience-chamber, full of tapestry, ormolu brass, *Sèvres* china, and sunshine. But of its grandeur the ambassador would grow weary, and every quarter-hour he would come out into the hall crowded with waiting English and Americans. There, assisted by M. Charles, who is as invaluable to our ambassadors to France as are Frank and Edward Hodson to our ambassadors to London, he would hold an impromptu reception. It was interesting to watch the ex-governor of Ohio clear that hall and send everybody away smiling. Having talked to his ambassador instead of to a secretary, each went off content. In the hall one morning I found a noble lord of high degree chuckling with pleasure.

"This is the difference between your ambassadors and ours," he said. "An English ambassador won't let you in to see him; your American ambassador comes out to see you." However true that may be, it was extremely fortunate that when war came we should have had a man at the storm-centre so admirably efficient.

Our embassy was not embarrassed nor was it greatly helped by the presence in Paris of two other American ambassadors: Mr. Sharp, the ambassador-elect, and Mr. Robert Bacon, the ambassador that was. That at such a crisis these gentlemen should have chosen to come to Paris and remain there showed that for an ambassador tact is not absolutely necessary.

Mr. Herrick was exceedingly fortunate in his secretaries, Robert Woods Bliss and Arthur H. Frazier. Their training in the diplomatic service made them most valuable. With him, also, as a volunteer counsellor, was H. Perceval Dodge, who, after serving in diplomatic posts in six countries, was thrown out of the service by Mr. Bryan to make room for a lawyer from Danville, Ky. Dodge was sent over to assist in distributing the money voted by Congress, and Herrick, knowing his record, signed him on to help him in the difficult task of running the affairs of the embassies of four countries, three of which were at war.

Dodge, Bliss, and Frazier were able to care for these embassies because, though young in years, in the diplomatic service they have had training and experience.

In this crisis they proved the need of it. For the duties they were, and still are, called upon to perform it is not enough that a man should have edited a democratic newspaper or stumped the State for Bryan. A knowledge of languages, of foreign countries, and of foreigners, their likes and their prejudices, good manners, tact, and training may not, in the eyes of the administration, seem necessary, but, in helping the ninety million people in whose interest the diplomat is sent abroad, these qualifications are not insignificant.

One might say that Brand Whitlock, who is so splendidly holding the fort at Brussels, in the very centre of the conflict, is not a trained diplomat. But he started with an excellent knowledge of the French language, and during the eight years in which he was mayor of Toledo he must have learned something of diplomacy, responsibility, and of the way to handle men—even German military governors. He is, in fact, the right man in the right place. In Belgium all men, Belgians, Americans, Germans, speak well of him. In one night he shipped out of Brussels, in safety and comfort, five thousand Germans; and when the German army advanced upon that city it was largely due to him and to the Spanish minister, the Marquis Villalobar, that Brussels did not meet the fate of Antwerp. He has a direct way of going at things.

One day, while the Belgian Government still was in Brussels and Whitlock in charge of the German legation, the chief justice called upon him. It was suspected, he said, that on the roof of the German legation, concealed in the chimney, was a wireless outfit. He came to suggest that the American minister, representing the German interests, and the chief justice should appoint a joint commission to investigate the truth of the rumour, to take the testimony of witnesses, and make a report.

"Wouldn't it be quicker," said Whitlock, "if you and I went up on the roof and looked down the chimney?"

The chief justice was surprised but delighted. Together they clambered over the roof of the German legation. They found that the wireless outfit was a rusty weathervane that creaked.

When the government moved to Antwerp Whitlock asked permission to remain at the capital. He believed that in Brussels he could be of greater service to both Americans and Belgians. And while diplomatic corps moved from Antwerp to Ostend, and from Ostend to

Brand Whitlock, four times mayor of Toledo, and now United States minister in Brussels

Havre, he and Villalobar stuck to their posts. What followed showed Whitlock was right. Today from Brussels he is directing the efforts of the rest of the world to save the people of that city and of Belgium from death by starvation. In this he has the help of his wife, who was Miss Ella Brainerd, of Springfield, Ill., M. Gaston de Levai, a Belgian gentleman, and Miss Caroline S. Larner, who was formerly a secretary in the State Department, and who, when the war started, was on a vacation in Belgium. She applied to Whitlock to aid her to return home; instead, much to her delight, he made her one of the legation staff. His right-hand man is Hugh C. Gibson, his first secretary, a diplomat of experience. It is a pity that to the legation in Brussels no military attaché was accredited. He need not have gone out to see the war; the war would have come to him.

As it was, Gibson saw more of actual warfare than did any or all of our twenty-eight military men in Paris. It was his duty to pass frequently through the firing-lines on his way to Antwerp and London. He was constantly under fire. Three times his automobile was hit by bullets. These trips were so hazardous that Whitlock urged that he should take them. It is said he and his secretary used to toss for it. Gibson told me he was disturbed by the signs the Germans placed between Brussels and Antwerp, stating that "automobiles looking as though they were on reconnoissance" would be fired upon. He asked how an automobile looked when it was on reconnoissance.

Gibson is one of the few men who, after years in the diplomatic service, refuses to take himself seriously. He is always smiling, cheerful, always amusing, but when the dignity of his official position is threatened he can be serious enough. When he was *chargé d'affaires* in Havana a young Cuban journalist assaulted him. That journalist is still in jail. In Brussels a German officer tried to blue-pencil a cable Gibson was sending to the State Department. Those who witnessed the incident say it was like a buzz-saw cutting soft pine.

When the present administration turned out the diplomats it spared the consuls-general and consuls. It was fortunate for the State Department that it showed this self-control, and fortunate for thousands of Americans who, when the war-cloud burst, were scattered all over Europe. Our consuls rose to the crisis and rounded them up, supplied them with funds, special trains, and letters of identification, and when they were arrested rescued them from jail. Under fire from shells and during days of bombardment the American consuls in France and Belgium remained at their posts and protected the people of many nationalities confided to their care. Only one showed the white feather. He first removed himself from his post, and then was removed still farther from it by the State Department. All the other American consuls of whom I heard in Belgium, France, and England were covering themselves with glory and bringing credit to their country. Nothing disturbed their calm, and at no hour could you catch them idle or reluctant to help a fellow countryman.

Their office hours were from twelve to twelve, and each consulate had taken out an all-night license and thrown away the key. With four other Americans I was forced to rout one consul out of bed at two in the morning. He was Colonel Albert W. Swalm, of Iowa, but of late years our representative at Southampton. That port was in the military zone, and before an American could leave it for Havre it was necessary that his passport should be *viséed* in London by the French and Belgian consuls-general and in Southampton by Colonel Swalm. We arrived in Southampton at two in the morning to learn that the boat left at four, and that unless, in the interval, we obtained the autograph and seal of Colonel Swalm she would sail without us.

In the darkness we set forth to seek our consul, and we found that, difficult as it was to leave the docks by sea, it was just as difficult by land. In war time two o'clock in the morning is no hour for honest men to prowl around wharfs. So we were given to understand by very wide-awake sentries with bayonets, policemen, and enthusiastic special constables. But at last we reached the consulate and laid siege. One man pressed the electric button, kicked the door, and pounded with the knocker, others hurled pebbles at the upper windows, and the fifth stood in the road and sang: "Oh, say, can you see, by the dawn's early light?"

A policeman arrested us for throwing stones at the consular sign. We explained that we had hit the sign by accident while aiming at the windows, and that in any case it was the inalienable right of Americans, if they felt like it, to stone their consul's sign. He said he always had understood we were a free people, but, "without meaning any disrespect to you, sir, throwing stones at your consul's coat of arms is almost, as you might say, sir, making too free." He then told us Colonel Swalm lived in the suburbs, and in a taxicab started us toward him.

Scantily but decorously clad, Colonel Swalm received us, and greeted us as courteously as though we had come to present him with a loving-cup. He acted as though our pulling him out of bed at two in the morning was intended as a compliment. For affixing the seal to our passports he refused any fee. We protested that the consuls-general of other nations were demanding fees. "I know," he said, "but I have never thought it right to fine a man for being an American."

Of our ambassadors and representatives in countries in Europe other than France and Belgium I have not written, because during this war I have not visited those countries. But of them, also, all men speak well. At the last election one of them was a candidate for the United States Senate. He was not elected. The reason is obvious.

Our people at home are so well pleased with their ambassadors in Europe that, while the war continues, they would keep them where they are.

CHAPTER 9

"Under Fire"

One cold day on the Aisne, when the Germans had just withdrawn to the east bank and the Allies held the west, the French soldiers built huge bonfires and huddled around them. When the "Jack Johnsons," as they call the six-inch howitzer shells that strike with a burst of black smoke, began to fall, sooner than leave the warm fires the soldiers accepted the chance of being hit by the shells. Their officers had to order them back. I saw this and wrote of it. A friend refused to credit it. He said it was against his experience. He did not believe that, for the sake of keeping warm, men would chance being killed.

But the incident was quite characteristic. In times of war you constantly see men, and women, too, who, sooner than suffer discomfort or even inconvenience, risk death. The psychology of the thing is, I think, that a man knows very little about being dead but has a very acute knowledge of what it is to be uncomfortable. His brain is not able to grasp death but it is quite capable of informing him that his fingers are cold. Often men receive credit for showing coolness and courage in times of danger when, in reality, they are not properly aware of the danger and through habit are acting automatically. The girl in Chicago who went back into the Iroquois Theatre fire to rescue her rubber overshoes was not a heroine. She merely lacked imagination. Her mind was capable of appreciating how serious for her would be the loss of her overshoes but not being burned alive.

At the Battle of Velestinos, in the Greek-Turkish War, John F. Bass, of *The Chicago Daily News*, and myself got into a trench at the foot of a hill on which later the Greeks placed a battery. All day the Turks bombarded this battery with a cross-fire of shrapnel and rifle-bullets which did not touch our trench but cut off our return to Velestinos. Sooner than pass through this crossfire, all day we crouched in the trench until about sunset, when it came on to rain. We exclaimed with dismay. We had neglected to bring our *ponchos*. "If we don't get back to the village at once," we assured each other, "we will get wet!" So we raced through half a mile of falling shells and bullets and, before the rain fell, got under cover. Then Bass said: "For twelve hours we stuck to that trench because we were afraid if we left it we would be killed. And the only reason we ever did leave it was because we were more afraid of catching cold!"

In the same war I was in a trench with some infantrymen, one of whom never raised his head. Whenever he was ordered to fire he would shove his rifle-barrel over the edge of the trench, shut his eyes, and pull the trigger. He took no chances. His comrades laughed at him and swore at him, but he would only grin sheepishly and burrow deeper. After several hours a friend in another trench held up a bag of tobacco and some cigarette-papers and in pantomime "dared" him to come for them. To the intense surprise of every one he scrambled out of our trench and, exposed against the sky-line, walked to the other trench and, while he rolled a handful of cigarettes, drew the fire of the enemy. It was not that he was brave; he had shown that he was not. He was merely stupid. Between death and cigarettes, his mind could not rise above cigarettes.

Why the same kind of people are so differently affected by danger is very hard to understand. It is almost impossible to get a line on it. I was in the city of Rheims for three days and two nights while it was being bombarded. During that time fifty thousand people remained in the city and, so far as the shells permitted, continued about their business. The other fifty thousand fled from the city and camped out along the road to Paris. For five miles outside Rheims they lined both edges of that road like people waiting for a circus parade. With them they brought rugs, blankets, and loaves of bread, and from daybreak until night fell and the shells ceased to fall they sat in the hay-fields and along the grass gutters of the road. Some of them were most intelligent-looking and had the manner and clothes of the rich.

There was one family of five that on four different occasions on our way to and from Paris we saw seated on the ground at a place certainly five miles away from any spot where a shell had fallen. They were all in deep mourning, but as they sat in the hay-field around a wicker tea basket and wrapped in steamer-rugs they were comic. Their lives were no more valuable than those of thousands of their fellow townsfolk who in Rheims were carrying on the daily routine. These kept the shops open or in the streets were assisting the Red Cross.

One elderly gentleman told me how he had been seized by the Germans as a hostage and threatened with death by hanging. With forty other first citizens, from the 4th to the 12th of September he had been in jail. After such an experience one would have thought that between himself and the Germans he would have placed as many miles as possible, but instead he was strolling around the Place du Parvis Notre-Dame, in front of the cathedral. For the French officers who, on sightseeing bent, were motoring into Rheims from the battle line he was acting as a sort of guide. Pointing with his umbrella, he would say: "On the left is the new Palace of Justice, the *façade* entirely destroyed; on the right you see the palace of the archbishop, completely wrecked. The shells that just passed over us have apparently fallen in the garden of the Hôtel Lion d'Or." He was as cool as the conductor on a "Seeing Rheims" observation-car.

He was matched in coolness by our consul, William Bardel. The American consulate is at No. 14 Rue Kellermann. That morning a shell had hit the chestnut-tree in the garden of his neighbour, at No. 12, and had knocked all the chestnuts into the garden of the consulate. "It's an ill wind that blows nobody good," said Mr. Bardel.

In the bombarded city there was no rule as to how anyone would act. One house would be closed and barred, and the inmates would be either in their own cellar or in the caves of the nearest champagne company. To those latter they would bring books or playing-cards and, among millions of dust-covered bottles, by candle-light, would wait for the guns to cease. Their neighbours sat in their shops or stood at the doors of their houses or paraded the streets. Past them their friends were hastening, trembling with terror. Many women sat on the front steps, knitting, and with interested eyes watched their acquaintances fleeing toward the Paris gate. When overhead a shell passed they would stroll, still knitting, out into the middle of the street to see where the shell struck.

By the noise it was quite easy to follow the flight of the shells. You were tricked by the sound into almost believing you could see them. The six-inch shells passed with a whistling roar that was quite terrifying. It was as though just above you invisible telegraph-wires had jangled, and their rush through the air was like the roar that rises to the car window when two express-trains going in opposite directions pass at sixty miles an hour. When these sounds assailed them the people flying from the city would scream. Some of them, as though they had been hit, would fall on their knees. Others were sobbing and praying aloud. The tears rolled down their cheeks. In their terror there was nothing ludicrous; they were in as great physical pain as were some of the hundreds in Rheims who had been hit. And yet others of their fellow townsmen living in the same street, and with the same allotment of brains and nerves, were treating the bombardment with the indifference they would show to a summer shower.

We had not expected to spend the night in Rheims, so, with Ashmead Bartlett, the military expert of the *London Daily Telegraph*, I went into a chemist's shop to buy some soap. The chemist, seeing I was an American, became very much excited. He was overstocked with an American shaving-soap, and he begged me to take it off his hands. He would let me have it at what it cost him. He did not know where he had placed it, and he was in great alarm lest we would leave his shop before he could unload it on us. From both sides of the town French artillery were firing in salvoes, the shocks shaking the air; over the shop of the chemist shrapnel was whining, and in the street the howitzer shells were opening up subways. But his mind was intent only on finding that American shaving-soap.

I was anxious to get on to a more peaceful neighbourhood. To French soap, to soap "made in Germany," to neutral American soap I was indifferent. Had it not been for the presence of Ashmead Bartlett I would have fled. To die, even though clasping a cake of American soap, seemed less attractive than to live unwashed. But the chemist had no time to consider shells. He was intent only on getting rid of surplus stock.

The majority of people who are afraid are those who refuse to consider the doctrine of chances. The chances of their being hit may be one in ten thousand, but they disregard the odds in their favour and fix their minds on that one chance against them. In their imagination it grows larger and larger. It looms red and bloodshot, it hovers over them; wherever they go it follows, menacing, threatening, filling them with terror. In Rheims there were one hundred thousand people, and by shells one thousand were killed or wounded. The chances against were a hundred to one. Those who left the city undoubtedly thought the odds were not good enough.

Those who on account of the bombs that fell from the German aeroplanes into Paris left that city had no such excuse. The chance of any one person being hit by a bomb was one in several millions. But even with such generous odds in their favour, during the days the bomb-dropping lasted many thousands fled. They were obsessed by that one chance against them. In my hotel in Paris my landlady had her mind fixed on that one chance, and regularly every afternoon when the aeroplanes were expected she would go to bed. Just as regularly her husband would take a pair of opera-glasses and in the Rue de la Paix hopefully scan the sky.

One afternoon while we waited in front of Cook's an aeroplane sailed overhead, but so far above us that no one knew whether it was a French air-ship scouting or a German one preparing to launch a bomb. A man from Cook's, one of the interpreters, with a horrible knowledge of English, said: "Taube or not Taube; that is the question." He was told he was inviting a worse death than from a bomb. To illustrate the attitude of mind of the Parisian, there is the story of the street *gamin* who for some time, from the Garden of the Tuileries, had been watching a German aeroplane threatening the city. Finally, he exclaimed impatiently:

"Oh, throw your bomb! You are keeping me from my dinner."

A soldier under fire furnishes few of the surprises of conduct to which the civilian treats you. The soldier has no choice. He is tied by the leg, and whether the chances are even or ridiculously in his favour he must accept them. The civilian can always say, "This is no place for me," and get up and walk away. But the soldier cannot say that. He and his officers, the Red Cross nurses, doctors, ambulance-bearers, and even the correspondents have taken some kind of oath or signed some kind of contract that makes it easier for them than for the civilian to stay on the job. For them to go away would require more courage than to remain.

Indeed, although courage is so highly regarded, it seems to be of all virtues the most common. In six wars, among men of nearly every race, colour, religion, and training, I have seen but four men who failed to show courage. I have seen men who were scared, sometimes whole regiments, but they still fought on; and that is the highest courage, for they were fighting both a real enemy and an imaginary one.

There is a story of a certain politician general of our army who, under a brisk fire, turned on one of his staff and cried:

"Why, major, you are scared, sir; you are scared!"

"I am," said the major, with his teeth chattering, "and if you were as scared as I am you'd be twenty miles in the rear."

In this war the onslaughts have been so terrific and so unceasing, the artillery fire especially has been so entirely beyond human experience, that the men fight in a kind of daze. Instead of arousing fear the tumult acts as an anaesthetic. With forests uprooted, houses smashing about them, and unseen express-trains hurtling through space, they are too stunned to be afraid. And in time they become fed up on battles and to the noise and danger grow callous.

On the Aisne I saw an artillery battle that stretched for fifteen miles. Both banks of the river were wrapped in smoke; from the shells villages miles away were in flames, and two hundred yards in front of us the howitzer shells were bursting in black fumes. To this the French soldiers were completely indifferent. The hills they occupied had been held that morning by the Germans, and the trenches and fields were strewn with their accoutrement. So all the French soldiers who were not serving the guns wandered about seeking souvenirs. They had never a glance for the villages burning crimson in the bright sunlight or for the falling "Jack Johnsons."

They were intent only on finding a spiked helmet, and when they came upon one they would give a shout of triumph and hold it up for their comrades to see. And their comrades would laugh delightedly and race toward them, stumbling over the furrows. They were as happy and eager as children picking wild flowers.

It is not good for troops to sup entirely on horrors and also to breakfast and lunch on them. So after in the trenches one regiment has been pounded it is withdrawn for a day or two and kept in reserve. The English Tommies spend this period of recuperating in playing football and cards. When the English learned this they forwarded so many thousands of packs of cards to the distributing depot that the War Office had to request them not to send any more. When the English officers are granted leave of absence they do not waste their energy on football, but motor into Paris for a bath and lunch. At eight they leave the trenches along the Aisne and by noon arrive at Maxim's, Voisin's, or La Rue's. Seldom does warfare present a sharper contrast. From a breakfast of "bully" beef, eaten from a tin plate, with in their nostrils the smell of camp-fires, dead horses, and unwashed bodies, they find themselves seated on red velvet cushions, surrounded by mirrors and walls of white and gold, and spread before them the most immaculate silver, linen, and glass. And the odours that assail them are those of truffles, white wine, and "*artechant sauce mousseline.*"

It is a delight to hear them talk. The point of view of the English is so sane and fair. In risking their legs or arms, or life itself, they see nothing heroic, dramatic, or extraordinary. They talk of the war as they would of a cricket-match or a day in the hunting-field. If things are going wrong they do not whine or blame, nor when fortune smiles are they unduly jubilant. And they are so appallingly honest and frank. A piece of shrapnel had broken the arm of one of them, and we were helping him to cut up his food and pour out his Scotch and soda.

Instead of making a hero or a martyr of himself, he said confidingly: "You know, I had no right to be hit. If I had been minding my own business I wouldn't have been hit. But Jimmie was having a hell of a time on top of a hill, and I just ran up to have a look in. And the beggars got me. Served me jolly well right. What?"

I met one subaltern at La Rue's who had been given so many commissions by his brother officers to bring back tobacco, soap, and underclothes that all his money save five *francs* was gone. He still had two days' leave of absence, and, as he truly pointed out, in Paris even in war time five *francs* will not carry you far. I offered to be his banker, but he said he would first try elsewhere. The next day I met him on the *boulevards* and asked what kind of a riotous existence he found possible on five *francs*.

"I've had the most extraordinary luck," he said. "After I left you I met my brother. He was just in from the front, and I got all his money."

"Won't your brother need it?" I asked.

"Not at all," said the subaltern cheerfully. "He's shot in the legs, and they've put him to bed. Rotten luck for him, you might say, but how lucky for me!"

Had he been the brother who was shot in both legs he would have treated the matter just as light-heartedly.

One English major, before he reached his own firing-line, was hit by a bursting shell in three places. While he was lying in the American ambulance hospital at Neuilly the doctor said to him:

"This cot next to yours is the only one vacant. Would you object if we put a German in it?"

"By no means," said the major; "I haven't seen one yet."

The stories the English officers told us at La Rue's and Maxim's by contrast with the surroundings were all the more gruesome. Seeing them there it did not seem possible that in a few hours these same fit, suntanned youths in khaki would be back in the trenches, or scouting in advance of them, or that only the day before they had been dodging death and destroying their fellow men.

Maxim's, which now reminds one only of the last act of *The Mer-*

British marines in the trenches outside of Antwerp

ry Widow, was the meeting-place for the French and English officers from the front; the American military *attachés* from our embassy, among whom were soldiers, sailors, aviators, marines; the doctors and volunteer nurses from the American ambulance, and the correspondents who by night dined in Paris and by day dodged arrest and other things on the firing-line, or as near it as they could motor without going to jail. For these Maxim's was the clearing-house for news of friends and battles. Where once were the supper-girls and the ladies of the gold-mesh vanity-bags now were only men in red and blue uniforms, men in khaki, men in bandages. Among them were English lords and French princes with titles that dated from Agincourt to Waterloo, where their ancestors had met as enemies. Now those who had succeeded them, as allies, were, over a sole Marguery, discussing air-ships, armoured automobiles, and *mitrailleuses*.

At one table Arthur H. Frazier, of the American embassy, would be telling an English officer that a captain of his regiment who was supposed to have been killed at Courtrai had, like a homing pigeon, found his way to the hospital at Neuilly and wanted to be reported "safe" at Lloyds. At another table a French lieutenant would describe a raid made by the son of an American banker in Paris who is in command of an armed automobile. "He swept his gun only once—so," the Frenchman explained, waving his arm across the champagne and the broiled lobster, "and he caught a general and two staff officers. He cut them in half." Or at another table you would listen to a group of English officers talking in wonder of the Germans' wasteful advance in solid formation.

"They were piled so high," one of them relates, "that I stopped firing. They looked like gray worms squirming about in a bait-box. I can shoot men coming at me on their feet, but not a mess of arms and legs."

"I know," assents another; "when we charged the other day we had to advance over the Germans that fell the night before, and my men were slipping and stumbling all over the place. The bodies didn't give them any foothold."

"My sergeant yesterday," another relates, "turned to me and said: 'It isn't cricket. There's no game in shooting into a target as big as that. It's just murder.' I had to order him to continue firing."

They tell of it without pose or emotion. It is all in the day's work. Most of them are young men of wealth, of ancient family, cleanly bred gentlemen of England, and as they nod and leave the restaurant we know that in three hours, wrapped in a greatcoat, each will be sleeping in the earth trenches, and that the next morning the shells will wake him.

CHAPTER 10

The Waste of War

In this war, more than in other campaigns, the wastefulness is apparent. In other wars, what to the man at home was most distressing was the destruction of life. He measured the importance of the conflict by the daily lists of killed and wounded. But in those wars, except human life, there was little else to destroy. The war in South Africa was fought among hills of stone, across vacant stretches of prairie. Not even trees were destroyed, because there were no trees. In the district over which the armies passed there were not enough trees to supply the men with firewood. In Manchuria, with the Japanese, we marched for miles without seeing even a mud village, and the approaches to Port Arthur were as desolate as our Black Hills. The Italian-Turkish War was fought in the sands of a desert, and in the Balkan War few had heard of the cities bombarded until they read they were in flames. But this war is being waged in that part of the world best known to the rest of the world.

Every summer hundreds of thousands of Americans, on business or on pleasure bent, travelled to the places that now daily are being taken or retaken or are in ruins. At school they had read of these places in their history books and later had visited them. In consequence, in this war they have a personal and an intelligent interest. It is as though of what is being destroyed they were part owners.

Toward Europe they are as absentee landlords. It was their pleasure-ground and their market. And now that it is being laid low the utter wastefulness of war is brought closer to this generation than ever before. Loss of life in war has not been considered entirely wasted, because the self-sacrifice involved ennobled it. And the men who went out to war knew what they might lose. Neither when, in the pursuits of peace, human life is sacrificed is it counted as wasted. The pioneers who were killed by the Indians or who starved to death in what then were deserts helped to carry civilization from the Atlantic to the Pacific. Only ten years ago men were killed in learning to control the "horseless wagons," and now sixty-horsepower cars are driven by women and young girls. Later the air-ship took its toll of human life. Nor, in view of the possibilities of the air-ships in the future, can it be said those lives were wasted.

But, except life, there was no other waste. To perfect the automobile and the air-ship no women were driven from home and the homes destroyed. No churches were bombarded. Men in this country who after many years had built up a trade in Europe were not forced to close their mills and turn into the streets hundreds of working men and women.

It is in the by-products of the war that the waste, cruelty, and stupidity of war are most apparent. It is the most innocent who suffer and those who have the least offended who are the most severely punished. The German Emperor wanted a place in the sun, and, having decided that the right moment to seize it had arrived, declared war. As a direct result, Mary Kelly, a telephone girl at the Wistaria Hotel, in New York, is looking for work. It sounds like an O. Henry story, but, except for the name of the girl and the hotel, it is not fiction. She told me about it one day on my return to New York, on Broadway.

"I'm looking for work," she said, "and I thought if you remembered me you might give me a reference. I used to work at Sherry's and at the Wistaria Hotel. But I lost my job through the war." How the war in Europe could strike at a telephone girl in New York was puzzling; but Mary Kelly made it clear.

"The Wistaria is very popular with Southerners," she explained, "They make their money in cotton and blow it in New York. But now they can't sell their cotton, and so they have no money, and so they can't come to New York. And the hotel is run at a loss, and the proprietor discharged me and the other girl, and the bellboys are tending the switchboard. I've been a month trying to get work. But everybody gives me the same answer. They're cutting down the staff on account of the war. I've walked thirty miles a day looking for a job, and I'm nearly all in. How long do you think this war will last?" This telephone girl looking for work is a tiny by-product of war. She is only one instance of efficiency gone to waste.

The reader can think of a hundred other instances. In his own life he can show where in his pleasures, his business, in his plans for the future the war has struck at him and has caused him inconvenience, loss, or suffering. He can then appreciate how much greater are the loss and suffering to those who live within the zone of fire. In Belgium and France the vacant spaces are very few, and the shells fall among cities and villages lying so close together that they seem to touch hands. For hundreds of years the land has been cultivated, the fields, gardens, orchards tilled and lovingly cared for.

The roads date back to the days of Caesar. The stone farmhouses, as well as the stone churches, were built to endure. And for centuries, until this war came, they had endured. After the battle of Waterloo some of these stone farmhouses found themselves famous. In them Napoleon or Wellington had spread his maps or set up his cot, and until this war the farmhouses of Mont-Saint-Jean, of Caillou, of Haie-Sainte, of the Belle-Alliance remained as they were on the day of the great battle a hundred years ago. They have received no special care, the elements have not spared them nor caretakers guarded them. They still were used as dwellings, and it was only when you recognized them by having seen them on the post-cards that you distinguished them from thousands of other houses, just as old and just as well preserved, that stretched from Brussels to Liége.

But a hundred years after this war those other houses will not be shown on picture postcards. King Albert and his staff may have spent the night in them, but the next day Von Kluck and his army passed, and those houses that had stood for three hundred years were destroyed. In the papers you have seen many pictures of the shattered roofs and the streets piled high with fallen walls and lined with gaping cellars over which once houses stood. The walls can be rebuilt, but what was wasted and which cannot be rebuilt are the labour, the saving, the sacrifices that made those houses not mere walls but homes.

A house may be built in a year or rented overnight; it takes longer than that to make it a home. The farmers and peasants in Belgium had spent many hours of many days in keeping their homes beautiful, in making their farms self-supporting. After the work of the day was finished they had planted gardens, had reared fruit-trees, built arbours; under them at mealtime they sat surrounded by those of their own household. To buy the horse and the cow they had pinched and saved; to make the gardens beautiful and the fields fertile they had sweated and slaved, the women as well as the men; even the watch-dog by day was a beast of burden.

When, in August, I reached Belgium between Brussels and Liége,

British officers in trench on the Aisne

the whole countryside showed the labour of these peasants. Unlike the American farmer, they were too poor to buy machines to work for them, and with scythes and sickles in hand they cut the grain; with heavy flails they beat it. All that you saw on either side of the road that was fertile and beautiful was the result of their hard, unceasing personal effort. Then the war came, like a cyclone, and in three weeks the labour of many years was wasted. The fields were torn with shells, the grain was in flames, torches destroyed the villages, by the roadside were the carcasses of the cows that had been killed to feed the invader, and the horses were carried off harnessed to gray gun-carriages.

These were the things you saw on every side, from Brussels to the German border. The peasants themselves were huddled beneath bridges. They were like vast camps of gypsies, except that, less fortunate than the gypsy, they had lost what he neither possesses nor desires, a home. As the enemy advanced the inhabitants of one village would fly for shelter to the next, only by the shells to be whipped farther forward; and so, each hour growing in number, the refugees fled toward Brussels and the coast. They were an army of tramps, of women and children tramps, sleeping in the open fields, beneath the hayricks seeking shelter from the rain, living on the raw turnips and carrots they had plucked from the deserted vegetable gardens. The peasants were not the only ones who suffered. The rich and the noble-born were as unhappy and as homeless. They had credit, and in the banks they had money, but they could not get at the money; and when a *château* and a farmhouse are in flames, between them there is little choice.

Three hours after midnight on the day the Germans began their three days' march through Brussels I had crossed the Square Rogier to send a despatch by one of the many last trains for Ostend. When I returned to the Palace Hotel, seated on the iron chairs on the sidewalk were a woman, her three children, and two maid servants. The woman was in mourning, which was quite new, for, though the war was only a month old, many had been killed, among them her husband. The day before, at Tirlemont, shells had destroyed her *château*, and she was on her way to England.

She had around her neck two long strings of pearls, the maids each held a small handbag, her boy clasped in his arms a forlorn and sleepy fox-terrier, and each of the little girls was embracing a birdcage. In one was a canary, in the other a parrot. That was all they had saved. In their way they were just as pathetic as the peasants sleeping under the hedges. They were just as homeless, friendless, just as much in need of food and sleep, and in their eyes was the same look of fear and horror. Bernhardi tells his countrymen that war is glorious, heroic, and for a nation an economic necessity. Instead, it is stupid, unintelligent. It creates nothing; it only wastes.

If it confined itself to destroying forts and cradles of barbed wire then it would be sufficiently hideous. But it strikes blindly, brutally; it tramples on the innocent and the beautiful. It is the bull in the china shop and the mad dog who snaps at children who are trying only to avoid him. People were incensed at the destruction in Louvain of the library, the Catholic college, the Church of St. Pierre that dated from the thirteenth century. These buildings belonged to the world, and over their loss the world was rightfully indignant, but in Louvain there were also shops and manufactories, hotels and private houses. Each belonged, not to the world, but to one family. These individual families made up a city of forty-five thousand people. In two days there was not a roof left to cover one of them. The trade those people had built up had been destroyed, the "goodwill and fixings," the stock on the shelves and in the storerooms, the goods in the shop-windows, the portraits in the drawing-room, the souvenirs and family heirlooms, the love-letters, the bride's veil, the baby's first worsted shoes, and the will by which some one bequeathed to his beloved wife all his worldly goods.

War came and sent all these possessions, including the will and the worldly goods, up into the air in flames. Most of the people of Louvain made their living by manufacturing church ornaments and brewing beer. War was impartial, and destroyed both the beer and the church ornaments. It destroyed also the men who made them, and it drove the women and children into concentration camps. When first I visited Louvain it was a brisk, clean, prosperous city. The streets were spotless, the shop-windows and *cafés* were modern, rich-looking, inviting, and her great churches and Hôtel de Ville gave to the city grace and dignity. Ten days later, when I again saw it, Louvain was in darkness, lit only by burning buildings. Rows and rows of streets were lined with black, empty walls. Louvain was a city of the past, another Pompeii, and her citizens were being led out to be shot.

The fate of Louvain was the fate of Vise, of Malines, of Tirlemont, of Liége, of hundreds of villages and towns, and by the time this is printed it will be the fate of hundreds of other towns over all of Europe. In this war the waste of horses is appalling. Those that first entered Brussels with the German army had been bred and trained for the purposes of war, and they were magnificent specimens. Everyone who saw them exclaimed ungrudgingly in admiration. But by the time the army reached the approaches of Paris the forced marches had so depleted the stock of horses that for remounts the Germans were seizing all they met. Those that could not keep up were shot. For miles along the road from Meaux to Soissons and Rheims their bodies tainted the air.

They had served their purposes, and after six weeks of campaigning the same animals that in times of peace would have proved faithful servants for many years were destroyed that they might not fall into the hands of the French. Just as an artillery-man spikes his gun, the Germans on their retreat to the Aisne River left in their wake no horse that might assist in their pursuit. As they withdrew they searched each stable yard and killed the horses. In village after village I saw horses lying in the stalls or in the fields still wearing the harness of the plough, or in groups of three or four in the yard of a barn, each with a bullet-hole in its temple. They were killed for fear they might be useful.

Waste can go no further. Another example of waste were the motor- trucks and automobiles. When the war began the motor-trucks of the big department stores and manufacturers and motor-buses of London, Paris, and Berlin were taken over by the different armies. They had cost them from two thousand to three thousand dollars each, and in times of peace, had they been used for the purposes for which they were built, would several times over have paid for themselves. But war gave them no time to pay even for their tires. You saw them by the roadside, cast aside like empty cigarette-boxes. A few hours' tinkering would have set them right. They were still good for years of service. But an army in retreat or in pursuit has no time to waste in repairing motors. To waste the motor is cheaper.

Between Villers-Cotterets and Soissons the road was strewn with high-power automobiles and motor-trucks that the Germans had been forced to destroy. Something had gone wrong, something that at other times could easily have been mended. But with the French in pursuit there was no time to pause, nor could cars of such value be left to the enemy. So they had been set on fire or blown up, or allowed to drive head-on into a stone wall or over an embankment. From the road above we could see them in the field below, lying like giant turtles on their backs. In one place in the forest of Villers was a line of fifteen trucks, each capable of carrying five tons. The gasoline to feed them had become exhausted, and the whole fifteen had been set on fire. In war this is necessary, but it was none the less waste. When an army takes the field it must consider first its own safety; and to embarrass the enemy everything else must be sacrificed. It cannot consider the feelings or pockets of railroad or telegraph companies. It cannot hesitate to destroy a bridge because that bridge cost five hundred thousand dollars. And it does not hesitate.

Motoring from Paris to the front these days is a question of avoiding roads rendered useless because a broken bridge has cut them in half. All over France are these bridges of iron, of splendid masonry, some decorated with statues, some dating back hundreds of years, but now with a span blown out or entirely destroyed and sprawling in the river. All of these material things—motorcars, stone bridges, railroad-tracks, telegraph-lines—can be replaced. Money can restore them. But money cannot restore the noble trees of France and Belgium, eighty years old or more, that shaded the roads, that made beautiful the parks and forests. For military purposes they have been cut down or by artillery fire shattered into splinters. They will again grow, but eighty years is a long time to wait.

Nor can money replace the greatest waste of all—the waste in "killed, wounded, and missing." The waste of human life in this war is so enormous, so far beyond our daily experience, that disasters less appalling are much easier to understand. The loss of three people in an automobile accident comes nearer home than the fact that at the battle of Sezanne thirty thousand men were killed. Few of us are trained to think of men in such numbers—certainly not of dead men in such numbers. We have seen thirty thousand men together only during the world's series or at the championship football matches. To get an idea of the waste of this war we must imagine all of the spectators at a football match between Yale and Harvard suddenly stricken dead.

We must think of all the wives, children, friends affected by the loss of those thirty thousand, and we must multiply those thirty thousand by hundreds, and imagine these hundreds of thousands lying dead in Belgium, in Alsace-Lorraine, and within ten miles of Paris. After the Germans were repulsed at Meaux and at Sezanne the dead of both armies were so many that they lay intermingled in layers three and four deep. They were buried in long pits and piled on top of each other like cigars in a box. Lines of fresh earth so long that you mistook them for trenches intended to conceal regiments were in reality graves.

Some bodies lay for days uncovered until they had lost all human semblance. They were so many you ceased to regard them even as corpses. They had become just a part of the waste, a part of the shattered walls, uprooted trees, and fields ploughed by shells. What once had been your fellow men were only bundles of clothes, swollen and shapeless, like scarecrows stuffed with rags, polluting the air.

The wounded were hardly less pitiful. They were so many and so thickly did they fall that the ambulance service at first was not sufficient to handle them. They lay in the fields or forests sometimes for a day before they were picked up, suffering unthinkable agony. And after they were placed in cars and started back toward Paris the tortures continued. Some of the trains of wounded that arrived outside the city had not been opened in two days. The wounded had been without food or water. They had not been able to move from the positions in which in torment they had thrown themselves. The foul air had produced gangrene. And when the cars were opened the stench was so fearful that the Red Cross people fell back as though from a blow.

For the wounded Paris is full of hospitals—French, English, and American. And the hospitals are full of splendid men. Each one once had been physically fit or he would not have been passed to the front; and those among them who are officers are finely bred, finely educated, or they would not be officers. But each matched his good health, his good breeding, and knowledge against a broken piece of shell or steel bullet, and the shell or bullet won. They always will win. Stephen Crane called a wound "the red badge of courage." It is all of that. And the man who wears that badge has all my admiration. But I cannot help feeling also the waste of it. I would have a standing army for the same excellent reason that I insure my house; but, except in self-defence, no war. For war—and I have seen a lot of it—is waste. And waste is unintelligent.

CHAPTER 11

War Correspondents

The attitude of the newspaper reader toward the war correspondent who tries to supply him with war news has always puzzled me.

One might be pardoned for suggesting that their interests are the same. If the correspondent is successful, the better service he renders the reader. The more he is permitted to see at the front, the more news he is allowed to cable home, the better satisfied should be the man who follows the war through the "extras."

But what happens is the reverse of that. Never is the "constant reader" so delighted as when the war correspondent gets the worst of it. It is the one sure laugh. The longer he is kept at the base, the more he is bottled up, "deleted," censored, and made prisoner, the greater is the delight of the man at home. He thinks the joke is on the war correspondent. I think it is on the "constant reader." If, at breakfast, the correspondent fails to supply the morning paper with news, the reader claims the joke is on the news-gatherer. But if the milkman fails to leave the milk, and the baker the rolls, is the joke on the milkman and the baker or is it on the "constant reader"? Which goes hungry?

The explanation of the attitude of the "constant reader" to the reporters seems to be that he regards the correspondent as a prying busybody, as a sort of spy, and when he is snubbed and suppressed he feels he is properly punished. Perhaps the reader also resents the fact that while the correspondent goes abroad, he stops at home and receives the news at second hand. Possibly he envies the man who has a front seat and who tells him about it. And if you envy a man, when that man comes to grief it is only human nature to laugh.

You have seen unhappy small boys outside a baseball park, and one happy boy inside on the highest seat of the grand stand, who calls down to them why the people are yelling and who has struck out. Do the boys on the ground love the boy in the grand stand and are they grateful to him? No.

Does the fact that they do not love him and are not grateful to him for telling them the news distress the boy in the grand stand? No. For no matter how closely he is bottled up, how strictly censored, "deleted," arrested, searched, and persecuted, as between the man at home and the correspondent, the correspondent will always be the more fortunate. He is watching the march of great events, he is studying history in the making, and all he sees is of interest. Were it not of interest he would not have been sent to report it. He watches men acting under the stress of all the great emotions. He sees them inspired by noble courage, pity, the spirit of self-sacrifice, of loyalty, and pride of race and country.

In Cuba I saw Captain Robb Church of our army win the Medal of Honour, in South Africa I saw Captain Towse of the Scot Greys win his Victoria Cross. Those of us who watched him knew he had won it just as surely as you know when a runner crosses the home plate and scores. Can the man at home from the crook play or the home run obtain a thrill that can compare with the sight of a man offering up his life that other men may live?

When I returned to New York every second man I knew greeted me sympathetically with: "So, you had to come home, hey? They wouldn't let you see a thing." And if I had time I told him all I saw was the German, French, Belgian, and English armies in the field, Belgium in ruins and flames, the Germans sacking Louvain, in the Dover Straits dreadnoughts, cruisers, torpedo destroyers, submarines, hydroplanes; in Paris bombs falling from air-ships and a city put to bed at 9 o'clock; battle-fields covered with dead men; fifteen miles of artillery firing across the Aisne at fifteen miles of artillery; the bombardment of Rheims, with shells lifting the roofs as easily as you would lift the cover of a chafing-dish and digging holes in the streets, and the cathedral on fire; I saw hundreds of thousands of soldiers from India, Senegal, Morocco, Ireland, Australia, Algiers, Bavaria, Prussia, Scotland, saw them at the front in action, saw them marching over the whole northern half of Europe, saw them wounded and helpless, saw thousands of women and children sleeping under hedges and haystacks with on every side of them their homes blazing in flames or crashing in ruins.

That was a part of what I saw. What during the same two months did the man at home see? If he were lucky he saw the Braves win the world's series, or the Vernon Castles dance the fox trot.

British and Belgian officers arranging plans for the defence of Antwerp.

The war correspondents who were sent to this war knew it was to sound their death-knell. They knew that because the newspapers that had no correspondents at the front told them so; because the General Staff of each army told them so; because every man they met who stayed at home told them so. Instead of taking their death-blow lying down they went out to meet it. In other wars as rivals they had fought to get the news; in this war they were fighting for their professional existence, for their ancient right to stand on the firing-line, to report the facts, to try to describe the indescribable. If their death-knell sounded they certainly did not hear it. If they were licked they did not know it. In the twenty-five years in which I have followed wars, in no other war have I seen the war correspondents so well prove their right to march with armies.

The happy days when they were guests of the army, when news was served to them by the men who made the news, when Archibald Forbes and Frank Millet shared the same mess with the future *Czar* of Russia, when MacGahan slept in the tent with Skobeleff and Kipling rode with Roberts, have passed. Now, with every army the correspondent is as popular as a floating mine, as welcome as the man dropping bombs from an air-ship. The hand of everyone is against him. "Keep out! This means you!" is the way they greet him. Added to the dangers and difficulties they must overcome in any campaign, which are only what give the game its flavour, they are now hunted, harassed, and imprisoned. But the new conditions do not halt them. They, too, are fighting for their place in the sun.

I know one man whose name in this war has been signed to despatches as brilliant and as numerous as those of any correspondent, but which for obvious reasons is not given here. He was arrested by one army, kept four days in a cell, and then warned if he was again found within the lines of that army he would go to jail for six months; one month later he was once more arrested, and told if he again came near the front he would go to prison for two years. Two weeks later he was back at the front. Such a story causes the teeth of all the members of the General Staff to gnash with fury. You can hear them exclaiming: "If we caught that man we would treat him as a spy." And so unintelligent are they on the question of correspondents that they probably would.

When Orville Wright hid himself in South Carolina to perfect his flying-machine he objected to what he called the "spying" of the correspondents. One of them rebuked him. "You have discovered something," he said, "in which the whole civilized world is interested. If it is true you have made it possible for man to fly, that discovery is more important than your personal wishes. Your secret is too valuable for you to keep to yourself. We are not spies. We are civilization demanding to know if you have something that more concerns the whole world than it can possibly concern you."

As applied to war, that point of view is equally just. The army calls for your father, husband, son—calls for your money. It enters upon a war that destroys your peace of mind, wrecks your business, kills the men of your family, the man you were going to marry, the son you brought into the world. And to you the army says: "This is our war. We will fight it in our own way, and of it you can learn only what we choose to tell you. We will not let you know whether your country is winning the fight or is in danger, whether we have blundered and the soldiers are starving, whether they gave their lives gloriously or through our lack of preparation or inefficiency are dying of neglected wounds." And if you answer that you will send with the army men to write letters home and tell you, not the plans for the future and the secrets of the army, but what are already accomplished facts, the army makes reply: "No, those men cannot be trusted. They are spies."

Not for one moment does the army honestly think those men are spies. But it is the excuse nearest at hand. It is the easiest way out of a situation every army, save our own, has failed to treat with intelligence. Every army knows that there are men today acting, or anxious to act, as war correspondents who can be trusted absolutely, whose loyalty and discretion are above question, who no more would rob their army of a military secret than they would rob a till. If the army does not know that, it is unintelligent. That is the only crime I impute to any general staff—lack of intelligence.

When Captain Granville Fortescue, of the Hearst syndicate, told the French general that his word as a war correspondent was as good as that of any general in any army he was indiscreet, but he was merely stating a fact. The answer of the French general was to put him in prison. That was not an intelligent answer.

The last time I was arrested was at Romigny, by General Asebert. I had on me a three-thousand-word story, written that morning in Rheims, telling of the wanton destruction of the cathedral. I asked the General Staff, for their own good, to let the story go through. It stated only facts which I believed were they known to civilized people would cause them to protest against a repetition of such outrages. To get the story on the wire I made to Lieutenant Lucien Frechet and Major Klotz, of the General Staff, a sporting offer. For every word of my despatch they censored I offered to give them for the Red Cross of France five *francs*. That was an easy way for them to subscribe to the French wounded three thousand dollars.

To release his story Gerald Morgan, of the *London Daily Telegraph*, made them the same offer. It was a perfectly safe offer for Gerald to make, because a great part of his story was an essay on Gothic architecture. Their answer was to put both of us in the Cherche-Midi prison. The next day the censor read my story and said to Lieutenant Frechet and Major Klotz: "But I insist this goes at once. It should have been sent twenty-four hours ago."

Than the courtesy of the French officers nothing could have been more correct, but I submit that when you earnestly wish to help a man to have him constantly put you in prison is confusing. It was all very well to dissemble your love. But why did you kick me downstairs?

There was the case of Luigi Barzini. In Italy Barzini is the D'Annunzio of newspaper writers. Of all Italian journalists he is the best known. On September 18, at Romigny, General Asebert arrested Barzini, and for four days kept him in a cow stable. Except what he begged from the *gendarmes*, he had no food, and he slept on straw. When I saw him at the headquarters of the General Staff under arrest I told them who he was, and that were I in their place I would let him see all there was to see, and let him, as he wished, write to his people of the excellence of the French army and of the inevitable success of the Allies. With Italy balancing on the fence and needing very little urging to cause her to join her fortunes with France, to choose that moment to put Italian journalists in a cow yard struck me as dull.

In this war the foreign offices of the different governments have been willing to allow correspondents to accompany the army. They know that there are other ways of killing a man than by hitting him with a piece of shrapnel. One way is to tell the truth about him. In this entire war nothing hit Germany so hard a blow as the publicity given to a certain remark about a scrap of paper. But from the government the army would not tolerate any interference. It said: "Do you want us to run this war or do you want to run it?" Each army of the Allies treated its own government much as Walter Camp would treat the Yale faculty if it tried to tell him who should play right tackle.

As a result of the ban put upon the correspondents by the armies, the English and a few American newspapers, instead of sending into the field one accredited representative, gave their credentials to a dozen. These men had no other credentials. The letter each received stating that he represented a newspaper worked both ways. When arrested it helped to save him from being shot as a spy, and it was almost sure to lead him to jail. The only way we could hope to win out was through the good nature of an officer or his ignorance of the rules. Many officers did not know that at the front correspondents were prohibited.

As in the old days of former wars we would occasionally come upon an officer who was glad to see someone from the base who could tell him the news and carry back from the front messages to his friends and family. He knew we could not carry away from him any information of value to the enemy, because he had none to give. In a battle front extending one hundred miles he knew only his own tiny unit. On the Aisne a general told me the shrapnel smoke we saw two miles away on his right came from the English artillery, and that on his left five miles distant were the Canadians. At that exact moment the English were at Havre and the Canadians were in Montreal.

In order to keep at the front, or near it, we were forced to make use of every kind of trick and expedient. An English officer who was acting as a correspondent, and with whom for several weeks I shared the same automobile, had no credentials except an order permitting him to pass the policemen at the British War Office. With this he made his way over half of France. In the corner of the pass was the seal or coat of arms of the War Office. When a sentry halted him he would, with great care and with an air of confidence, unfold this permit, and with a proud smile point at the red seal. The sentry, who could not read English, would invariably salute the coat of arms of his ally, and wave us forward.

That we were with allied armies instead of with one was a great help. We would play one against the other. When a French officer halted us we would not show him a French pass but a Belgian one, or one in English, and out of courtesy to his ally he would permit us to proceed. But our greatest asset always was a newspaper. After a man has been in a dirt trench for two weeks, absolutely cut off from the entire world, and when that entire world is at war, for a newspaper he will give his shoes and his blanket.

The Paris papers were printed on a single sheet and would pack as close as banknotes. We never left Paris without several hundred of them, but lest we might be mobbed we showed only one. It was the duty of one of us to hold this paper in readiness. The man who was to show the pass sat by the window. Of all our worthless passes our rule was always to show first the one of least value. If that failed we brought out a higher card, and continued until we had reached the ace. If that proved to be a two-spot, we all went to jail.

Whenever we were halted, invariably there was the knowing individual who recognized us as newspaper men, and in order to save his country from destruction clamoured to have us hung. It was for this pest that the one with the newspaper lay in wait. And the instant the pest opened his lips our man in reserve would shove the *Figaro* at him. "Have you seen this morning's paper?" he would ask sweetly. It never failed us. The suspicious one would grab at the paper as a dog snatches at a bone, and our chauffeur, trained to our team-work, would shoot forward.

When after hundreds of delays we did reach the firing-line, we always announced we were on our way back to Paris and would convey there postal cards and letters. If you were anxious to stop in any one place this was an excellent excuse. For at once every officer and soldier began writing to the loved ones at home, and while they wrote you knew you would not be molested and were safe to look at the fighting.

It was most wearing, irritating, nerve-racking work. You knew you were on the level. In spite of the General Staff you believed you had a right to be where you were. You knew you had no wish to pry into military secrets; you knew that toward the allied armies you felt only admiration—that you wanted only to help. But no one else knew that; or cared. Every hundred yards you were halted, cross-examined, searched, put through a third degree. It was senseless, silly, and humiliating. Only a professional crook with his thumb-prints and photograph in every station-house can appreciate how from minute to minute we lived. Under such conditions work is difficult. It does not make for efficiency to know that any man you meet is privileged to touch you on the shoulder and send you to prison.

This is a world war, and my contention is that the world has a right to know, not what is going to happen next, but at least what has happened. If men have died nobly, if women and children have cruelly and needlessly suffered, if for no military necessity and without reason cities have been wrecked, the world should know that.

Those who are carrying on this war behind a curtain, who have enforced this conspiracy of silence, tell you that in their good time the truth will be known. It will not. If you doubt this, read the accounts of this war sent out from the Yser by the official "eyewitness" or "observer" of the English General Staff. Compare his amiable gossip in early Victorian phrases with the story of the same battle by Percival Phillips; with the descriptions of the fall of Antwerp by Arthur Ruhl, and the retreat to the Marne by Robert Dunn.

Some men are trained to fight, and others are trained to write. The latter can tell you of what they have seen so that you, safe at home at the breakfast table, also can see it. Any newspaper correspondent would rather send his paper news than a descriptive story. But news lasts only until you have told it to the next man, and if in this war the correspondent is not to be permitted to send the news I submit he should at least be permitted to tell what has happened in the past. This war is a world enterprise, and in it every man, woman, and child is an interested stockholder. They have a right to know what is going forward. The directors' meetings should not be held in secret.

With the French in France and Salonika

Richard Harding Davis

GENERAL SARRAIL, COMMANDING THE ALLIED ARMIES IN GREECE, MAKING HIS FIRST LANDING IN SALONIKA.

Contents

Preface	137
President Poincaré Thanks America	141
The Mud Trenches of Artois	155
The Zigzag Front of Champagne	165
From Paris to the Piræus	175
Why King Constantine is Neutral	182
With the Allies in Salonika	189
Two Boys Against an Army	209
The French-British Front in Serbia	216
Verdun and St. Mihiel	227
War in the Vosges	240
Hints For Those Who Want to Help	246
London, a Year Later	258
Letters From the Front	272

To the Memory
Of
Justus Miles Forman

Preface

This book was written during the three last months of 1915 and the first month of this year in the form of letters from France, Greece, Serbia, and England. The writer visited ten of the twelve sectors of the French front, seeing most of them from the first trench, and was also on the French-British front in the Balkans. Outside of Paris the French cities visited were Verdun, Amiens, St. Die, Arras, Chalons, Nancy, and Rheims. What he saw served to strengthen his admiration for the French army and, as individuals and as a nation, for the French people, and to increase his confidence in the ultimate success of their arms.

This success he believes would come sooner were all the fighting concentrated in Europe. To scatter the forces of the Allies in expeditions overseas, he submits, only weakens the main attack and the final victory. At the present moment, outside of her armies for defence in England and for offense in Flanders, Great Britain is supporting armies in Egypt, German East Africa, Salonika, and Mesopotamia. No one who has seen in actual being one of these vast expeditions, any one of which in the past would have commanded the interest of the entire world, can appreciate how seriously they cripple the main offensive. Each robs it of hundreds of thousands of men needed in the trenches, of the transports required to carry those men, of war-ships to convoy them, of hospital ships to mend them, of medical men, medical stores, aeroplanes, motor-trucks, ambulances, machine-guns, field-guns, siege-guns, and millions upon millions of rounds of ammunition.

Transports that from neutral ports should be carrying bully beef, grain, and munitions, are lying idle at a rent per day of many hundreds of thousands of pounds, in the harbours of Moudros, Salonika, Aden, Alexandria, in the Persian Gulf, and scattered along both coasts of

Africa. They are guarded by war-ships withdrawn from duty in the Channel and North Sea. What, in lives lost, these expeditions have cost both France and Great Britain, we know; what they have cost in millions of money, it would be impossible even to guess.

For these excursions far afield it is not the military who are responsible. There is the highest authority for believing neither General Joffre nor Lord Kitchener approves of them. They are efforts launched for political effect by loyal and well-meaning, but possibly mistaken, members of the two governments. By them these expeditions were sent forth to seize some place in the sun already held by Germany, to prevent other places falling into her hands, or in the hope of turning some neutral power into an ally. It was merely dancing to Germany's music. It postponed and weakened the main attack.

This war should be fought in France. If it is, Germany will be utterly defeated; she cannot long survive such another failure as Verdun, or even should she eventually occupy Verdun could she survive such a victory. When she no longer is a military threat all she possessed before the war, and whatever territory she has taken since she began the war, will automatically revert to the Allies. It then will be time enough to restore to Belgium, Serbia, Poland, and other rightful owners the possessions of which Germany has robbed them. If you surprise a burglar, his pockets stuffed with the family jewels, would you first attempt to recover the jewels, or to subdue the burglar? Before retrieving your possessions would it not be better strategy to wait until the burglar is down and out, and the police are adjusting the handcuffs?

In the first chapter of this book is reprinted a letter I wrote from Paris to the papers of the Wheeler Syndicate, stating that in no part of Europe was our country popular. It was a hint given from one American speaking in confidence to another, and as from one friend to another. It was not so received. To my suggestion that in Europe we are losing friends, the answer invariably was: "We should worry!" That is not a good answer. With a nation it surely should be as with the individuals who compose it. If, when an individual is told he has lost the good opinion of his friends, he sings, "I don't care, I don't care!" he exhibits only bad manners.

The other reply made to the warning was personal abuse. That also is the wrong answer. To kill the messenger of ill tidings is an ancient prerogative; but it leads nowhere. If it is true that we are losing our friends we should try to find out whose fault it is that we lost them, and our wish should be to bring our friends back.

Men of different countries of Europe repeatedly told me that all of a century must elapse before America can recover the prestige she has lost since this war began. My answer was that it was unintelligent to judge ninety million people by the acts, or lack of action, of one man, and that to recover our lost prestige will take us no longer than is required to get rid of that man. As soon as we elect a new President and a new Congress, who are not necessarily looking for trouble, but who will not crawl under the bed to avoid it, our lost prestige will return.

In the meantime, that France and her Allies succeed should be the hope and prayer of every American. The fight they are waging is for the things the real, unhyphenated American is supposed to hold most high and most dear. Incidentally, they are fighting his fight, for their success will later save him, unprepared as he is to defend himself, from a humiliating and terrible thrashing. And every word and act of his now that helps the Allies is a blow against frightfulness, against despotism, and in behalf of a broader civilization, a nobler freedom, and a much more pleasant world in which to live.

Richard Harding Davis.

April 11, 1916.

CHAPTER 1

President Poincaré Thanks America

Paris, October, 1915.

While still six hundred miles from the French coast the passengers on the *Chicago* of the French line entered what was supposed to be the war zone.

In those same waters, just as though the reputation of the Bay of Biscay was not sufficiently scandalous, two ships of the line had been torpedoed.

So, in preparation for what the captain tactfully called an "accident," we rehearsed abandoning ship.

It was like the fire-drills in our public schools. It seemed a most sensible precaution, and one that in times of peace, as well as of war, might with advantage be enforced on all passenger-ships.

In his proclamation Commandant Mace of the *Chicago* borrowed an idea from the New York Fire Department. It was the warning Commissioner Adamson prints on theatre programmes, and which casts a gloom over patrons of the drama by instructing them to look for the nearest fire-escape.

Each passenger on the *Chicago* was assigned to a life-boat. He was advised to find out how from any part of the ship at which he might be caught he could soonest reach it.

Women and children were to assemble on the boat deck by the boat to which they were assigned. After they had been lowered to the water, the men—who, meanwhile, were to be segregated on the deck below them—would descend by rope ladders.

Entrance to a boat was by ticket only. The tickets were six inches square and bore a number. If you lost your ticket you lost your life. Each of the more imaginative passengers insured his life by fastening the ticket to his clothes with a safety-pin.

Two days from land there was a full-dress rehearsal, and for the first time we met those with whom we were expected to put to sea in an open boat.

Apparently those in each boat were selected by lot. As one young doctor in the ambulance service put it: "The society in my boat is not at all congenial."

The only other persons originally in my boat were Red Cross nurses of the Post unit and infants. In trampling upon them to safety I foresaw no difficulty.

But at the dress rehearsal the purser added six dark and dangerous-looking Spaniards. It developed later that by profession they were bull-fighters. Any man who is not afraid of a bull is entitled to respect. But being cast adrift with six did not appeal.

One could not help wondering what would happen if we ran out of provisions and the bull-fighters grew hungry. I tore up my ticket and planned to swim.

Some of the passengers took the rehearsal to heart, and, all night, fully dressed, especially as to boots, tramped the deck. As the promenade-deck is directly over the cabins, not only they did not sleep but neither did anyone else.

The next day they began to see periscopes. For this they were not greatly to be blamed. The sea approach to Bordeaux is flagged with black buoys supporting iron masts that support the lights, and in the rain and fog they look very much like periscopes.

But after the passengers had been thrilled by the sight of twenty of them, they became so bored with false alarms that had a real submarine appeared they were in a mood to invite the captain on board and give him a drink.

While we still were anxiously keeping watch, a sail appeared upon the horizon. Even the strongest glasses could make nothing of it. A young, very young Frenchman ran to the bridge and called to the officers: "Gentlemen, will you please tell me what boat it is that I see?"

Had he asked the same question of an American captain while that officer was on the bridge, the captain would have turned his back. An English captain would have put him in irons.

But the French captain called down to him: "She is pilot-boat No. 28. The pilot's name is Jean Baptiste. He has a wife and four children in Bordeaux, and others in Brest and Havre. He is fifty years old and has a red nose and a wart on his chin. Is there anything else you would like to know?"

At daybreak, as the ship swept up the Gironde to Bordeaux, we had our first view of the enemy.

We had passed the vineyards and those *châteaux* the names of which every wine-card in every part of the world helps to keep famous and familiar, and had reached the outskirts of the city. Here the banks are close together, so close that one almost can hail those on shore; but there was a heavy rain and the mist played tricks.

When I saw a man in a black overcoat with the brass buttons wider apart across the chest than at the belt line, like those of our traffic police in summer-time, I thought it was a trick of the mist. Because the uniform that, by a nice adjustment of buttons, tries to broaden the shoulders and decrease the waist, is not being worn much in France. Not if a French sharpshooter sees it first.

But the man in the overcoat was not carrying a rifle on his shoulder. He was carrying a bag of cement, and from the hull of the barge others appeared, each with a bag upon his shoulder. There was no mistaking them. Nor their little round caps, high boots, and field uniforms of gray-green.

It was strange that the first persons we should see since we left the wharf at the foot of Fifteenth Street, North River, the first we should see in France, should not be French people, but German soldiers.

Bordeaux had the good taste to burn down when the architect who designed the Place de la Concorde, in Paris, and the buildings facing it was still alive; and after his designs, or those of his pupils, Bordeaux was rebuilt. So wherever you look you see the best in what is old and the smartest in what is modern.

Certainly when to that city President Poincaré and his cabinet moved the government, they gave it a resting-place that was both dignified and charming. To walk the streets and wharfs is a continual delight. One is never bored. It is like reading a book in which there are no dull pages.

Everywhere are the splendid buildings of Louis XV, statues, parks, monuments, churches, great arches that once were the outer gates, and many miles of quays redolent, not of the sea, but of the wine to which the city gives her name.

But today to walk the streets of Bordeaux saddens as well as delights. There are so many wounded. There are so many women and children all in black. It is a relief when you learn that the wounded are from different parts of France, that they have been sent to Bordeaux to recuperate and are greatly in excess of the proportion of wounded you would find in other cities.

But the women and children in black are not convalescents. Their wounds heal slowly, or not at all.

At the wharfs a white ship with gigantic American flags painted on her sides and with an American flag at the stern was unloading horses. They were for the French artillery and cavalry, but they were so glad to be free of the ship that their future state did not distress them.

Instead, they kicked joyously, scattering the sentries, who were jet-black *Turcos*. As one of them would run from a plunging horse, the others laughed at him with that contagious laugh of the darky that is the same all the world over, whether he hails from Mobile or Tangiers, and he would return sheepishly, with eyes rolling, protesting the horse was a "*boche*."

Officers, who looked as though in times of peace they might be gentlemen jockeys, were receiving the remounts and identifying the brands on the hoof and shoulder that had been made by their agents in America.

If the veterinary passed the horse, he was again marked, this time with regimental numbers, on the hoof with a branding-iron, and on the flanks with white paint. In ten days he will be given a set of shoes, and in a month he will be under fire.

Colonel Count René de Montjou, who has been a year in America buying remounts, and who returned on the *Chicago*, discovered that one of the horses was a *substitut*, and a very bad *substitut* he was. His teeth had been filed, but the French officers saw that he was all of eighteen years old.

The young American who, in the interests of the contractor, was checking off the horses, refused to be shocked. Out of the corner of his thin lips he whispered confidentially:

"Suppose he is a ringer," he protested; "suppose he is eighteen years old, what's the use of their making a holler? What's it matter how old he is, if all they're going to do with him is to get him shot?"

That night at the station, as we waited for the express to Paris, many recruits were starting for the front. There seemed to be thousands of them, all new; new sky-blue uniforms, new soup-tureen helmets, new shoes.

They were splendidly young and vigorous looking, and to the tale that France now is forced to call out only old men and boys they gave the lie. With many of them, to say farewell, came friends and family. There was one group that was all comedy, a handsome young man under thirty, his mother and a young girl who might have been his wife or sister.

They had brought him food for the journey; chocolate, a long loaf, tins of sardines, a bottle of wine; and the fun was in trying to find any pocket, bag, or haversack not already filled. They were all laughing, the little, fat mother rather mechanically, when the whistle blew.

It was one of those shrill, long-drawn whistles without which in Europe no train can start. It had a peevish, infantile sound, like the squeak of a nursery toy. But it was as ominous as though someone had fired a siege-gun.

The soldiers raced for the cars, and the one in front of me, suddenly grown grave, stooped and kissed the fat, little mother.

She was still laughing; but at his embrace and at the meaning of it, at the thought that the son, who to her was always a baby, might never again embrace her, she tore herself from him sobbing and fled—fled blindly as though to escape from her grief.

Other women, their eyes filled with sudden tears, made way, and with their fingers pressed to their lips turned to watch her.

The young soldier kissed the wife, or sister, or sweetheart, or whatever she was, sketchily on one ear and shoved her after the fleeing figure.

"*Guardez mama!*" he said.

It is the tragedy that will never grow less, and never grow old.

One who left Paris in October, 1914, and returned in October, 1915, finds her calm, confident; her social temperature only a little below normal.

A year ago the gray-green tidal wave of the German armies that threatened to engulf Paris had just been checked. With the thunder of their advance Paris was still shaken. The withdrawal of men to the front, and of women and children to Bordeaux and the coast, had left the city uninhabited. The streets were as deserted as the Atlantic City board walk in January. For miles one moved between closed shops. Along the Aisne the lines had not been dug in, and hourly from the front ambulances, carrying the wounded and French and British officers unwashed from the trenches, in mud-covered, bullet-scarred cars, raced down the echoing boulevards. In the few restaurants open, you met men who that morning had left the firing-line, and who after *déjeuner*, and the purchase of soap, cigarettes, and underclothes, by sunset would be back on the job. In those days Paris was inside the "fire-lines." War was in the air; you smelled it, saw it, heard it.

President Poincaré on a visit to the front

Today a man from Mars visiting Paris might remain here a week, and not know that this country is waging the greatest war in history. When you walk the crowded streets it is impossible to believe that within forty miles of you millions of men are facing each other in a death grip. This is so, first, because a great wall of silence has been built between Paris and the front, and, second, because the spirit of France is too alive, too resilient, occupied with too many interests, to allow any one thing, even war, to obsess it. The people of France have accepted the war as they accept the rigours of winter. They may not like the sleet and snow of winter, but they are not going to let the winter beat them. In consequence, the shop windows are again dressed in their best, the kiosks announce comedies, *revues*, operas; in the gardens of the Luxembourg the beds are brilliant with autumn flowers, and the old gentlemen have resumed their games of croquet, the Champs-Élysées swarms with baby-carriages, and at the aperitif hour on the sidewalks there are no empty chairs. At many of the restaurants it is impossible to obtain a table.

It is not the Paris of the days before the war. It is not "gay Paris." But it is a Paris going about her "business as usual." This spirit of the people awakens only the most sincere admiration. It shows great calmness, great courage, and a confidence that, for the enemy of France, must be disquieting. Work for the wounded and for the families of those killed in action and who have been left without support continues. Only now, after a year of bitter experience, it is no longer hysterical. It has been systematized, made more efficient. It is no longer the work of amateurs, but of those who by daily practise have become experts.

In Paris the signs of war are not nearly as much in evidence as the activities of peace. There are many soldiers; but, in Paris, you always saw soldiers. The only difference is that now they wear bandages, or advance on crutches. And, as opposed to these evidences of the great conflict going on only forty miles distant, are the flower markets around the Madeleine, the crowds of women in front of the jewels, furs, and *manteaux* in the Rue de la Paix.

It is not that France is indifferent to the war. But that she has faith in her armies, in her generals. She can afford to wait. She drove the enemy from Paris; she is teaching French in Alsace; in time, when Joffre is ready, she will drive the enemy across her borders. In her faith in Joffre, she opens her shops, markets, schools, theatres. It is not callousness she shows, but that courage and confidence that are the forerunners of success.

But the year of war has brought certain changes. The search-lights have disappeared. It was found that to the enemy in the air they were less of a menace than a guide. So the great shafts of light that with majesty used to sweep the skies or cut a path into the clouds have disappeared. And nearly all other lights have disappeared. Those who drive motor-cars claim the pedestrians are careless; the pedestrians protest that the drivers of motor-cars are reckless. In any case, to cross a street at night is an adventure.

Something else that has disappeared is the British soldier. A year ago he swarmed, now he is almost entirely absent. Outside of the hospital corps, a British officer in Paris is an object of interest. In their place are many Belgians, almost too many Belgians. Their new khaki uniforms are unsoiled. Unlike the French soldiers you see, few are wounded. The answer probably is that as they cannot return to their own country, they must make their home in that of their ally. And the front they defend so valiantly is not so extended that there is room for all. Meanwhile, as they wait for their turn in the trenches, they fill the *boulevards* and *cafés*.

This is not true of the French officers. The few you see are convalescents, or on leave. It is not as it was last October, when Paris was part of the war zone. Up to a few days ago, until after seven in the evening, when the work of the day was supposed to be finished, an officer was not permitted to sit idle in a *café*. And now when you see one you may be sure he is recovering from a wound, or is on the General Staff, and for a few hours has been released from duty.

It is very different from a year ago when every officer was fresh from the trenches—and, fresh is not quite the word, either—and he would talk freely to an eager, sympathetic group of the battle of the night before. Now the wall of silence stretches around Paris. By posters it is even enforced upon you. Before the late minister of war gave up his portfolio, by placards he warned all when in public places to be careful of what they said. "*Taisez-vous! Méfiez-vous. Les oreilles ennemies vous écoutent.*" "Be silent. Be distrustful. The ears of the enemies are listening." This warning against spies was placed in tramways, railroad-trains, cafés. A cartoonist refused to take the good advice seriously. His picture shows one of the women conductors in a street-car asking a passenger where he is going. The passenger points to the warning. "Silence," he says, "someone may be listening."

There are other changes. A year ago gold was king. To imagine any time or place when it is not is difficult. But today an American

TAISEZ=VOUS!
MÉFIEZ - VOUS!
Les oreilles ennemies
vous écoutent

REPRODUCTION OF PLACARD WARNING FRANCE AGAINST SPIES.

twenty-dollar bill gives you a higher rate of exchange than an American gold double-eagle. A thousand dollars in bills in Paris is worth thirty dollars more to you than a thousand dollars in gold. And to carry it does not make you think you are concealing a forty-five Colt. The decrease in value is due to the fact that you cannot take gold out of the country. That is true of every country in Europe, and of any kind of gold. At the border it is taken from you and in exchange you must accept bills. So, any one in Paris, wishing to travel, had best turn over his gold to the Bank of France. He will receive not only a good rate of exchange but also an engraved certificate testifying that he has contributed to the national defence.

Another curious vagary of the war that obtains now is the sudden disappearance of the copper *sou* or what ranks with our penny. Why it is scarce no one seems to know. The generally accepted explanation is that the copper has flown to the trenches where millions of men are dealing in small sums. But whatever the reason, the fact remains. In the stores you receive change in postage-stamps, and, on the underground railroad, where the people have refused to accept stamps in lieu of coppers, there are incipient riots. One night at a restaurant I was given change in stamps and tried to get even with the house by unloading them as his tip on the waiter. He protested eloquently. "Letters I never write," he explained. "To write letters makes me *ennui*. And yet if I wrote for a hundred years I could not use all the stamps my patrons have forced upon me."

These differences the year has brought about are not lasting, and are unimportant. The change that is important, and which threatens to last a long time, is the difference in the sentiment of the French people toward Americans.

Before the war we were not unduly flattering ourselves if we said the attitude of the French toward the United States was friendly. There were reasons why they should regard us at least with tolerance. We were very good customers. From different parts of France we imported wines and silks. In Paris we spent, some of us spent, millions on jewels and clothes. In automobiles and on Cook's tours every summer Americans scattered money from Brittany to Marseilles. They were the natural prey of Parisian hotel-keepers, restaurants, milliners, and dressmakers. We were a sister republic, the two countries swapped statues of their great men—we had not forgotten Lafayette, France honoured Paul Jones.

A year ago, in the comic papers, between John Bull and Uncle Sam, it was not Uncle Sam who got the worst of it. Then the war came and with it, in the feeling toward ourselves, a complete change. A year ago we were almost one of the Allies, much more popular than Italians, more sympathetic than the English. Today we are regarded, not with hostility, but with amazed contempt.

This most regrettable change was first brought about by President Wilson's letter calling upon Americans to be neutral. The French could not understand it. From their point of view it was an unnecessary affront. It was as unexpected as the cut direct from a friend; as unwarranted, as gratuitous, as a slap in the face. The millions that poured in from America for the Red Cross, the services of Americans in hospitals, were accepted as the offerings of individuals, not as representing the sentiment of the American people. That sentiment, the French still insist in believing, found expression in the letter that called upon all Americans to be neutral, something which to a Frenchman is neither fish, fowl, nor good red herring.

We lost caste in other ways. We supplied France with munitions, but, as a purchasing agent for the government put it to me, we are not losing much money by it, and, until the French Government protested, and the protest was printed all over the United States, some of our manufacturers supplied articles that were worthless. Doctor Charles W. Cowan, an American who in winter lives in Paris and Nice and spends his summers in America, showed me the half section of a shoe of which he said sixty thousand pairs had been ordered, until it was found that part of each shoe was made of brown paper. Certainly part of the shoe he showed me was made of brown paper.

When an entire people, men, women, and children, are fighting for their national existence, and their individual home and life, to have such evidences of Yankee smartness foisted upon them does not make for friendship. It inspired contempt. This unpleasant sentiment was strengthened by our failure to demand satisfaction for the lives lost on the *Lusitania*, while at the same time our losses in dollars seemed to distress us so deeply. But more harmful and more unfortunate than any other word or act was the statement of President Wilson that we might be "too proud to fight." This struck the French not only as proclaiming us a cowardly nation, but as assuming superiority over the man who not only would fight, but who was fighting. And as at that moment several million Frenchmen were fighting, it was natural that they should laugh. Every nation in Europe laughed. In an Italian cartoon Uncle Sam is shown, hat in hand, offering a "note" to the German Emperor and in another shooting Haitians.

The legend reads: "He is too proud to fight the *Kaiser*, but not too proud to kill niggers." In London, "Too Proud to Fight" is in the music-halls the line surest of raising a laugh, and the recruiting-stations show pictures of fat men, effeminates, degenerates, and cripples labelled: "These Are Too Proud to Fight! Are You?"

The change of sentiment toward us in France is shown in many ways. To retail them would not help matters. But as one hears of them from Americans who, since the war began, have been working in the hospitals, on distributing committees, in the banking-houses, and as diplomats and consuls, that our country is most unpopular is only too evident.

It is the greater pity because the real feeling of our people toward France in this war is one of enthusiastic admiration. Of all the Allies, Americans probably hold for the French the most hearty good-feeling, affection, and good-will. Through the government at Washington this feeling has been ill-expressed, if not entirely concealed. It is unfortunate. Mr. Kipling, whose manners are his own, has given as a toast: "Damn all neutrals." The French are more polite. But when this war is over we may find that in twelve months we have lost friends of many years. That over all the world we have lost them.

That does not mean that for the help Americans have given France and her Allies, the Allies are ungrateful. That the French certainly are not ungrateful I was given assurance by no less an authority than the President of the republic. His assurance was conveyed to the American people in a message of thanks. It is also a message of good-will.

It recognizes and appreciates the sympathy shown to France in her present fight for liberty and civilization by those Americans who remember that when we fought for our liberty France was not neutral, but sent us Lafayette and Rochambeau, ships and soldiers. It is a message of thanks from President Poincaré to those Americans who found it less easy to be neutral than to be grateful.

It was my good fortune to be presented by Paul Benazet, a close personal friend of the President, and both an officer of the army and a deputy. As a deputy before the war he helped largely in passing the bills that called for three years of military service and for heavier artillery. As an officer he won the Legion of Honour and the Cross of War. Besides being a brilliant writer, M. Benazet is also an accomplished linguist, and as President Poincaré does not express himself readily in English, and as my French is better suited to restaurants than palaces, he acted as our interpreter.

The arrival of important visitors, M. Cambon, the former ambassador to the United States, and the new prime minister, M. Briand, delayed our reception, and while we waited we were escorted through the official rooms of the Élysée. It was a half-hour of most fascinating interest, not only because the vast salons were filled with what, in art, is most beautiful, but because we were brought back to the ghosts of other days.

What we actually saw were the best of Gobelin tapestries, the best of *Sèvres* china, the best of mural paintings. We walked on silken carpets, bearing the *fleur-de-lis*. We sat on sofas of embroidery as fine as an engraving and as rich in colour as a painting by Morland. The bright autumn sunshine illuminated the ormulu brass of the First Empire, gilt eagles, crowns, cupids, and the only letter of the alphabet that always suggests one name.

Those which we brought back to the rooms in which once they lived, planned, and plotted were the ghosts of Mme. de Pompadour, Louis XVI, Murat, Napoleon I, and Napoleon III. We could imagine the first Emperor standing with his hands clasped behind him in front of the marble fireplace, his figure reflected in the full-length mirrors, his features in gold looking down at him from the walls and ceilings. We intruded even into the little room opening on the rose garden, where for hours he would pace the floor.

But, perhaps, what was of greatest interest was the remarkable adjustment of these surroundings, royal and imperial, to the simple and dignified needs of a republic.

France is a military nation and at war, but the evidences of militarism were entirely absent. Our own White House is not more empty of uniforms. One got the impression that he was entering the house of a private gentleman—a gentleman of great wealth and taste.

We passed at last through four rooms, in which were the secretaries of the President, and as we passed, the *major-domo* spoke our names, and the different gentlemen half rose and bowed. It was all so quiet, so calm, so free from telephones and typewriters, that you felt that, by mistake, you had been ushered into the library of a student or a Cabinet minister.

Then in the fourth room was the President. Outside this room we were presented to M. Sainsere, the personal secretary of the President, and without further ceremony M. Benazet opened the door, and in the smallest room of all, introduced me to M. Poincaré. His portraits have rendered his features familiar, but they do not give sufficiently the impression I received of kindness, firmness, and dignity.

He returned to his desk and spoke in a low voice of peculiar charm. As though the better to have the stranger understand, he spoke slowly, selecting his words.

"I have a great admiration," he said, "for the effectiveness with which Americans have shown their sympathy with France. They have sent doctors, nurses, and volunteers to drive the ambulances to carry the wounded. I have visited the hospitals at Neuilly and other places; they are admirable.

"The one at Juilly was formerly a college, but with ingenuity they have converted it into a hospital, most complete and most valuable. The American colony in Paris has shown a friendship we greatly appreciate. Your ambassador I have met several times. Our relations are most pleasant, most sympathetic."

I asked if I might repeat what he had said. The President gave his assent, and, after a pause, as though, now that he knew he would be quoted, he wished to emphasize what he had said, continued:

"My wife, who distributes articles of comfort, sent to the wounded and to families in need, tells me that Americans are among the most generous contributors. Many articles come anonymously—money, clothing, and comforts for the soldiers, and layettes for their babies. We recognize and appreciate the manner in which, while preserving a strict neutrality, your country men and women have shown their sympathy."

The President rose and on leaving I presented a letter from ex-President Roosevelt. It was explained that this was the second letter for him I had had from Colonel Roosevelt, but that when I was a prisoner with the Germans, I had judged it wise to swallow the first one, and that I had requested Colonel Roosevelt to write the second one on thin paper. The President smiled and passed the letter critically between his thumb and forefinger.

"This one," he said, "is quite digestible."

I carried away the impression of a kind and distinguished gentleman, who, in the midst of the greatest crisis in history, could find time to dictate a message of thanks to those he knew were neutrals only in name.

CHAPTER 2

The Mud Trenches of Artois

Amiens, October, 1915.

In England it is "business as usual"; in France it is "war as usual." The English tradesman can assure his customers that with such an "old-established" firm as his not even war can interfere; but France, with war actually on her soil, has gone further and has accepted war as part of her daily life. She has not merely swallowed, but digested it. It is like the line in Pinero's play, where one woman says she cannot go to the opera because of her neuralgia. Her friend replies: "You can have neuralgia in my box as well as anywhere else." In that spirit France has accepted the war. The neuralgia may hurt, but she does not take to her bed and groan. Instead, she smiles cheerfully and goes about her duties—even sits in her box at the opera.

As we approached the front this was even more evident than in Paris, where signs of war are all but invisible. Outside of Amiens we met a regiment of Scots with the pipes playing and the cold rain splashing their bare legs. To watch them we leaned from the car window. That we should be interested seemed to surprise them; no one else was interested. A year ago when they passed it was "Roses, roses, all the way"—or at least cigarettes, chocolate, and red wine. Now, in spite of the skirling bagpipes, no one turned his head; to the French they had become a part of the landscape.

A year ago the roads at every two hundred yards were barricaded. It was a continual hurdle-race. Now, except at distances of four or five miles, the barricades have disappeared. One side of the road is reserved for troops, the other for vehicles. The vehicles we met—for the most part two-wheeled hooded carts—no longer contained peasants flying from dismantled villages. Instead, they were on the way to market with garden-truck, pigs, and calves. On the drivers' seat the peasant whistled cheerily and cracked his whip. The long lines of London buses, that last year advertised soap, mustard, milk, and music-halls, and which now are a decorous gray; the ambulances; the great guns drawn by motor-trucks with caterpillar wheels, no longer surprise him.

The English ally has ceased to be a stranger, and in the towns and villages of Artois is a "paying guest." It is for him the shop-windows are dressed. The names of the towns are Flemish; the names of the streets are Flemish; the names over the shops are Flemish; but the goods for sale are marmalade, tinned kippers, *The Daily Mail*, and the *Pink 'Un*.

"Is it your people who are selling these things?" I asked an English officer.

The question amused him.

"Our people won't think of it until the war is over," he said, "but the French are different.

"They are capable, adaptable, and obliging. If one of our men asks these shopkeepers for anything they haven't got they don't say, 'We don't keep it'; they get him to write down what it is he wants, and send for it."

It is the better way. The Frenchman does not say, "War is ruining me"; he makes the war help to support him, and at the same time gives comfort to his ally.

A year ago in the villages the old men stood in disconsolate groups with their hands in their pockets. Now they are briskly at work. They are working in the fields, in the vegetable-gardens, helping the Territorials mend the roads. On every side of them were the evidences of war—in the fields abandoned trenches, barbed-wire entanglements, shelters for fodder and ammunition, hangars for repairing aeroplanes, vast slaughter-houses, parks of artillery; and on the roads endless lines of lorries, hooded ambulances, marching soldiers.

To us those were of vivid interest, but to the French peasant they are in the routine of his existence. After a year of it war neither greatly distresses nor greatly interests him. With one hand he fights; with the other he ploughs.

We had made a bet as to which would see the first sign of real war, and the sign of it that won and that gave general satisfaction, even to the man who lost, was a group of German soldiers sweeping the streets of St. Pol. They were guarded only by one of their own number, and they looked fat, sleek, and contented. When, on our return from the trenches, we saw them again, we knew they were to be greatly envied. Between standing waist-high in mud in a trench and being drowned in it, buried in it, blown up or asphyxiated, the post of crossing-sweeper becomes a sinecure.

The next sign of war was more thrilling. It was a race between a French aeroplane and German shrapnel. To us the bursting shells looked like five little cotton balls. Since this war began shrapnel, when it bursts, has invariably been compared to balls of cotton, and as that is exactly what it looks like, it is again so described. The balls of cotton did not seem to rise from the earth, but to pop suddenly out of the sky.

A moment later five more cotton balls popped out of the sky. They were much nearer the aeroplane. Others followed, leaping after it like the spray of succeeding waves. But the aeroplane steadily and swiftly conveyed itself out of range and out of sight.

To say where the trenches began and where they ended is difficult. We were passing through land that had been retrieved from the enemy. It has been fought for inch by inch, foot by foot. To win it back thousands of lives had been thrown like dice upon a table. There were vast stretches of mud, of fields once cultivated, but now scarred with pits, trenches, rusty barbed-wires. The roads were rivers of clay. They were lined with dugouts, cellars, and caves. These burrows in the earth were supported by beams, and suggested a shaft in a disused mine. They looked like the tunnels to coal-pits. They were inhabited by a race of French unknown to the boulevards—men, bearded, deeply tanned, and caked with clay. Their uniforms were like those of football players on a rainy day at the end of the first half.

We were entering what had been the village of Ablain, and before us rose the famous heights of Mont de Lorette. To scale these heights seemed a feat as incredible as scaling our Palisades or the sheer cliff of Gibraltar. But they had been scaled, and the side toward us was crawling with French soldiers, climbing to the trenches, descending from the trenches, carrying to the trenches food, ammunition, and fuel for the fires.

A cold rain was falling and had turned the streets of Ablain and all the roads to it into swamps. In these were islands of bricks and lakes of water of the solidity and colour of melted chocolate. Whatever you touched clung to you. It was a land of mud, clay, liquid earth. A cold wind whipped the rain against your face and chilled you to the bone. All you saw depressed and chilled your spirit.

To the *poilus*, who, in the face of such desolation, joked and laughed with the civilians, you felt you owed an apology, for your automobile was waiting to whisk you back to a warm dinner, electric lights, red wine, and a dry bed. The men we met were cavemen. When night came they would sleep in a hole in the hill fit for a mud-turtle or a muskrat.

They moved in streets of clay two feet across. They were as far removed from civilization, as in the past they have known it, as though they had been cast adrift upon an island of liquid mud. Wherever they looked was desolation, ruins, and broken walls, jumbles of bricks, tunnels in mud, caves in mud, graves in mud.

In other wars the "front" was something almost human. It advanced, wavered, and withdrew. At a single bugle-call it was electrified. It remained in no fixed place, but, like a wave, enveloped a hill, or with galloping horses and cheering men overwhelmed a valley. In comparison, this trench work did not suggest war. Rather it reminded you of a mining-camp during the spring freshet, and for all the attention the cavemen paid to them, the reports of their "seventy-fives" and the "Jack Johnsons" of the enemy bursting on Mont de Lorette might have come from miners blasting rock.

What we saw of these cave-dwellers was only a few feet of a moat that for three hundred miles like a miniature canal is cut across France. Where we stood we could see of the three hundred miles only mud walls, so close that we brushed one with each elbow. By looking up we could see the black, leaden sky. Ahead of us the trench twisted, and an arrow pointed to a first-aid dressing-station. Behind us was the winding entrance to a shelter deep in the earth, reinforced by cement and corrugated iron, and lit by a candle.

From a trench that was all we could see of the war, and that is all millions of fighting men see of it—wet walls of clay as narrow as a grave, an arrow pointing to a hospital, earthen steps leading to a shelter from sudden death, and overhead the rain-soaked sky and perhaps a great bird at which the enemy is shooting snowballs.

In northern France there are many buried towns and villages. They are buried in their own cellars. Arras is still uninterred. She is the corpse of a city that waits for burial, and day by day the German shells are trying to dig her grave. They were at it yesterday when we visited Arras, and this morning they will be hammering her again.

Seven centuries before this war Arras was famous for her tapestries, so famous that in England a piece of tapestry was called an arras. Now she has given her name to a battle—to different battles—that began with the great bombardment of October a year ago, and each day since then have continued. On one single day, June 26, the Germans threw into the city shells in all sizes, from three to sixteen inches, and to the number of ten thousand. That was about one for each house.

This bombardment drove 2,700 inhabitants into exile, of whom 1,200 have now returned. The army feeds them, and in response they have opened shops that the shells have not already opened, and supply the soldiers with tobacco, postcards, and from those gardens not hidden under bricks and cement, fruit and vegetables. In the deserted city these civilians form an inconspicuous element. You can walk for great distances and see none of them. When they do appear in the empty streets they are like ghosts. Every day the shells change one or two of them into real ghosts. But the others still stay on. With the dogs nosing among the fallen bricks, and the pigeons on the ruins of the cathedral, they know no other home.

As we entered Arras the silence fell like a sudden change of temperature. It was actual and menacing. Every corner seemed to threaten an ambush. Our voices echoed so loudly that unconsciously we spoke in lower tones. The tap of the captain's walking-stick resounded like the blow of a hammer. The emptiness and stillness was like that of a vast cemetery, and the grass that had grown through the paving-stones deadened the sound of our steps. This silence was broken only by the barking of the French seventy-fives, in parts of the city hidden to us, the boom of the German guns in answer, and from overhead by the aeroplanes. In the absolute stillness the whirl of their engines came to us with the steady vibrations of a loom.

In the streets were shell holes that had been recently filled and covered over with bricks and fresh earth. It was like walking upon newly made graves. On either side of us were gaping cellars into which the houses had dumped themselves or, still balancing above them, were walls prettily papered, hung with engravings, paintings, mirrors, quite intact. These walls were roofless and defenceless against the rain and snow. Other houses were like those toy ones built for children, with the front open. They showed a bed with pillows, shelves supporting candles, books, a washstand with basin and pitcher, a piano, and a reading-lamp.

In one house four stories had been torn away, leaving only the attic sheltered by the peaked roof. To that height no one could climb, and exposed to view were the collection of trunks and boxes familiar to all attics. As a warning against rough handling, one of these, a woman's

"OF ANOTHER HOUSE THE ROOF ONLY REMAINED, FROM UNDER IT THE REST OF THE BUILDING HAD BEEN SHOT AWAY."

hat-box, had been marked "Fragile." Secure and serene, it smiled down sixty feet upon the mass of iron and bricks it had survived.

Of another house the roof only remained; from under it the rest of the building had been shot away. It was as though after a soldier had been blown to pieces, his helmet still hung suspended in mid-air.

In other streets it was the front that was intact, but when our captain opened the street door we faced a cellar. Nothing beside remained. Or else we stepped upon creaky floors that sagged, through rooms swept by the iron brooms into vast dust heaps. From these protruded wounded furniture—the leg of a table, the broken arm of a chair, a headless statue.

From the *débris* we picked the many little heirlooms, souvenirs, possessions that make a home. Photographs with written inscriptions, postcards bearing good wishes, ornaments for the centre-table, ornaments for the person, images of the church, all crushed, broken, and stained. Many shop-windows were still dressed invitingly as they were when the shell burst, but beyond the goods exposed for sale was only a deep hole.

The pure deviltry of a shell no one can explain. Nor why it spares a looking-glass and wrecks a wall that has been standing since the twelfth century.

In the cathedral the stone roof weighing hundreds of tons had fallen, and directly beneath where it had been hung an enormous glass chandelier untouched. A shell loves a shining mark. To what is most beautiful it is most cruel. The Hôtel de Ville, which was counted among the most presentable in the north of France, that once rose in seven arches in the style of the Renaissance, the shells marked for their own.

And all the houses approaching it from the German side they destroyed. Not even those who once lived in them could say where they stood. There is left only a mess of bricks, tiles, and plaster. They suggest the homes of human beings as little as does a brickyard.

We visited what had been the headquarters of General de Wignacourt. They were in the garden of a house that opened upon one of the principal thoroughfares, and the floor level was twelve feet under the level of the flower-beds. To this subterranean office there are two entrances, one through the cellar of the house, the other down steps from the garden. The steps were beams the size of a railroad-tie. Had they not been whitewashed they would look like the shaft leading to a coal-pit.

THE STONE ROOF OVER THIS GLASS CHANDELIER IN THE ARRAS CATHEDRAL WAS DESTROYED BY SHELLS, AND THE CHANDELIER NOT TOUCHED

A soldier who was an artist in plaster had decorated the entrance to the shaft with an ornamental façade worthy of any public building. Here, secure from the falling walls and explosive shells, the general by telephone directed his attack. The place was as dry, as clean, and as compact as the admiral's quarters on a ship of war. The switchboard connected with batteries buried from sight in every part of the unburied city, and in an adjoining room a soldier cook was preparing a most appetizing luncheon.

Above us was three yards of cement, rafters, and earth, and crowning them grass and flowers. When the owner of the house returns he will find this addition to his residence an excellent refuge from burglars or creditors.

Personally we were glad to escape into the open street. Between being hit by a shell and buried under twelve feet of cement the choice was difficult.

We lunched in a charming house, where the table was spread in the front hall. The bed of the officer temporarily occupying the house also was spread in the hall, and we were curious to know, but too proud to ask, why he limited himself to such narrow quarters. Our captain rewarded our reticence. He threw back the heavy curtain that concealed the rest of the house, and showed us that there was no house. It had been deftly removed by a shell.

The owner of the house had run away, but before he fled, fearing the Germans might enter Arras and take his money, he had withdrawn it and hidden it in his garden. The money amounted to two hundred and fifty thousand dollars. He placed it in a lead box, soldered up the opening, and buried the box under a tree. Then he went away and carelessly forgot *which* tree.

During a lull in the bombardment, he returned, and until two o'clock in the morning dug frantically for his buried treasure. The soldier who guarded the house told me the difference in the way the soldiers dig a trench and the way our absent host dug for his lost money was greatly marked. I found the leaden box cast aside in the dog-kennel. It was the exact size of a suitcase. As none of us knows when he may not have to bury a quarter of a million dollars hurriedly, it is a fact worth remembering. Any ordinary suitcase will do. The soldier and I examined the leaden box carefully. But the owner had not overlooked anything.

When we reached the ruins of the cathedral, we did not need darkness and falling rain to depress us further, or to make the scene more desolate. One lacking in all reverence would have been shocked. The wanton waste, the senseless brutality in such destruction would have moved a statue. Walls as thick as the ramparts of a fort had been blown into powdered chalk. There were great breaches in them through which you could drive an omnibus. In one place the stone roof and supporting arches had fallen, and upon the floor, where for two hundred years the people of Arras had knelt in prayer, was a mighty barricade of stone blocks, twisted candelabra, broken praying-chairs, torn vestments, shattered glass. Exposed to the elements, the chapels were open to the sky. The rain fell on sacred emblems of the Holy Family, the saints, and apostles. Upon the altars the dust of the crushed walls lay inches deep.

The destruction is too great for present repair. They can fill the excavations in the streets and board up the shattered show-windows, but the cathedral is too vast, the destruction of it too nearly complete. The sacrilege must stand. Until the war is over, until Arras is free from shells, the ruins must remain uncared for and uncovered. And the cathedral, by those who once came to it for help and guidance, will be deserted.

But not entirely deserted. The pigeons that built their nests under the eaves have descended to the empty chapels, and in swift, graceful circles sweep under the ruined arches. Above the dripping of the rain, and the surly booming of the cannon, their contented cooing was the only sound of comfort. It seemed to hold out a promise for the better days of peace.

CHAPTER 3

The Zigzag Front of Champagne

Paris, October, 1915.

In Artois we were "personally conducted." In a way, we were the guests of the war department; in any case, we tried to behave as such. It was no more proper for us to see what we were not invited to see than to bring our own wine to another man's dinner.

In Champagne it was entirely different. I was alone with a car and a chauffeur and a blue slip of paper. It permitted me to remain in a "certain place" inside the war zone for ten days. I did not believe it was true. I recalled other trips over the same roads a year before which finally led to the Cherche-Midi prison, and each time I showed the blue slip to the *gendarmes* I shivered. But the gendarmes seemed satisfied, and as they permitted us to pass farther and farther into the forbidden land, the chauffeur began to treat me almost as an equal. And so, with as little incident as one taxis from Madison Square to Central Park, we motored from Paris into the sound of the guns.

At the "certain place" the general was absent in the trenches, but the chief of staff asked what I most wanted to see. It was as though the fairy godmother had given you one wish. I chose Rheims, and to spend the night there. The chief of staff waved a wand in the shape of a second piece of paper, and we were in Rheims. To a colonel we presented the two slips of paper, and, in turn, he asked what was wanted. A year before I had seen the cathedral when it was being bombarded, when it still was burning. I asked if I might revisit it.

"And after that?" said the colonel.

It was much too good to be real.

I would wake and find myself again in Cherche-Midi prison.

Outside, the sounds of the guns were now very close. They seemed to be just around the corner, on the roof of the next house.

"Of course, what I really want is to visit the first trench."

It was like asking a Mason to reveal the mysteries of his order, a priest to tell the secrets of the confessional. The colonel commanded the presence of Lieutenant Blank. With alarm I awaited his coming. Did a military prison yawn, and was he to act as my escort? I had been too bold. I should have asked to see only the third trench.

At the order the colonel gave, Lieutenant Blank expressed surprise. But his colonel, with a shrug, as though ridding himself of all responsibility, showed the blue slip. It was a pantomime, with which by repetition, we became familiar. In turn each officer would express surprise; the other officer would shrug, point to the blue slip, and we would pass forward.

The cathedral did not long detain us. Outside, for protection, it was boarded up, packed tightly in sand-bags; inside, it had been swept of broken glass, and the paintings, tapestries, and the carved images on the altars had been removed. A professional sacristan spoke a set speech, telling me of things I had seen with my own eyes—of burning rafters that spared the Gobelin tapestries, of the priceless glass trampled underfoot, of the dead and wounded Germans lying in the straw that had given the floor the look of a barn. Now it is as empty of decoration as the Pennsylvania railroad-station in New York. It is a beautiful shell waiting for the day to come when the candles will be relit, when the incense will toss before the altar, and the gray walls glow again with the colours of tapestries and paintings. The windows only will not bloom as before. The glass destroyed by the Emperor's shells, all the king's horses and all the king's men cannot restore.

The professional guide, who is already so professional that he is exchanging German cartridges for tips, supplied a morbid detail of impossible bad taste. Among the German wounded there was a major (I remember describing him a year ago as looking like a college professor) who, when the fire came, was one of these the priests could not save, and who was burned alive. Marks on the gray surface of a pillar against which he reclined and grease spots on the stones of the floor are supposed to be evidences of his end, a torture brought upon him by the shells of his own people.

Mr. Kipling has written that there are many who "hope and pray these signs will be respected by our children's children." Mr. Kipling's hope shows an imperfect conception of the purposes of a cathedral. It is a house dedicated to God, and on earth to peace and good-will among men. It is not erected to teach generations of little children to gloat over the fact that an enemy, even a German officer, was by accident burned alive.

Personally, I feel the sooner those who introduced "frightfulness" to France, Belgium, and the coasts of England are hunted down and destroyed the better. But the stone-mason should get to work, and remove those stains from the Rheims cathedral. Instead, for our children's children, would not a tablet to Edith Cavell be better, or one to the French priest, Abbé Thinot, who carried the wounded Germans from the burning cathedral, and who later, while carrying French wounded from the field of battle, was himself hit three times, and of his wounds died?

I hinted to the lieutenant that the cathedral would remain for some time, but that the trenches would soon be ploughed into turnip-beds.

So, we moved toward the trenches. The officer commanding them lived in what he described as the deck of a battleship sunk underground. It was a happy simile. He had his conning-tower, in which, with a telescope through a slit in a steel plate, he could sweep the countryside. He had a fire-control station, executive offices, wardroom, cook's galley, his own cabin, equipped with telephones, electric lights, and running water. There was a carpet on the floor, a gay coverlet on the four-poster bed, photographs on his dressing-table, and flowers. All of these were buried deep underground. A puzzling detail was a perfectly good brass lock and key on his door. I asked if it were to keep out shells or burglars. And he explained that the door with the lock in tact had been blown off its hinges in a house of which no part was now standing. He had borrowed it, as he had borrowed everything else in the subterranean war-ship, from the near-by ruins.

He was an extremely light-hearted and courteous host, but he frowned suspiciously when he asked if I knew a correspondent named Senator Albert Beveridge. I hastily repudiated Beveridge. I knew him not, I said, as a correspondent, but as a politician who possibly had high hopes of the German vote. "He dined with us," said the colonel, "and then wrote against France." I suggested it was at their own risk if they welcomed those who already had been with the Germans, and who had been received by the German Emperor. This is no war for neutrals.

Then began a walk of over a mile through an open drain. The walls were of chalk as hard as flint. Unlike the mud trenches in Artois, there were no slides to block the miniature canal. It was as firm and compact as a whitewashed stone cell. From the main drain on either side ran other drains, *cul-de-sacs*, cellars, trap-doors, and ambushes. Overhead hung balls of barbed-wire that, should the French troops withdraw, could be dropped and so block the trench behind them. If you raised your head they playfully snatched off your cap. It was like ducking under innumerable bridges of live wires.

The drain opened at last into a wrecked town. Its ruins were complete. It made Pompeii look like a furnished flat. The officer of the day joined us here, and to him the lieutenant resigned the post of guide. My new host wore a steel helmet, and at his belt dangled a mask against gas. He led us to the end of what had been a street, and which was now barricaded with huge timbers, steel doors, like those to a gambling house, intricate cat's cradles of wire, and solid steel plates.

To go back seemed the only way open. But the officer in the steel cap dived through a slit in the iron girders, and as he disappeared, beckoned. I followed down a well that dropped straight into the very bowels of the earth. It was very dark, and only crosspieces of wood offered a slippery footing. Into the darkness, with hands pressed against the well, and with feet groping for the log steps, we tobogganed down, down, down. We turned into a tunnel, and, by the slant of the ground, knew we were now mounting. There was a square of sunshine, and we walked out, and into a graveyard. It was like a dark change in a theatre. The last scene had been the ruins of a town, a gate like those of the Middle Ages, studded with bolts, reinforced with steel plates, guarded by men-at-arms in steel *casques*, and then the dark change into a graveyard, with grass and growing flowers, gravel walks, and hedges.

The graves were old, the monuments and urns above them moss-covered, but one was quite new, and the cross above it said that it was the grave of a German aviator. As they passed it the French officers saluted. We entered a trench as straight as the letter Z. And at each twist and turn we were covered by an eye in a steel door. An attacking party advancing would have had as much room in which to dodge that eye as in a bath-tub. One man with his magazine rifle could have halted a dozen. And when in the newspapers you read that one man has captured twenty prisoners, he probably was looking at them through the peep-hole in one of those steel doors.

We zigzagged into a cellar, and below the threshold of some one's front door. The trench led directly under it. The house into which the door had opened was destroyed; possibly those who once had entered by it also were destroyed, and it now swung in air with men crawling like rats below it, its half-doors banging and groaning; the wind, with ghostly fingers, opening them to no one, closing them on nothing. The trench wriggled through a garden, and we could see flung across the narrow strip of sky above us, the branch of an apple-tree, and with one shoulder brushed the severed roots of the same tree. Then the trench led outward, and we passed beneath railroad tracks, the ties reposing on air, and supported by, instead of supporting, the iron rails.

We had been moving between garden walls, cellar walls; sometimes hidden by ruins, sometimes diving like moles into tunnels. We remained on no one level, or for any time continued in any one direction. It was entirely fantastic, entirely unreal. It was like visiting a new race of beings, who turn day into night; who, like bats, molochs, and wolves, hide in caves and shun the sunlight.

By the ray of an electric torch we saw where these underground people store their food. Where, against siege, are great casks of water, dungeons packed with ammunition, more dungeons, more ammunition. We saw, always by the shifting, pointing finger of the electric torch, sleeping quarters underground, dressing stations for the wounded underground. In niches at every turn were gas-extinguishers. They were as many, as much as a matter of course, as fire-extinguishers in a modern hotel. They were exactly like those machines advertised in seed catalogues for spraying fruit-trees. They are worn on the back like a knapsack. Through a short rubber hose a fluid attacks and dissipates the poison gases.

The sun set, and we proceeded in the light of a full moon. It needed only this to give to our journey the unreality of a nightmare. Long since I had lost all sense of direction. It was not only a maze and labyrinth, but it held to no level. At times, concealed by walls of chalk, we walked erect, and then, like woodchucks, dived into earthen burrows. For a long distance we crawled, bending double through a tunnel. At intervals lamps, as yet unlit, protruded from either side, and to warn us of these from the darkness a voice would call, "attention à gauche," "attention à droite." The air grew foul and the pressure on the ear-drums like that of the subway under the North River. We came out and drew deep breaths as though we had been long under water.

We were in the first trench. It was, at places, from three hundred to forty yards distant from the Germans. No one spoke, or only in whispers. The moonlight turned the men at arms into ghosts. Their silence added to their unreality. I felt like Rip Van Winkle hemmed in by the goblin crew of Hendrik Hudson. From somewhere near us, above or below, to the right or left the "seventy-fives," as though aroused by the moon, began like terriers to bark viciously. The officer in the steel *casque* paused to listen, fixed their position, and named them. How he knew where they were, how he knew where he was himself, was all part of the mystery. Rats, jet black in the moonlight, scurried across the open places, scrambled over our feet, ran boldly between them. We had scared them, perhaps, but not half so badly as they scared me.

We pushed on past sentinels, motionless, silent, fatefully awake. The moonlight had turned their blue uniforms white and flashed on their steel helmets. They were like men in armour, and so still that only when you brushed against them, cautiously as men change places in a canoe, did you feel they were alive. At times, one of them thinking something in the gardens of barb-wire had moved, would loosen his rifle, and there would be a flame and flare of red, and then again silence, the silence of the hunter stalking a wild beast, of the officer of the law, gun in hand, waiting for the breathing of the burglar to betray his presence.

The next morning I called to make my compliments to General Franchet d'Espéray. He was a splendid person—as alert as a steel lance. He demanded what I had seen.

"Nothing!" he protested. "You have seen nothing. When you return from Serbia, come to Champagne again and I myself will show you something of interest."

I am curious to see what he calls "something of interest."

"I wonder what's happening in Buffalo?"

There promised to be a story for someone to write a year after the war. It would tell how quickly Champagne recovered from the invasion of the Germans. But one need not wait until after the war. The story can be written now.

We know that the enemy was thrown back across the Aisne.

We know that the enemy drove the French and English before him until at the Forest of Montmorency, the Hun was within ten and at Claye within fifteen miles of Paris.

But today, by any outward evidence, he would have a hard time to prove it. And that is not because when he advanced he was careful not to tramp on the grass or to pick the flowers. He did not obey even the warnings to automobilists: "Attention *les enfants!*"

On the contrary, as he came, he threw before him thousands of tons of steel and iron. Like a cyclone he uprooted trees, unroofed houses; like a tidal wave he excavated roads that had been built by the

General Franchet d'Espéray.
"He was a splendid person, as alert as a steel lance."

Romans, swept away walls, and broke the backs of stone bridges that for hundreds of years had held their own against swollen rivers.

A year ago I followed the German in his retreat from Claye through Meaux, Château Thierry to Soissons, where, on the east bank of the Aisne, I watched the French artillery shell his guns on the hills opposite. The French then were hot upon his heels. In one place they had not had time to remove even their own dead, and to avoid the bodies in the open road the car had to twist and turn.

Yesterday, coming back to Paris from the trenches that guard Rheims, I covered the same road. But it was not the same. It seemed that I must surely have lost the way. Only the iron signs at the crossroads, and the map used the year before and scarred with my own pencil marks, were evidences that again I was following mile by mile and foot by foot the route of that swift advance and riotous retreat.

A year before the signs of the retreat were the road itself, the houses facing it, and a devastated countryside. You knew then, that, of these signs, some would at once be effaced. They had to be effaced, for they were polluting the air. But until the villagers returned to their homes, or to what remained of their homes, the bloated carcasses of horses blocked the road, the bodies of German soldiers, in death mercifully unlike anything human and as unreal as fallen scarecrows, sprawled in the fields.

But while you knew these signs of the German raid would be removed, other signs were scars that you thought would be long in healing. These were the stone arches and buttresses of the bridges, dynamited and dumped into the mud of the Marne and Ourcq, *châteaux* and villas with the roof torn away as deftly as with one hand you could rip off the lid of a cigar-box, or with a wall blown in, or out, in either case exposing indecently the owner's bedroom, his wife's *boudoir*, the children's nursery.

Other signs of the German were villages with houses wrecked, the humble shops sacked, garden walls levelled, fields of beets and turnips uprooted by his shells, or where he had snatched sleep in the trampled mud, strewn with demolished haystacks, vast trees split clean in half as though by lightning, or with nothing remaining but the splintered stump. That was the picture of the roads and countryside in the triangle of Soissons, Rheims, and Meaux, as it was a year ago.

And I expected to see the wake of that great retreat still marked by ruins and devastation.

But I had not sufficiently trusted to the indomitable spirit of the

French, in their intolerance of waste, their fierce, yet ordered energy.

Today the fields are cultivated up to the very butts of the French batteries. They are being put to bed, and tucked in for the long winter sleep. For miles the furrows stretch over the fields in unbroken lines. Ploughs, not shells, have drawn them.

They are gray with fertilizers, strewn with manure; the swiftly dug trenches of a year ago have given way to the peaked mounds in which turnips wait transplanting. Where there were vast stretches of mud, scarred with intrenchments, with the wheel tracks of guns and ammunition carts, with stale, ill-smelling straw, the carcasses of oxen and horses, and the bodies of men, is now a smiling landscape, with miles of growing grain, green vegetables, green turf.

In Champagne the French spirit and nature, working together, have wiped out the signs of the German raid. It is as though it had never been. You begin to believe it was only a bad dream, an old wife's tale to frighten children.

The car moved slowly, but, look no matter how carefully, it was most difficult to find the landfalls I remembered.

Near Feret Milton there was a *château* with a lawn that ran to meet the Paris road. It had been used as a German emergency hospital, and previously by them as an outpost. The long windows to the terrace had been wrecked, the terrace was piled high with bloodstained uniforms, hundreds of boots had been tossed from an upper story that had been used as an operating-room, and mixed with these evidences of disaster were monuments of empty champagne-bottles.

That was the picture I remembered. Yesterday, like a mantle of moss, the lawn swept to the road, the long windows had been replaced and hung with yellow silk, and, on the terrace, where I had seen the blood-stained uniforms, a small boy, maybe the son and heir of the *château*, with hair flying and bare legs showing, was joyfully riding a tricycle.

Neufchelles I remembered as a village completely wrecked and inhabited only by a very old man, and a cat, that, as though for company, stalked behind him.

But today Neufchelles is a thriving, contented, commonplace town. Splashes of plaster, less weather-stained than the plaster surrounding them, are the only signs remaining of the explosive shells. The stone-mason and the plasterer have obliterated the work of the guns, the tiny shops have been refilled, the tide of life has flowed back, and in the streets the bareheaded women, their shoulders wrapped in black woollen shawls, gather to gossip, or, with knitting in hand, call to each other from the doorways.

There was the stable of a large villa in which I had seen five fine riding-horses lying on the stones, each with a bullet-hole over his temple. In the retreat they had been destroyed to prevent the French using them as remounts.

This time, as we passed the same stable-yard, fresh horses looked over the half-doors, the lofts were stuffed with hay; in the corner, against the coming of winter, were piled many cords of wood, and rival *chanticleers*, with their *harems*, were stalking proudly around the stable-yard, pecking at the scattered grain. It was a picture of comfort and content. It continued like that all the way.

Even the giant poplars that line the road for four miles out of Meaux to the west, and that had been split and shattered, are now covered with autumn foliage, the scars are overgrown and by doctor nature the raw spots have been cauterized and have healed.

The stone bridges, that at Meaux and beyond the Château Thierry sprawled in the river, again have been reared in air. People have already forgotten that a year ago to reach Soissons from Meaux the broken bridges forced them to make a *détour* of fifty miles.

The lesson of it is that the French people have no time to waste upon post mortems. With us, fifty years after the event, there are those who still talk of Sherman's raid through Columbia, who are so old that they hum hymns of hate about it. How much wiser, how much more proud, is the village of Neufchelles!

Not fifty, but only one year has passed since the Germans wrecked Neufchelles, and already it has been rebuilt and repopulated—not after the war has for half a century been at an end, but while war still endures, while *it is but twenty miles distant!* What better could illustrate the spirit of France or better foretell her final victory?

CHAPTER 4

From Paris to the Piræus

Athens, November, 1915.

At home we talk glibly of a world war. But beyond speculating in munitions and as to how many Americans will be killed by the next submarine, and how many notes the President will write about it, we hardly appreciate that this actually is a war of the world, that all over the globe, every ship of state, even though it may be trying to steer a straight course, is being violently rocked by it. Even the individual, as he moves from country to country, is rocked by it, not violently, but continuously. It is in loss of time and money he feels it most. And as he travels, he learns, as he cannot learn from a map, how far-reaching are the ramifications of this war, in how many different ways it affects everyone. He soon comes to accept whatever happens as directly due to the war—even when the deck steward tells him he cannot play shuffle-board because, owing to the war, there is no chalk.

In times of peace to get to this city from Paris did not require more than six days, but now, owing to the war, in making the distance we wasted fifteen. That is not counting the time in Paris required by the police to issue the passport, without which no one can leave France. At the prefecture of police I found a line of people—French, Italians, Americans, English—in columns of four and winding through gloomy halls, down dark stairways, and out into the street. I took one look at the line and fled to Mr. Thackara, our consul-general, and, thanks to him, was not more than an hour in obtaining my *laisser-passer*. The police assured me I might consider myself fortunate, as the time they usually spent in preparing a passport was two days.

It was still necessary to obtain a *visé* from the Italian consulate permitting me to enter Italy, from the Greek consulate to enter Greece, and, as my American passport said nothing of Serbia, from Mr. Thackara two more *visés*, one to get out of France, and another to invade Serbia. Thanks to the war, in obtaining all these autographs two more days were wasted. In peace times one had only to go to Cook's and buy a ticket. In those days there was no more delay than in reserving a seat for the theatre.

War followed us south. The windows of the wagon-lit were plastered with warnings to be careful, to talk to no strangers; that the enemy was listening. War had invaded even Aix-les-Bains, most lovely of summer pleasure-grounds. As we passed, it was wrapped in snow; the Cat's Tooth, that towers between Aixe and Chambéry, and that lifts into the sky a great cross two hundred feet in height, was all white, the pine-trees around the lake were white, the streets were white, the Casino des Fleurs, the Cercle, the hotels. And above each of them, where once was only good music, good wines, beautiful flowers, and *baccarat*, now droop innumerable Red Cross flags. Against the snow-covered hills they were like little splashes of blood.

War followed us into Italy. But from the war as one finds it in England and France it differed. Perhaps we were too far west, but except for the field uniforms of green and the new scabbards of gun-metal, and, at Turin, four aeroplanes in the air at the same time, you might not have known that Italy was one of the Allies. For one thing, you saw no wounded. Again, perhaps, it was because we were too far south and west, and that the fighting in Tyrol is concentrated. But Bordeaux is farther from the battle-line of France than is Naples from the Italian front, and the multitudes of wounded in Bordeaux, the multitudes of women in black in Bordeaux, make one of the most appalling, most significant pictures of this war. In two days in Naples I did not see one wounded man. But I saw many Germans and German signs, and no one had scratched Mumm off the wine-card. A country that is one of the Allies, and yet not at war with Germany, cannot be taken very seriously. Indeed, in England the War Office staff speak of the Italian *communiqués* as the "weather reports."

In Naples the foreigners accuse Italy of running with the hare and the hounds. They asked what is her object in keeping on friendly terms with the bitterest enemy of the Allies. Is there an understanding that after the war she and Germany will together carve slices off of Austria? Whatever her ulterior object may be, her present war spirit does not impress the visitor. It is not the spirit of France and England. One man said to me: "Why can't you keep the Italian-Americans in America? Over there they earn money, and send millions of it to Italy.

When they come here to fight, not only that money stops, but we have to feed and pay them."

It did not sound grateful. Nor as though Italy were seriously at war. You do not find France and England, or Germany, grudging the man who returns to fight for his country his rations and pay. And Italy pays her soldiers five cents a day. Many of the reservists and volunteers from America who answered the call to arms are bitterly disappointed. It was their hope to be led at once to the firing-line. Instead, after six months, they are still in camp. The families some brought with them are in great need. They are not used to living on five cents a day. An Italian told me the heaviest drain upon the war-relief funds came from the families of these Italian-Americans, stranded in their own country. He also told me his chief duty was to meet them on their arrival.

"But haven't they money when they arrive from America?" I asked.

"That's it," he said *naïvely*. "I'm at the wharf to keep their countrymen from robbing them of it."

At present in Europe you cannot take gold out of any country that is at war. As a result, gold is less valuable than paper, and when I exchanged my double-eagles for paper I lost.

On the advice of the wisest young banker in France I changed, again at a loss, the French paper into Bank of England notes. But when I arrived in Salonika I found that with the Greeks English banknotes were about as popular as English troops, and that had I changed my American gold into American notes, as was my plan, I would have been passing rich. That is what comes of associating with bankers.

At the Italian frontier, a French gentleman had come to the door of the compartment, raised his hat to the inmates, and asked if we had any gold. Forewarned, we had not; and, taking our word for it, he again raised his hat and disappeared. But, on leaving Naples, it was not like that. In these piping times of war your baggage is examined when you depart as well as when you arrive. You get it coming and going. But the Greek steamer was to weigh anchor at noon, and at noon all the port officials were at *déjeuner*; so, sooner than wait a week for another boat, the passengers went on board and carried their bags with them. It was unpardonable.

It was an affront the port officials could not brook. They had been disregarded. Their dignity had been flouted. What was worse, they had not been tipped. Into the dining-saloon of the Greek steamer, where we were at luncheon, they burst like Barbary pirates. They shrieked, they yelled. Nobody knew who they were, or what they wanted. Nor did they enlighten us. They only beat upon the tables, clanked their swords, and spoiled our lunch. Why we were abused, or of what we were accused, we could not determine. We vaguely recognized our names, and stood up, and, while they continued to beat upon the tables, a Greek steward explained they wanted our gold. I showed them my bank-notes, and was allowed to return to my garlic and veal. But the English cigarette king, who each week sends some millions of cigarettes to the Tommies in the trenches, proposed to make a test case of it.

"I have on me," he whispered, "four English sovereigns. I am not taking them out of Italy, because until they crossed the border in my pocket, they were not in Italy, and as I am now leaving Italy, one might say they have never been in Italy. It's as though they were in bond. I am a British subject, and this is not Italian, but British, gold. I shall refuse to surrender my four sovereigns. I will make it a test case."

The untipped port officials were still jangling their swords, so I advised the cigarette king to turn in his gold. Even a Greek steamer is better than an Italian jail.

"I will make of it a test case," he repeated.

"Let George do it," I suggested.

At that moment, in the presence of all the passengers, they were searching the person of another British subject, and an Ally. He was one of Lady Paget's units. He was in uniform, and, as they ran itching fingers over his body, he turned crimson, and the rest of us, pretending not to witness his humiliation, ate ravenously of goat's cheese.

The cigarette king, breathing defiance, repeated: "I will make of it a test case."

"Better let George do it," I urged.

And when his name was called, a name that is as well known from Kavalla to Smyrna in tobacco-fields, sweetmeat shops, palaces, and mosques, as at the Ritz and the Gaiety, the cigarette king wisely accepted for his four sovereigns Italian *lire*. At their rate of exchange, too.

Later, off Capri, he asked: "When you advised me to let George make a test case of it, to which of our fellow passengers did you refer?"

In the morning the *Adriaticus* picked up the landfall of Messina, but, instead of making fast to the quay, anchored her length from it. This appeared to be a port regulation. It enables the boatman to earn a living by charging passengers two *francs* for a round trip of fifty yards. As the wrecked city seems to be populated only by boatmen, rowing passengers ashore is the chief industry.

The stricken seaport looks as though as recently as last week the German army had visited it. In France, although war still continues, towns wrecked by the Germans are already rebuilt. But Messina, after four years of peace, is still a ruin. But little effort has been made to restore it. The postcards that were printed at the moment of the earthquake show her exactly as she is today. With, in the streets, no sign of life, with the inhabitants standing idle along the quay, shivering in the rain and snow, with for a background crumbling walls, gaping cellars, and hills buried under acres of fallen masonry, the picture was one of terrible desolation, of neglect and inefficiency.

The only structures that had obviously been erected since the earthquake were the "ready-to-wear" shacks sent as a stop-gap from America. One should not look critically at a gift-house, but they are certainly very ugly. In Italy, where every spot is a "location" for moving-pictures, where the street corners are backgrounds for lovers' trysts and assassinations, where even poverty is picturesque, and each landscape "composes" into a beautiful and wondrous painting, the zinc shacks, in rigid lines, like the barracks of a mining-camp, came as a shock.

Sympathetic Americans sent them as only a temporary shelter until Messina rose again. But it was explained, as there is no rent to pay, the Italians, instead of rebuilding, prefer to inhabit the ready-to-wear houses. How many tourists the mere view of them will drive away no one can guess.

People who linger in Naples, and by train to Reggio join the boat at Messina, never admit that they followed that route to avoid being seasick. Seasickness is an illness of which no one ever boasts. He may take pride in saying: "I've an awful cold!" or "I've such a headache I can't see!" and will expect you to feel sorry. But he knows, no matter how horribly he suffers from *mal de mer*, he will receive no sympathy. In a *Puck* and *Punch* way he will be merely comic. So, the passengers who come over the side at Messina always have an excuse other than that they were dodging the sea. It is usually that they lost their luggage at Naples and had to search for it. As the Italian railroads, which are operated by the government, always lose your luggage, it is an admirable excuse. So, also, is the one that you delayed in order to visit the ruins of Pompeii. The number of people who have visited Pompeii solely because the Bay of Naples was in an ugly mood will never be counted.

Among those who joined at Messina were the French princess, who talked American much too well to be French, and French far too well to be an American, two military *attachés*, the King's messenger, and the Armenian, who was by profession an olive merchant, and by choice a manufacturer and purveyor of rumours. He was at once given an opportunity to exhibit his genius. The Italians held up our ship, and would not explain why. So the rumour man explained. It was because Greece had joined the Germans, and Italy had made a prize of her. Ten minutes later, he said Greece had joined the Allies, and the Italians were holding our ship until they could obtain a convoy of torpedo-boats. Then it was because two submarines were waiting for us outside the harbour. Later, it was because the Allies had blockaded Greece, and our Greek captain would not proceed, not because he was detained by Italians, but by fear.

Every time the rumour man appeared in the door of the smoking-room he was welcomed with ironic cheers. But he was not discouraged. He would go outside and stand in the rain while he hatched a new rumour, and then, in great excitement, dash back to share it. War levels all ranks, and the passengers gathered in the smoking-room playing solitaire, sipping muddy Turkish coffee, and discussing the war in seven languages, and everybody smoked—especially the women. Finally the military *attachés*, Sir Thomas Cunningham and Lieutenant Boulanger, put on the uniforms of their respective countries and were rowed ashore to protest. The rest of us paced the snow-swept decks and gazed gloomily at the wrecked city. Out of the fog a boat brought two Sisters of the Poor, wrapped in the black cloaks of their order. They were petitioners for the poor of Messina, and everybody in the smoking-room gave them a *franc*. Because one of them was Irish and because it was her fate to live in Messina, I gave her ten *francs*. Meaning to be amiable, she said: "Ah, it takes the English to be generous!"

I said I was Irish.

The King's messenger looked up from his solitaire and, also wishing to be amiable, asked: "What's the difference?"

The Irish sister answered him.

"Nine *francs*," she said.

After we had been prisoners of war for twenty-four hours John Bass of the Chicago *Daily News* suggested that if we remained longer at Messina our papers would say we thought the earthquake was news, and had stopped to write a story about it. So, we sent a telegram to our consul.

The American consul nearest was George Emerson Haven at Catania, by train three hours distant. We told him for twenty-four hours we had been prisoners, and that unless we were set free he was to declare war on Italy. The telegram was written not for the consul to read, but for the benefit of the port authorities. We hoped it might impress them. We certainly never supposed they would permit our ultimatum to reach Mr. Haven. In any case, the ship was allowed to depart. But whether the commandant of the port was alarmed by our declaration of war, or the unusual spectacle of the British *attaché*, "Tommy" Cunningham, in khaki while three hundred miles distant from any firing-line, we will never know.[1] But the rumour man knew, and explained.

"We had been delayed," he said, "because Italy had declared war on Greece, and did not want the food on board our ship to enter that country."

The cigarette king told him if the food on board was the same food we had been eating, to bring it into any country was a proper cause for war.

At noon we passed safely between Scylla and Charybdis, and the following morning were in Athens.

---

1. Later we were sorry we had not been held longer in captivity. The telegram reached our consul, and that gentleman at once journeyed to Messina not only to rescue us, but to invite us to a Thanksgiving Day dinner. A consul like that is wasted on the Island of Sicily. The State Department is respectfully urged to promote him to the mainland.

CHAPTER 5

Why King Constantine is Neutral

Athens, November, 1915.

We are not allowed to tell what the situation is here. But, in spite of the censor, I am going to tell what the situation is. It is involved. That is not because no one will explain it. In Greece at present, explaining the situation is the national pastime. Since arriving yesterday I have had the situation explained to me by members of the Cabinet, guides to the Acropolis, generals in the army, Teofani, the cigarette king, three ministers plenipotentiary, the man from St. Louis who is over here to sell aeroplanes, the man from Cook's, and "extra people," like soldiers in cafés, brigands in petticoats, and peasants in peaked shoes with tassels. They asked me not to print their names, which was just as well, as I cannot spell them. They each explained the situation differently, but all agree it is involved.

To understand it, you must go back to Helen of Troy, take a running jump from the Greek war for independence and Lord Byron to Mr. Gladstone and the Bulgarian atrocities, note the influence of the German Emperor at Corfu, appreciate the intricacies of Russian diplomacy in Belgrade, the rise of Enver Pasha and the Young Turks, what Constantine said to Venizelos about giving up Kavalla, and the cablegram Prince Danilo, of "Merry Widow" fame, sent to his cousin of Italy. By following these events, the situation is as easy to grasp as an eel that has swallowed the hook and cannot digest it.

For instance, Mr. Poneropolous, the well-known contractor who sells shoes to the army, informs me the Greeks as one man want war. They are even prepared to fight for it. On the other hand, Axon Skiadas, the popular barber of the Hôtel Grande Bretagne, who has just been called to the colours, assures me no patriot would again plunge this country into conflict.

The diplomats also disagree, especially as to which of them is responsible for the failure of Greece to join the Allies. The one who is to blame for that never is the one who is talking to you. The one who is talking is always the one who, had they followed his advice, could have saved the "situation." They did not, and now it is involved, not to say addled. The military *attaché* of Great Britain volunteered to set the situation before me in a few words. After explaining for two hours, he asked me to promise not to repeat what he had said. I promised. Another diplomat, who was projected into the service by William Jennings Bryan, said if he told all he knew about the situation "the world would burst." Those are his exact words. It would have been an event of undoubted news value, and as a news-gatherer I should have coaxed his secret from him, but it seemed as though the world is in trouble enough as it is, and if it must burst I want it to burst when I am nearer home. So I switched him off to the St. Louis convention, where he was probably more useful than he will ever be in the Balkans.

While everyone is guessing, the writer ventures to make a guess. It is that Greece will remain neutral, or will join the Allies. Without starving to death she cannot join the Germans. Greece is non-supporting. What she eats comes in the shape of wheat from outside her borders, from the grain-fields of Russia, Egypt, Bulgaria, France, and America. When Denys Cochin, the French minister to Athens, had his interview with the King, the latter became angry and said, "We can get along without France's money," and Cochin said: "That is true, but you cannot get along without France's wheat."

The Allies are not going to bombard Greek ports or shell the Acropolis. They will not even blockade the ports. But their fleets—French, Italian, English—will stop all ships taking foodstuffs to Greece. They have just released seven grain ships from America, that were held up at Malta, and ships carrying food to Greece have been stopped at points as far away as Gibraltar. As related in the last chapter, the Greek steamer on which we sailed from Naples was held up at Messina for twenty-four hours until her cargo was overhauled. As we had nothing in the hold more health-sustaining than hides and barbed-wire, we were allowed to proceed.

Whatever course Greece follows, her dependence upon others for food explains her act. Today (November 29) there is not enough wheat in the country to feed the people for, some say three—the most optimistic, ten—days. Should she decide to join Germany she would starve. It would be deliberate suicide. The French and Italian fleets are

King Constantine of Greece and commander-in-chief of her armies.
In two years he led his people to victory in two wars. If now they desire peace and in this big war the right to remain neutral, he thinks they have earned that right.

at Malta, less than a day distant; the English fleet is off the Gallipoli peninsula. Fifteen hours' steaming could bring it to Salonika. Greece is especially vulnerable from the sea. She is all islands, coast towns, and seaports. The German navy could not help her. It will not leave the Kiel Canal. The Austrian navy cannot leave the Adriatic. Should Greece decide against the Allies, their combined war-ships would pick up her islands and blockade her ports. In a week she would be starving. The railroad from Bulgaria to Salonika, over which in peace times comes much wheat from Roumania, would be closed to her. Even if the Germans and Bulgarians succeeded in winning it to the coast, they could get no food for Greece farther than that. They have no war-ships, and the Gulf of Salonika is full of those of the Allies.

The position of King Constantine is very difficult. He is supposed to be strongly pro-German, and the reason for his sympathy that is given here is the same as is accepted in America. Every act of his is supposed to be inspired by family influences, when, as he has stated publicly through his friend Walter Harris of the *London Times*, he is pro-English, and has been actuated solely by what he thought was best for his own people. Indeed, there are many who believe if the terms upon which Greece might join the Allies had been left to the King instead of to Venizelos, Greece now would be with the Entente.

Or, if Greece remained neutral, no one could better judge whether neutrality was or was not best for her than Constantine. In the three years before the World War, he had led his countrymen through two wars, and if both, as King and commander of her armies, he thought they needed rest and peace, he was entitled to that opinion. Instead, he was misrepresented and abused. His motives were assailed; he was accused of being dominated by his Imperial brother-in-law. At no time since the present war began has he been given what we would call a "square deal." The writer has followed the career of Constantine since the Greek-Turkish war of 1897, when they "drank from the same canteen," and as Kings go, or until they all do go, respects him as a good King.

To his people he is generous, kind, and considerate; as a general he has added to the territory of Greece many miles and seaports; he is fond of his home and family, and in his reign there has been no scandal, no Knights of the Round Table, such as disgraced the German court, no Tripoli massacre, no Congo atrocities, no Winter Garden or La Scala favourites. Venizelos may or may not be as unselfish a patriot. But justly or not, it is difficult to disassociate what Venizelos wants for

Greece with what he wants for Venizelos. The King is removed from any such suspicion. He is already a King, and except in continuing to be a good King, he can go no higher.

How Venizelos came so prominently into the game is not without interest. As long ago as when the two German cruisers escaped from Messina and were sold to Turkey, the diplomatic representatives of the Allies in the Balkans were instructed to see that Turkey and Germany did not get together, and that, as a balance of power in case of such a union, the Balkan States were kept in line. Instead of themselves attending to this, the diplomats placed the delicate job in the hands of one man. At the framing of the Treaty of London, of all the representatives from the Balkans, the one who most deeply impressed the other powers was M. Venizelos. And the task of keeping the Balkans neutral or with the Allies was left to him.

He has a dream of a Balkan "band," a union of all the Balkan principalities. It obsesses him. And to bring that dream true he was willing to make concessions which King Constantine, who considered only what was good for Greece, and was not concerned with a Balkan alliance, thought most unwise. Venizelos also was working for the good of Greece, but he was convinced it could come to her only through the union. He was willing to give Kavalla to Bulgaria in exchange for Asia Minor, from the Dardanelles to Smyrna. But the King would not consent. As a buffer against Turkey, he considered Kavalla of the greatest strategic value, and he had the natural pride of a soldier in holding on to land he himself had added to his country. But in his opposition to Venizelos in this particular, credit was not given him for acting in the interests of Greece, but of playing into the hands of Germany.

Another step he refused to take, which refusal the Allies attributed to his pro-German leanings, was to attack the Dardanelles. In the wars of 1912-13 the King showed he was an able general. With his staff he had carefully considered an attack upon the Dardanelles. He submitted this plan to the Allies, and was willing to aid them if they brought to the assault 400,000 men. They claim he failed them. He did fail them, but not until after they had failed him by bringing thousands of men instead of the tens of thousands he knew were needed.

The Dardanelles expedition was not required to prove the courage of the French and British. Beyond furnishing fresh evidence of that, it has been a failure. And in refusing to sacrifice the lives of his subjects the military judgment of Constantine has been vindicated. He was willing to attack Turkey through Kavalla and Thrace, because by that route he presented an armed front to Bulgaria. But, as he pointed out, if he sent his army to the Dardanelles, he left Kavalla at the mercy of his enemy. In his mistrust of Bulgaria he has certainly been justified.

Greece is not at war, but in outward appearance she is as firmly on a war footing as is France or Italy. A man out of uniform is conspicuous, and all day regiments pass through the streets carrying the campaign kit and followed by the medical corps, the mountain batteries, and the transport wagons. In the streets the crowds are cheering Denys Cochin, the special ambassador from France. He makes speeches to them from the balcony of our hotel, and the mob wave flags and shout "*Zito! Zito!*"

In a play Colonel Savage produced, I once wrote the same scene and placed it in the same hotel in Athens. In Athens the local colour was superior to ours, but George Marion stage-managed the mob better than did the Athens police.

Athens is in a perplexed state of mind. She does not know if she wants to go to war or wants peace. She does not know if she should go to war, on which side she wants to fight. People tell you frankly that their heart-beats are with France, but that they are afraid of Germany.

"If Germany wins," they asked, "what will become of us? The Germans already are in Monastir, twenty miles from our border. They have driven the Serbians, the French, and the British out of Serbia, and they will make our King a German *vassal*."

"Then, why don't you go out and fight for your King?" I asked.

"He won't let us," they said.

When the army of a country is mobilized, it is hard to understand that that country is neutral. You expect to see evidences of her partisanship for one cause or the other. But in Athens, from a shop-window point of view, both the Allies and the Germans are equally supported. There are just as many pictures of the German generals as of Joffre, as many post-cards of the German Emperor as of King George and King Albert. After Paris, it is a shock to see German books, portraits of German statesmen, composers, and musicians. In one shop-window conspicuously featured, evidently with intent, is an engraving showing Napoleon III surrendering to Bismarck. In the principal bookstore, books in German on German victories, and English and French pamphlets on German atrocities stand shoulder to shoulder. The choice is with you.

Meanwhile, on every hand are the signs of a nation on the brink of war; of armies of men withdrawn from trades, professions, homes; of men marching and drilling in squads, companies, brigades. At times the columns are so long that in passing the windows of the hotel they take an hour. All these fighting men must be fed, clothed, paid, and while they are waiting to fight, whether they are goatherds or piano-tuners or shopkeepers, their business is going to the devil.

CHAPTER 6

With the Allies in Salonika

Salonika, December, 1915.
We left Athens on the first ship that was listed for Salonika. She was a strange ship. During many years on various vessels in various seas, she was the most remarkable. Every Greek loves to gamble; but for some reason, or for that very reason, for him to gamble on shore is by law made difficult. In consequence, as soon as the *Hermoupolis* raised anchor she became a floating gambling-hell. There were twenty-four first-class passengers who were in every way first class; Greek officers, bankers, merchants, and deputies, and their time on the steamer from eleven each morning until four the next morning was spent in dealing *baccarat*.

When the stewards, who were among the few persons on board who did not play, tried to spread a table-cloth and serve food, they were indignantly rebuked. The most untiring players were the captain and the ship's officers. Whenever they found that navigating their ship interfered with their *baccarat* we came to anchor. We should have reached Salonika in a day and a half. We arrived after four days. And all of each day and half of each night we were anchored in midstream while the captain took the bank. The hills of Eubœa and the mainland formed a giant funnel of snow, through which the wind roared. It swept the ship from bow to stern, turning to ice the woodwork, the velvet cushions, even the blankets. Fortunately, it was not the kind of a ship that supplied sheets, or we would have frozen in our berths. Outside of the engine-room, which was aft, there was no heat of any sort, but undaunted, the gamblers, in caps and fur coats, their breath rising in icy clouds, crouched around the table, their frozen fingers fumbling with the cards.

There were two charming Italians on board, a father and son—the father absurdly youthful, the boy incredibly wise. They operate a chain of banks through the Levant. They watched the game but did not play. The father explained this to me. "My dear son is a born gambler," he said. "So, in order that I may set him an example, I will not play until after he has gone to sleep."

Later, the son also explained. "My dear father," he whispered, "is an inveterate gambler. So, in order that I may reprove him, I do not gamble. At least not until he has gone to bed." At midnight I left them still watching each other. The next day the son said: "I got no sleep last night. For some reason, my dear father was wakeful, and it was four o'clock before he went to his cabin."

When we reached Volo the sun was shining, and as the day was so beautiful, the gamblers remained on board and played *baccarat*. The rest of us explored Volo. On the mountains above it the Twenty-Four Villages were in sight, nestling on the knees of the hills. Their red-tiled houses rose one above the other, the roof of one on a line with the door-step of the neighbour just overhead. Their white walls, for Volo is a summer resort, were merged in the masses of snow, but in Volo itself roses were still blooming, and in every garden the trees were heavy with oranges. They were so many that they hid the green leaves, and against the walls of purple, blue, and Pompeian red, made wonderful splashes of a gorgeous gold.

Apparently the captain was winning, for he sent word he would not sail until midnight, and nine of his passengers dined ashore. We were so long at table, not because the dinner was good, but because there was a charcoal brazier in the room, that we missed the moving-pictures. So the young Italian banker was sent to bargain for a second and special performance. In the Levant there always is one man who works, and one man who manages him. A sort of impresario. Even the boatmen and bootblacks have a manager who arranges the financial details. It is difficult to buy a newspaper without dealing through a third party. The moving-picture show, being of importance, had seven managers. The young Italian, undismayed, faced all of them. He wrangled in Greek, Turkish, French, and Italian, and they all talked to him at the same time. Finally the negotiations came to an end, but our ambassador was not satisfied.

"They got the best of me," he reported to us. "They are going to give the show over again, and we are to have the services of the pianist, the orchestra of five, and the lady vocalist. But I had to agree to pay for the combined entertainment entirely too much."

"How much?" I asked.

"Eight *drachmas*," he said apologetically, "or, in your money, one dollar and fifty-two cents."

"Each?" I said.

He exclaimed in horror: "No, divided among the nine of us!"

No wonder Volo is a popular summer resort, even in December.

The next day, after sunset, we saw the snow-capped peak of Mount Olympus and the lamps of a curving water-front, the long rows of green air ports that mark the French hospital ships, the cargo lights turned on the red crosses painted on their sides, the gray, grim battleships of England, France, Italy, and Greece, and a bustling torpedo-boat took us in tow, and guided us through the floating mines and into the harbour of Salonika.

If it is true that happy are the people without a history, then Salonika should be thoroughly miserable. Some people make history; others have history thrust upon them. Ever since the world began Salonika has had history thrust upon her. She aspired only to be a great trading seaport. She was content to be the place where the caravans from the Balkans met the ships from the shores of the Mediterranean, Egypt, and Asia Minor. Her wharfs were counters across which they could swap merchandise. All she asked was to be allowed to change their money. Instead of which, when any two nations of the Near East went to the mat to settle their troubles, Salonika was the mat.

If any country within a thousand-mile radius declared war on any other country in any direction whatsoever, the armies of both belligerents clashed at Salonika. They not only used her as a door-mat, but they used her hills to the north of the city for their battle-field. In the fighting, Salonika took no part. She merely loaned the hills. But she knew, whichever side won, two things would happen to her: She would pay a forced loan and subscribe to an entirely new religion. Three hundred years before Christ, the people of Salonika worshipped the mysterious gods who had their earthly habitation on the island of Thasos. The Greeks ejected them, and erected altars to Apollo and Aphrodite, the Egyptians followed and taught Salonika to fear Serapis; then came Roman gods and Roman generals; and then St. Paul.

The Jews set up synagogues, the Mohammedans reared minarets, the Crusaders restored the cross, the Tripolitans restored the crescent, the Venetians re-restored Christianity. Romans, Greeks, Byzantines, Persians, Franks, Egyptians, and Barbary pirates, all, at one time or another, invaded Salonika. She was the butcher's block upon which they carved history. Some ruled her only for months, others for years. Of the monuments to the religions forced upon her, the most numerous today are the synagogues of the Jews and the mosques of the Mohammedans. It was not only fighting men who invaded Salonika. Italy can count her great earthquakes on one hand; the United States on one finger. But a resident of Salonika does not speak of the "year of the earthquake." For him, it saves time to name the years when there was no earthquake. Each of those years was generally "the year of the great fire."

If it wasn't one thing, it was another. If it was not a tidal wave, it was an epidemic; if it was not a war, it was a blizzard. The trade of Asia Minor flows into Salonika and with it carries all the plagues of Egypt. Epidemics of cholera in Salonika used to be as common as yellow fever in Guayaquil. Those years the cholera came the people abandoned the seaport and lived on the plains north of Salonika, in tents. If the cholera spared them, the city was swept by fire; if there was no fire, there came a great frost. Salonika is on the same latitude as Naples, Madrid, and New York; and New York is not unacquainted with blizzards. Since the seventeenth century, last winter was said to be the coldest Salonika has ever known.

I was not there in the seventeenth century, but am willing to believe that last winter was the coldest since then; not only to believe it, but to swear to it. Of the frost in 1657 the Salonikans boast the cold was so severe that to get wood the people destroyed their houses. This December, when on the English and French front in Serbia, I saw soldiers using the same kind of fire-wood. They knew a mud house that is held together with beams and rafters can be rebuilt, but that you cannot rebuild frozen toes and fingers.

In thrusting history upon Salonika, the last few years have been especially busy. They gave her a fire that destroyed a great part of the city, and between 1911 and 1914 two cholera epidemics, the Italian-Turkish War, which, as Salonika was then Turkish, robbed her of hundreds of her best men, the Balkan-Turkish War, and the Second Balkan War. In this Salonika was part of the spoils, and Greece and Bulgaria fought to possess her. The Greeks won, and during one year she was at peace. Then, in 1914, the Great War came, and Serbia sent out an S. O. S. call to her Allies. At the Dardanelles, not eighteen hours away, the French and English heard the call. But to reach Serbia by the shortest route they must disembark at Salonika, a port belonging to Greece, a neutral power; and in moving north from Salonika into Serbia they

"In Salonika the water-front belongs to everybody."

must pass over fifty miles of neutral Greek territory.

Venizelos, prime minister of Greece, gave them permission. King Constantine, to preserve his neutrality, disavowed the act of his representative, and Venizelos resigned. From the point of view of the Allies, the disavowal came too late. As soon as they had received permission from the recognized Greek Government, they started, and, leaving the King and Venizelos to fight it out between them, landed at Salonika. The inhabitants received them calmly. The Greek officials, the colonel commanding the Greek troops, the Greek captain of the port, and the Greek collector of customs may have been upset; but the people of Salonika remained calm. They were used to it. Foreign troops were always landing at Salonika. The oldest inhabitant could remember, among others, those of Alexander the Great, Mark Antony, Constantine, the Sultan Murad, and several hundred thousand French and English who over their armour wore a red cross. So he was not surprised when, after seven hundred years, the French and English returned, still wearing the red cross.

One of the greatest assets of those who live in a seaport city is a view of their harbour. As a rule, that view is hidden from them by zinc sheds on the wharfs and warehouses. But in Salonika the water-front belongs to everybody. To the north it encloses the harbour in a great half-moon that from tip to tip measures three miles. At the western tip of this crescent are tucked away the wharfs for the big steamers, the bonded warehouses, the customs, the goods-sheds. The rest of the water-front is open to the people and to the small sailing vessels. For over a mile it is bordered by a stone quay, with stone steps leading down to the rowboats. Along this quay runs the principal street, and on the side of it that faces the harbour, in an unbroken row, are the hotels, the houses of the rich Turks and Jews, clubs, restaurants, cafés, and moving-picture theatres.

At night, when these places are blazing with electric lights, the curving water-front is as bright as Broadway—but Broadway with one-half of the street in darkness. On the dark side of the street, to the quay, are moored hundreds of sailing vessels. Except that they are painted and gilded differently, they look like sisters. They are fat, squat sisters with the lines of half a cantaloupe. Each has a single mast and a lateen-sail, like the Italian *felucca* and the sailing boats of the Nile. When they are moored to the quay and the sail is furled, each yard-arm, in a graceful, sweeping curve, slants downward. Against the sky, in wonderful confusion, they follow the edge of the half-moon; the masts

"On one side of the quay, a moving-picture palace, ... on the other a boat unloading fish."

a forest of dead tree trunks, the slanting yards giant quill pens dipping into an ink-well. Their hulls are rich in gilding and in colours—green, red, pink, and blue. At night the electric signs of a moving-picture palace on the opposite side of the street illuminate them from bow to stern. It is one of those bizarre contrasts you find in the Near East.

On one side of the quay a perfectly modern hotel, on the other a boat unloading fish, and in the street itself, with French automobiles and trolley-cars, men who still are beasts of burden, who know no other way of carrying a bale or a box than upon their shoulders. In Salonika even the trolley-car is not without its contrast. One of our "Jim Crow" street-cars would puzzle a Turk. He would not understand why we separate the white and the black man. But his own street-car is also subdivided. In each there are four seats that can be hidden by a curtain. They are for the women of his *harem*.

From the water-front Salonika climbs steadily up-hill to the row of hills that form her third and last line of defence. On the hill upon which the city stands are the walls and citadel built in the fifteenth century by the Turks, and in which, when the city was invaded, the inhabitants sought refuge. In aspect it is medieval; the rest of the city is modern and Turkish. The streets are very narrow; in many the second stories overhang them and almost touch, and against the skyline rise many minarets. But the Turks do not predominate. They have their quarter, and so, too, have the French and the Jews. In numbers the Jews exceed all the others. They form fifty-six *per cent* of a population composed of Greeks, Turks, Armenians, Bulgarians, Egyptians, French, and Italians.

The Jews came to Salonika the year America was discovered. To avoid the Inquisition they fled from Spain and Portugal and brought their language with them; and after five hundred years it still obtains. It has been called the Esperanto of the Salonikans. For the small shop-keeper, the cabman, the waiter, it is the common tongue. In such an environment it sounds most curious. When, in a Turkish restaurant, you order a dinner in the same words you last used in Vera Cruz, and the dinner arrives, it seems uncanny. But, in Salonika, the language most generally spoken is French. Among so many different races they found, if they hoped to talk business—and a Greek, an Armenian, and a Jew are not averse to talking business—a common tongue was necessary.

So, all those who are educated, even most sketchily, speak French. The greater number of newspapers are in French; and notices, adver-

Outside the Citadel, which is medieval, Salonika is modern and Turkish

tisements, and official announcements are printed in that language. It makes life in Salonika difficult. When a man attacks you in Turkish, Yiddish, or Greek, and you cannot understand him, there is some excuse, but when he instantly renews the attack in both French and Spanish, it is disheartening. It makes you regret that when you were in college the only foreign language you studied was football signals.

At any time, without the added presence of 100,000 Greeks and 170,000 French and English, Salonika appears overpopulated. This is partly because the streets are narrow and because in the streets everybody gathers to talk, eat, and trade. As in all Turkish cities, nearly every shop is an "open shop." The counter is where the window ought to be, and opens directly upon the sidewalk. A man does not enter the door of a shop, he stands on the sidewalk, which is only thirty-six inches wide, and makes his purchase through the window. This causes a crowd to collect. Partly because the man is blocking the sidewalk, but chiefly because there is a chance that something may be bought and paid for.

In normal times, if Salonika is ever normal, she has a population of 120,000, and every one of those 120,000 is personally interested in any one else who engages, or may be about to engage, in a money transaction. In New York, if a horse falls down there is at once an audience of a dozen persons; in Salonika the downfall of a horse is nobody's business, but a copper coin changing hands is everybody's. Of this local characteristic, John T. McCutcheon and I made a careful study; and the result of our investigations produced certain statistics. If in Salonika you buy a newspaper from a news-boy, of the persons passing, two will stop; if at an open shop you buy a package of cigarettes, five people will look over your shoulder; if you pay your cab-driver his fare, you block the sidewalk; and if you try to change a hundred-*franc* note, you cause a riot.

In each block there are nearly a half dozen money-changers; they sit in little shops as narrow as a doorway, and in front of them is a show-case filled with all the moneys of the world. It is not alone the sight of your hundred-*franc* note that enchants the crowd. That collects the crowd; but what holds the crowd is that it knows there are twenty different kinds of money, all current in Salonika, into which your note can be changed. And they know the money-changer knows that and that you do not. So each man advises you. Not because he does not want to see you cheated—between you and the money-changer he is neutral—but because he can no more keep out of a money deal than can a fly pass a sugar-bowl.

The men on the outskirts of the crowd ask: "What does he offer?"

The lucky ones in the front-row seats call back: "A hundred and eighteen *drachmas*." The rear ranks shout with indignation. "It is robbery!" "It is because he changes his money in Venizelos Street." "He is paying the money-changer's rent." "In the Jewish quarter they are giving nineteen." "He is too lazy to walk two miles for a *drachma*." "Then let him go to the Greek, Papanastassion."

A man in a *fez* whispers to you impressively: "*La livre turque est encore d'un usage fort courant. La valeur au pair est de francs vingt-deux.*"

But at this the Armenian shrieks violently. He scorns Turkish money and advises Italian *lire*. At the idea of lire the crowd howl. They hurl at you instead *francs, piastres, paras, drachmas, lepta, metalliks, mejidis, centimes,* and English shillings. The money-changer argues with them gravely. He does not send for the police to drive them away. He does not tell them: "This is none of your business." He knows better. In Salonika, it is their business.

In Salonika, after money, the thing of most consequence is conversation. Men who are talking always have the right of way. When two men of Salonika are seized with a craving for conversation, they feel, until that craving is satisfied, that nothing else is important. So, when the ruling passion grips them, no matter where they may meet, they stop dead in their tracks and talk. If possible they select the spot, where by standing still they can cause the greatest amount of inconvenience to the largest number of people. They do not withdraw from the sidewalk. On the contrary, as best suited for conversation, they prefer the middle of it, the doorway of a *café*, or the centre aisle of a restaurant. Of the people who wish to pass they are as unconscious as a Chinaman smoking opium is unconscious of the sightseers from uptown.

That they are talking is all that counts. They feel everyone else should appreciate that. Because the Allies failed to appreciate it, they gained a reputation for rudeness. A French car, flying the flag of the general, a squad of Tommies under arms, a motor-cyclist carrying despatches could not understand that a conversation on a street crossing was a sacred ceremony. So they shouldered the conversationalists aside or splashed them with mud. It was intolerable. Had they stamped into a mosque in their hobnailed boots, on account of their faulty religious training, the Salonikans might have excused them. But that a man driving an ambulance full of wounded should think he had the right to disturb a conversation that was blocking the traffic of only the entire water-front was a discourtesy no Salonikan could comprehend.

The wonder was that among so many mixed races the clashes were so few. In one place seldom have people of so many different nationalities met, and with interests so absolutely opposed. It was a situation that would have been serious had it not been comic. For causing it, for permitting it to continue, Greece was responsible. Her position was not happy. She was between the Allies and the Kaiser. Than Greece, no country is more vulnerable from an attack by sea; and if she offended the Allies, their combined fleets at Malta and Lemnos could seize all her little islands and seaports. If she offended the Kaiser, he would send the Bulgarians into eastern Thrace and take Salonika, from which only two years before Greece had dispossessed them. Her position was indeed most difficult. As the barber at the Grande Bretange in Athens told me: "It makes me a headache."

On many a better head than his it had the same effect. King Constantine, because he believed it was best for Greece, wanted to keep his country neutral. But after Venizelos had invited the Allies to make a landing-place and a base for their armies at Salonika, Greece was no longer neutral. If our government invited 170,000 German troops to land at Portland, and through Maine invade Canada, our neutrality would be lost. The neutrality of Greece was lost, but Constantine would not see that. He hoped, although 170,000 fighting men are not easy to hide, that the *Kaiser* also would not see it. It was a very forlorn hope.

The Allies also cherished a hope. It was that Constantine not only would look the other way while they slipped across his country, but would cast off all pretence of neutrality and join them. So, as far as was possible, they avoided giving offense. They assisted him in his pretence of neutrality. And that was what caused the situation. It was worthy of a comic opera. Before the return of the allied troops to Salonika, there were on the neutral soil of Greece, divided between Salonika and the front in Serbia, 110,000 French soldiers and 60,000 British. Of these, 100,000 were in Salonika.

The advanced British base was at Doiran and the French advanced base at Strumnitza railroad-station. In both places martial law existed. But at the main base, at Salonika, both armies were under the local authority of the Greeks. They submitted to the authority of the Greeks because they wanted to keep up the superstition that Salonika was a neutral port, when the mere fact that they were there proved she was not. It was a situation almost unparalleled in military history. At the base of a French and of a British army, numbering together 170,000 men, the generals who commanded them possessed less local authority than one Greek policeman. They were guests. They were invited guests of the Greek, and they had no more right to object to his other guests or to rearrange his house rules than would you have the right, when a guest in a strange club, to reprimand the servants.

The Allies had in the streets military police; but they held authority over only soldiers of their own country; they could not interfere with a Greek soldier, or with a civilian of any nation, and even the provost guard sent out at night was composed not alone of French and English but of an equal number of Greeks. I often wondered in what language they issued commands. As an instance of how strictly the Allies recognized the authority of the neutral Greek, and how jealously he guarded it, there was the case of the Entente Café. The proprietor of the Entente Café was a Greek. A British soldier was ill-treated in his *café*, and by the British commanding officer the place, so far as British soldiers and sailors were concerned, was declared "out of bounds." A notice to that effect was hung in the window. But it was a Greek policeman who placed it there.

In matters much more important, the fact that the Allies were in a neutral seaport greatly embarrassed them. They were not allowed to censor news despatches nor to examine the passports of those who arrived and departed. The question of the censorship was not so serious as it might appear. General Sarrail explained to the correspondents what might and what might not be sent, and though what we wrote was not read in Salonika by a French or British censor, General Sarrail knew it would be read by censors of the Allies at Malta, Rome, Paris, and London. Any news despatch that, unscathed, ran that gantlet, while it might not help the Allies certainly would not harm them. One cablegram of three hundred words, sent by an American correspondent, after it had been blue-pencilled by the Greek censors in Salonika and Athens, and by the four allied censors, arrived at his London office consisting entirely of "ands" and "thes."

So, if not from their censors, at least from the correspondents, the Allies were protected. But against the really serious danger of spies they were helpless. In New York the water-fronts are guarded. Unless he is known, no one can set foot upon a wharf. Night and day, against spies and German military *attachés* bearing explosive bombs, steamers loading munitions are surrounded by police, watchmen, and detectives.

But in Salonika the wharfs were as free to any one as a park bench, and the quay supplied every spy, German, Bulgarian, Turk or Austrian, with an uninterrupted view. To suppose spies did not avail themselves of this opportunity is to insult their intelligence. They swarmed. In solid formation spies lined the quay. For every landing-party of blue-jackets they formed a committee of welcome. Of every man, gun, horse, and box of ammunition that came ashore they kept tally.

On one side of the wharf stood "P. N. T. O.," principal naval transport officer, in gold braid, ribbons, and armlet, keeping an eye on every box of shell, gun-carriage, and caisson that was swung from a transport, and twenty feet from him, and keeping count with him, would be two dozen spies. And, to make it worse, the P. N. T. O. knew they were spies. The cold was intense and wood so scarce that to obtain it men used to row out two miles and collect the boxes thrown overboard from the transports and battleships.

Half of these men had but the slightest interest in kindling-wood; they were learning the position of each battleship, counting her guns, noting their calibre, counting the men crowding the rails of the transports, reading the insignia on their shoulder-straps, and, as commands and orders were wigwagged from ship to ship, writing them down. Other spies took the trouble to disguise themselves in rags and turbans, and, mixing with the Tommies, sold them sweetmeats, fruit, and cigarettes. The spy told the Tommy he was his ally, a Serbian refugee; and Tommy, or the *poilu*, to whom Bulgarians, Turks, and Serbians all look alike, received him as a comrade.

"You had a rough passage from Marseilles," ventures the spy.

"We come from the peninsula," says Tommy.

"Three thousand of you on such a little ship!" exclaims the sympathetic Serbian. "You must have been crowded!"

"Crowded as hell," corrects Tommy, "because there are five thousand of us." Over these common spies were master spies, Turkish and German officers from Berlin and Constantinople. They sat in the same restaurants with the French and English officers. They were in *mufti*, but had they appeared in uniform, while it might have led to a riot, in this neutral port they would have been entirely within their rights.

The clearing-houses for the spies were the consulates of Austria, Turkey, and Germany. From there what information the spies turned in was forwarded to the front. The Allies were helpless to prevent. How helpless may be judged from these quotations that are translated from *Phos*, a Greek newspaper published daily in Salonika, and which

"The quay supplied every spy—German, Bulgarian, Turk, or Austrian—with an uninterrupted view."

any one could buy in the streets. "The English and French forces mean to retreat. Yesterday six trains of two hundred and forty wagons came from the front with munitions." "The Allies' first line of defence will be at Soulowo, Doiran, Goumenitz. At Topsin and Zachouna intrenchments have not yet been started, but strong positions have been taken up at Chortiatis and Nihor." "Yesterday the landing of British reinforcements continued, amounting to 15,000. The guns and munitions were out of date. The position of the Allies' battleships has been changed. They are now inside the harbour."

The most exacting German General Staff could not ask for better service than that! When the Allies retreated from Serbia into Salonika everyone expected the enemy would pursue; and thousands fled from the city. But the Germans did not pursue, and the reason may have been because their spies kept them so well informed. If you hold four knaves and, by stealing a look at your opponent's hand, see he has four kings, to attempt to fight him would be suicide. So, in the end, the very freedom with which the spies moved about Salonika may have been for good. They may have prevented the loss of many lives.

During these strenuous days the position of the Greek army in Salonika was most difficult. There were of their soldiers nearly as many as there were French and British combined, and they resented the presence of the foreigners in their new city and they showed it. But they could not show it in such a way as to give offense, because they did not know but that on the morrow with the Allies they would be fighting shoulder to shoulder. And then, again, they did not know but that on the morrow they might be with the Germans and fighting against the Allies, gun to gun.

Not knowing just how they stood with anybody, and to show they resented the invasion of their newly won country by the Allies, the Greeks tried to keep proudly aloof. In this they failed. For anyone to flock by himself in Salonika was impossible. In a long experience of cities swamped by conventions, inaugurations, and coronations, of all I ever saw, Salonika was the most deeply submerged. During the Japanese-Russian War the Japanese told the correspondents there were no horses in Corea, and that before leaving Japan each should supply himself with one. Dinwiddie refused to obey. The Japanese warned him if he did not take a pony with him he would be forced to accompany the army on foot.

"There will always," replied Dinwiddie, "be a pony in Corea for Dinwiddie." It became a famous saying. When the alarmist tells you all the rooms in all the hotels are engaged; that people are sleeping on cots and billiard-tables; that there are no front-row seats for the Follies, no berths in any cabin of any steamer, remind yourself that there is always a pony in Corea for Dinwiddie. The rule is that the hotel clerk discovers a vacant room, a ticket speculator disgorges a front-row seat, and the ship's doctor sells you a berth in the sick bay. But in Salonika the rule failed.

As already explained, Salonika always is overcrowded. Suddenly, added to her 120,000 peoples, came 110,000 Greek soldiers, their officers, and with many of them their families, 60,000 British soldiers and sailors, 110,000 French soldiers and sailors, and no one knows how many thousand Serbian soldiers and refugees, both the rich and the destitute. The population was quadrupled; and four into one you can't. Four men cannot with comfort occupy a cot built for one, four men at the same time cannot sit on the same chair in a restaurant, four men cannot stand on that spot in the street where previously there was not room enough for one. Still less possible is it for three military motor-trucks to occupy the space in the street originally intended for one small donkey. Of Salonika, a local French author has written:

> When one enters the city he is conscious of a cry, continuous and piercing. A cry unique and monotonous, always resembling itself. It is the clamour of Salonika.

Everyone who has visited the East, where everyone lives in the streets, knows the sound. It is like the murmur of a stage mob. Imagine, then, that "clamour of Salonika" increased by the rumble and roar over the huge paving-stones of thousands of giant motor-trucks; by the beat of the iron-shod hoofs of cavalry, the iron-shod boots of men marching in squads, companies, regiments, the shrieks of peasants herding flocks of sheep, goats, turkeys, cattle; the shouts of bootblacks, boatmen, sweetmeat venders; newsboys crying the names of Greek papers that sound like "*Hi hippi hippi hi*," "*Teyang Teyang Teyah*"; by the tin horns of the trolley-cars, the sirens of automobiles, the warning whistles of steamers, of steam-launches, of donkey-engines; the creaking of cordage and chains on cargo-hoists, and by the voices of 300,000 men speaking different languages, and each, that he may be heard above it, adding to the tumult.

For once the alarmist was right. There were no rooms in any hotel. Early in the rush John McCutcheon, William G. Shepherd, John Bass, and James Hare had taken the quarters left vacant by the Austrian Club in the Hotel Olympus. The room was vast and overlooked the principal square of the city, where every Salonikan met to talk, and the only landing-place on the quay. From the balcony you could photograph, as it made fast, not forty feet from you, every cutter, gig, and launch of every war-ship. The late Austrian Club became the headquarters for lost and strayed Americans. For four nights, before I secured a room to myself by buying the hotel, I slept on the sofa. It was two feet too short, but I was very fortunate.

Outside, in the open halls on cots, were English, French, Greek, and Serbian officers. The place looked like a military hospital. The main *salon*, gilded and bemirrored, had lost its identity. At the end overlooking the water-front were Serbian ladies taking tea; in the centre of the salon at the piano a little Greek girl taking a music lesson; and at the other end, on cots, British officers from the trenches and Serbian officers who had escaped through the snows of Albania, their muddy boots, uniforms, and swords flung on the floor, slept the drugged sleep of exhaustion.

Meals were a continuous performance and interlocked. Except at midnight, dining-rooms, *cafés*, and restaurants were never aired, never swept, never empty. The dishes were seldom washed; the waiters—never. People succeeded each other at table in relays, one group giving their order while the other was paying the bill. To prepare a table, a waiter with a napkin swept everything on it to the floor. War prices prevailed. Even the necessities of life were taxed. For a sixpenny tin of English pipe tobacco I paid two dollars, and Scotch whiskey rose from four *francs* a bottle to fifteen.

On even a letter of credit it was next to impossible to obtain money, and the man who arrived without money in his belt walked the water-front. The refugees from Serbia who were glad they had escaped with their lives were able to sleep and eat only through the charity of others. Not only the peasants, but young girls and women of the rich, and more carefully nurtured class of Serbians were glad to sleep on the ground under tents.

The scenes in the streets presented the most curious contrasts. It was the East clashing with the West, and the uniforms of four armies—British, French, Greek, and Serbian—and of the navies of Italy, Russia, Greece, England, and France contrasted with the dress of civilians of every nation. There were the officers of Greece and Serbia in smart uniforms of many colours—blue, green, gray—with much gold and silver braid, and wearing swords which in this war are obsolete; there were English officers, generals of many wars, and red-cheeked boys from Eton, clad in businesslike khaki, with huge, cape-like collars of red fox or wolf skin, and carrying, in place of the sword, a hunting-crop or a walking-stick; there were English bluejackets and marines, Scotch Highlanders, who were as much intrigued over the petticoats of the *Evzones* as were the Greeks astonished at their bare legs; there were French *poilus* wearing the steel *casque*, French aviators in short, shaggy fur coats that gave them the look of a grizzly bear balancing on his hind legs; there were Jews in gabardines, old men with the noble faces of Sargent's apostles, robed exactly as was Irving as Shylock; there were the Jewish married women in sleeveless cloaks of green silk trimmed with rich fur, and each wearing on her head a cushion of green that hung below her shoulders; there were Greek priests with matted hair reaching to the waist, and Turkish women, their faces hidden in *yashmaks*, who looked through them with horror, or envy, at the English, Scotch, and American nurses, with their cheeks bronzed by snow, sleet, and sun, wearing men's hobnailed boots, men's blouses, and, across their breasts, war medals for valour.

All day long these people of all races, with conflicting purposes, speaking, or shrieking, in a dozen different tongues, pushed, shoved, and shouldered. At night, while the bedlam of sounds grew less, the picture became more wonderful. The lamps of automobiles would suddenly pierce the blackness, or the blazing doors of a cinema would show in the dark street, the vast crowd pushing, slipping, struggling for a foothold on the muddy stones. In the circle of light cast by the automobiles, out of the mass a single face would flash—a face burned by the sun of the Dardanelles or frost-bitten by the snows of the Balkans. Above it might be the gold visor and scarlet band of a "Brass Hat," staff-officer, the fur *kepi* of a Serbian refugee, the steel helmet of a French soldier, the "bonnet" of a Highlander, the white cap of a navy officer, the tassel of an *Evzone*, a red *fez*, a turban of rags.

This lasted until the Allies retreated upon Salonika, and the Greek army, to give them a clear field in which to fight, withdrew, 100,000 of them in two days, carrying with them tens of thousands of civilians—those who were pro-Germans, and Greeks, Jews, and Serbians. The civilians were flying before the expected advance of the Bulgar-German forces.

But the Central Powers, possibly well informed by their spies, did not attack. That was several months ago, and at this writing they have not yet attacked. What one man saw of the approaches to Salonika from the north leads him to think that the longer the attack of the Bulgar-Germans is postponed the better it will be—for the Bulgar-Germans.

CHAPTER 7

Two Boys Against an Army

Salonika, December, 1915.

On the day the retreat began from Krivolak, General Sarrail, commanding the Allies in Serbia, gave us permission to visit the French and English front. The French advanced position, and a large amount of ammunition, six hundred shells to each gun, were then at Krivolak, and the English base at Doiran. We left the train at Doiran, but our French "guide" had not informed the English a "*mission militaire*" was descending upon them, and in consequence at Doiran there were no conveyances to meet us. So, a charming English captain commandeered for us a vast motor-truck. Stretched above it were ribs to support a canvas top, and by clinging to these, as at home on the Elevated we hang to a strap, we managed to avoid being bumped out into the road.

The English captain, who seemed to have nothing else on his hands, volunteered to act as our escort, and on a splendid hunter galloped ahead of and at the side of the lorry, and, much like a conductor on a sight-seeing car, pointed out the objects of interest. When not explaining he was absent-mindedly jumping his horse over swollen streams, ravines, and fallen walls. We found him much more interesting to watch than the scenery.

The scenery was desolate and bleak. It consisted of hills that opened into other hills, from the summit of which more hills stretched to a horizon entirely of mountains. They did not form ridges but, like men in a crowd, shouldered into one another. They were of a soft rock and covered with snow, above which to the height of your waist rose scrub pine-trees and bushes of holly. The rain and snow that ran down their slopes had turned the land into a sea of mud, and had swamped the stone roads. In walking, for each step you took forward you skidded and slid several yards back. If you had an hour to spare you had time for a ten-minute walk.

In our motor-truck we circled Lake Doiran, and a mile from the station came to a stone obelisk. When we passed it our guide on horseback shouted to us that we had crossed the boundary from Greece, and were now in Serbia. The lake is five miles wide and landlocked, and the road kept close to the water's edge. It led us through little mud villages with houses of mud and wattle, and some of stone with tiled roofs and rafters, and beams showing through the cement. The second story projected like those of the Spanish blockhouses in Cuba, and the log forts from which, in the days when there were no hyphenated Americans, our forefathers fought the Indians.

Except for some fishermen, the Serbians had abandoned these villages, and they were occupied by English army service men and infantry. The "front," which was hidden away among the jumble of hills, seemed, when we reached it, to consist entirely of artillery. All along the road the Tommies were waging a hopeless war against the mud, shovelling it off the stone road to keep the many motor-trucks from skidding over a precipice, or against the cold making shelters of it, or washing it out of their uniforms and off their persons.

Shivering from ears to heels and with teeth rattling, for they had come from the Dardanelles, they stood stripped to the waist scrubbing their sun-tanned chests and shoulders with ice-water. It was a spectacle that inspired confidence. When a man is so keen after water to wash in that he will kick the top off a frozen lake to get it, a little thing like a barb-wire entanglement will not halt him.

The cold of those hills was like no cold I had ever felt. Officers who had hunted in northern Russia, in the Himalayas, in Alaska, assured us that never had they so suffered. The men we passed, who were in the ambulances, were down either with pneumonia or frostbite. Many had lost toes and fingers. And it was not because they were not warmly clad.[1]

Last winter in France had taught the war office how to dress the part; but nothing had prepared them for the cold of the Balkans. And

---

1. It has been charged that the British troops in the Balkans wore the same tropic uniforms they wore in the Dardanelles. This was necessarily true, when first they landed, but almost at once the winter uniform was issued to all of them. I saw no British or French soldier who was not properly and warmly clad, with overcoat, muffler, extra waistcoat, and gloves. And while all, both officers and men, cursed the cold, none complained that he had not been appropriately clothed to meet it.—R. H. D.

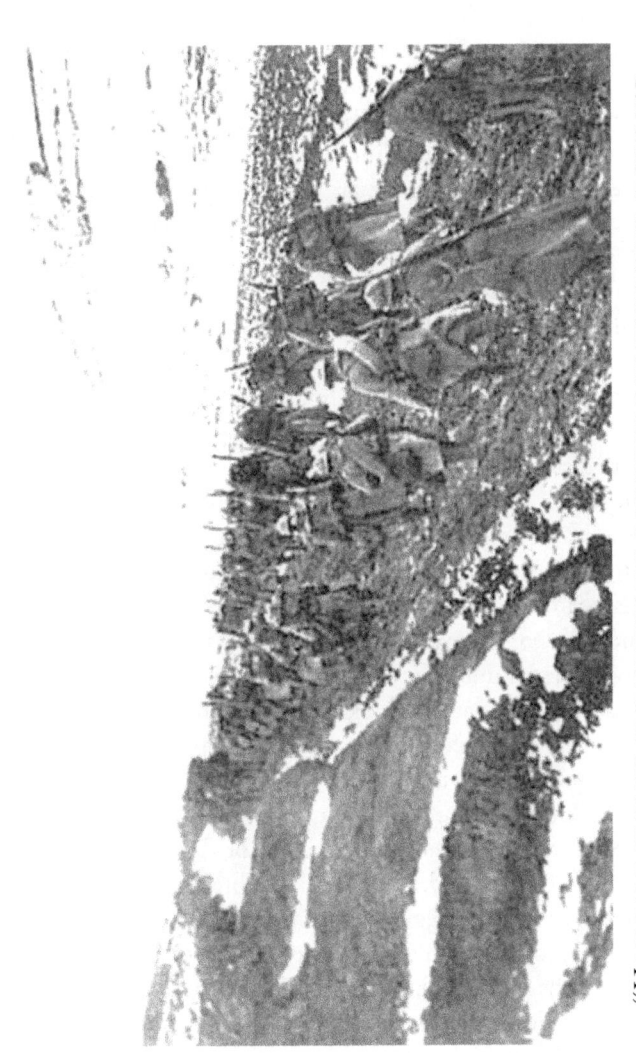

"Hills bare of trees, from which the snow that ran down their slopes had turned the road into a sea of mud."

to add to their distress, for it was all of that, there was no fire-wood. The hills were bare of trees, and such cold as they endured could not be fought with green twigs.

It was not the brisk, invigorating cold that invites you out of doors. It had no cheery, healthful appeal to skates, toboggans, and the jangling bells of a cutter. It was the damp, clammy, penetrating cold of a dungeon, of an unventilated ice-chest, of a morgue. Your clothes did not warm you, the heat of your body had to warm your clothes. And warm, also, all of the surrounding hills.

Between the road and the margin of the lake were bamboo reeds as tall as lances, and at the edge of these were gathered myriads of ducks. The fishermen were engaged in bombarding the ducks with rocks. They went about this in a methodical fashion. All around the lake, concealed in the reeds and lifted a few feet above the water they had raised huts on piles. In front of these huts was a ledge or balcony. They looked like overgrown bird-houses on stilts.

One fisherman waited in a boat to pick up the dead ducks, and the other hurled stones from a sling. It was the same kind of a sling as the one with which David slew Goliath. In Athens I saw small boys using it to throw stones at an electric-light pole. The one the fisherman used was about eight feet long. To get the momentum he whirled it swiftly above his head as a cowboy swings a lariat, and then let one end fly loose, and the stone, escaping, smashed into the mass of ducks. If it stunned or killed a duck the human water-spaniel in the boat would row out and retrieve it. To duck hunters at home the sport would chiefly recommend itself through the cheapness of the ammunition.

On the road we met relays of water-carts and wagons that had been up the hills with food for the gunners at the front; and engineers were at work repairing the stone bridges or digging *détours* to avoid those that had disappeared. They had been built to support no greater burden than a flock of sheep, an ox-cart, or what a donkey can carry on his back, and the assault of the British motor-trucks and French six-inch guns had driven them deep into the mud.

After ten miles we came to what a staff officer would call an "advanced base," but which was locally designated the "Dump." At the side of the road, much of it uncovered to the snow, were stores of ammunition, "bully beef," and barb-wire. The camp bore all the signs of a temporary halting place. It was just what the Tommies called it, a dump. We had not been told then that the Allies were withdrawing, but one did not have to be a military expert to see that there was excellent reason why they should.

They were so few. Whatever the force was against them, the force I saw was not strong enough to hold the ground, not that it covered, but over which it was sprinkled. There were outposts without supports, supports without reserves. A squad was expected to perform the duties of a company. Where a brigade was needed there was less than a battalion. Against the white masses of the mountains and the desolate landscape without trees, houses, huts, without any sign of human habitation, the scattered groups of khaki only accented the bleak loneliness.

At the dump we had exchanged for the *impromptu* motor-truck, automobiles of the French staff, and as "Jimmie" Hare and I were alone in one of them we could stop where we liked. So we halted where an English battery was going into action. It had dug itself into the side of a hill and covered itself with snow and pine branches. Somewhere on one of the neighbouring hills the "spotter" was telephoning the range. The gunners could not see at what they were firing. They could see only the high hill of rock and snow, at the base of which they stood shoulder high in their mud cellars. Ten yards to the rear of them was what looked like a newly made grave reverently covered with pine boughs. Through these a rat-faced young man, with the receivers of a telephone clamped to his ears, pushed his head.

"Eight degrees to the left, sir," he barked, "four thousand yards."

The men behind the guns were extremely young, but, like most artillerymen, alert, sinewy, springing to their appointed tasks with swift, catlike certainty. The sight of the two strangers seemed to surprise them as much as the man in the grave had startled us.

There were two boy officers in command, one certainly not yet eighteen, his superior officer still under twenty.

"I suppose you're all right," said the younger one. "You couldn't have got this far if you weren't all right."

He tried to scowl upon us, but he was not successful. He was too lonely, too honestly glad to see any one from beyond the mountains that hemmed him in. They stretched on either side of him to vast distances, massed barriers of white against a gray, sombre sky; in front of him, to be exact, just four thousand yards in front of him, were Bulgarians he had never seen, but who were always with their shells ordering to "move on," and behind him lay a muddy road that led to a rail-head, that led to transports, that led to France, to the Channel, and England. It was a long, long way to England. I felt like taking one

John T. McCutcheon.   John F. Bass.
          Richard Harding Davis.   James H. Hare.

of the boy officers under each arm, and smuggling him safely home to his mother.

"You don't seem to have any supports," I ventured.

The child gazed around him. It was growing dark and gloomier, and the hollows of the white hills were filled with shadows. His men were listening, so he said bravely, with a vague sweep of the hand at the encircling darkness, "Oh, they're about—somewhere. You might call this," he added, with pride, "an independent command."

You well might.

"Report when ready!" chanted his superior officer, aged nineteen.

He reported, and then the guns spoke, making a great flash in the twilight.

In spite of the light, Jimmie Hare was trying to make a photograph of the guns.

"Take it on the recoil," advised the child officer. "It's sure to stick. It always does stick."

The men laughed, not slavishly, because the officer had made a joke, but as companions in trouble, and because when you are abandoned on a mountainside with a lame gun that jams, you must not take it lying down, but make a joke of it.

The French chauffeur was pumping his horn for us to return, and I went, shamefacedly, as must the robbers who deserted the babes in the wood.

In farewell I offered the boy officer the best cigars for sale in Greece, which is the worse thing one can say of any cigar. I apologized for them, but explained he must take them because they were called the "King of England."

"I would take them," said the infant, "if they were called the 'German Emperor.'"

At the door of the car we turned and waved, and the two infants waved back. I felt I had meanly deserted them—that for his life the mother of each could hold me to account.

But as we drove away from the cellars of mud, the gun that stuck, and the "independent command," I could see in the twilight the flashes of the guns and two lonely specks of light.

They were the "King of England" cigars burning bravely.

CHAPTER 8

The French-British Front in Serbia

Salonika, December, 1915.

The chauffeur of an army automobile must make his way against cavalry, artillery, motor-trucks, motor-cycles, men marching, and ambulances filled with wounded, over a road torn by thousand-ton lorries and excavated by washouts and Jack Johnsons. It is therefore necessary for him to drive with care. So he drives at sixty miles an hour, and tries to scrape the mud from every wheel he meets.

In these days of his downfall the greatest danger to the life of the war correspondent is that he must move about in automobiles driven by military chauffeurs. The one who drove me from the extreme left of the English front up to hill 516, which was the highest point of the French front, told me that in peace times he drove a car to amuse himself. His idea of amusing himself was to sweep around a corner on one wheel, exclaim with horror, and throw on all the brakes with the nose of the car projecting over a precipice a thousand yards deep. He knew perfectly well the precipice was there, but he leaped at it exactly as though it were the finish line of the Vanderbilt cup race. If his idea of amusing himself was to make me sick with terror he must have spent a thoroughly enjoyable afternoon.

The approaches to hill 516, the base of the hill on the side hidden from the Bulgarians, and the trenches dug into it were crowded with the French. At that point of the line they greatly outnumbered the English. But it was not the elbow touch of numbers that explained their cheerfulness; it was because they knew it was expected of them. The famous scholar who wrote in our school geographies, "The French are a gay people, fond of dancing and light wines," established a tradition. And on hill 516, although it was to keep from freezing that they danced, and though the light wines were melted snow, they still kept up that tradition and were "gay."

They laughed at us in welcome, crawling out of their igloos on all fours like bears out of a cave; they laughed when we photographed them crowding to get in front of the camera, when we scattered among them copies of *L'Opinion*, when up the snow-clad hillside we skidded and slipped and fell. And if we peered into the gloom of the shelters, where they crouched on the frozen ground with snow dripping from above, with shoulders pressed against walls of icy mud, they waved spoons at us and invited us to share their soup. Even the dark-skinned, sombre-eyed men of the desert, the tall Moors and Algerians, showed their white teeth and laughed when a "seventy-five" exploded from an unsuspicious bush, and we jumped.

It was like a camp of Boy Scouts, picnicking for one day, and sure the same night of a warm supper and bed. But the best these *poilus* might hope for was months of ice, snow, and mud, of discomfort, colds, long marches carrying heavy burdens, the pain of frost-bite, and, worst of all, homesickness. They were sure of nothing: not even of the next minute. For hill 516 was dotted with oblong rows of stones with, at one end, a cross of green twigs and a soldier's cap.

The hill was the highest point of a ridge that looked down into the valleys of the Vardar and of Bodjinia. Toward the Bulgarians we could see the one village of Kosturino, almost indistinguishable against the snow, and for fifty miles, even with glasses, no other sign of life. Nothing but hills, rocks, bushes, and snow. When the "seventy-fives" spoke with their smart, sharp crack that always seems to say, "Take that!" and to add, with aristocratic insolence, "and be damned to you!" one could not guess what they were firing at. In Champagne, where the Germans were as near as from a hundred to forty yards; in Artois, where they were a mile distant, but where their trench was as clearly in sight as the butts of a rifle-range, you could understand. You knew that "that dark line over there" was the enemy.

A year before at Soissons you had seen the smoke of the German guns in a line fifteen miles long. In other little wars you had watched the shells destroy a blockhouse, a village, or burst upon a column of men. But from hill 516 you could see no enemy; only mountains draped in snow, silent, empty, inscrutable. It seemed ridiculous to be attacking fifty miles of landscape with tiny pills of steel. But although we could not see the Bulgars, they could see the flashes on hill 516, and from somewhere out of the inscrutable mountains shells burst and fell. They fell very close, within forty feet of us, and, like children being sent to bed just at dessert time, our hosts hurried us out of the trenches and drove us away.

While on "516" we had been in Bulgaria; now we returned to Serbia, and were halted at the village of Valandova. There had been a ceremony that afternoon. A general, whose name we may not mention, had received the *medaille militaire*. One of the French correspondents asked him in recognition of which of his victories it had been bestowed. The general possessed a snappy temper.

"The medal was given me," he said, "because I was the only general without it, and I was becoming conspicuous."

It had long been dark when we reached Strumnitza station, where we were to spend the night in a hospital tent. The tent was as big as a barn, with a stove, a cot for each, and fresh linen sheets. All these good things belong to the men we had left on hill 516 awake in the mud and snow. I felt like a burglar, who, while the owner is away, sleeps in his bed. There was another tent with a passageway filled with medical supplies connecting it with ours. It was in darkness, and we thought it empty until someone exploring found it crowded with wounded and men with frozen legs and hands.

For half an hour they had been watching us through the passageway, making no sign, certainly making no complaint. John Bass collected all our newspapers, candles, and boxes of cigarettes, which the hospital stewards distributed, and when we returned from dinner our neighbours were still wide awake and holding a smoking concert. But when in the morning the bugles woke us we found that during the night the wounded had been spirited away, and by rail transferred to the hospital ships. We should have known then that the army was in retreat. But it was all so orderly, so leisurely, that it seemed like merely a shifting from one point of the front to another.

We dined with the officers and they certainly gave no suggestion of men contemplating retreat, for the mess-hall in which dinner was served had been completed only that afternoon. It was of rough stones and cement, and the interior walls were covered with whitewash. The cement was not yet dry, nor, as John McCutcheon later discovered when he drew caricatures on it, neither was the whitewash. There were twenty men around the dinner-table, seated on ammunition-boxes and Standard Oil cans, and so close together you could use only one hand. So, you gave up trying to cut your food, and used the free hand solely in drinking toasts to the army, to France, and the Allies. Then, to each Ally individually. You were glad there were so many

HEADQUARTERS OF THE FRENCH COMMANDER IN GRAVEC, SERBIA.

Allies. For it was not Greek, but French wine, of the kind that comes from Rheims. And the army was retreating. What the French army offers its guests to drink when it is advancing is difficult to imagine.

We were waited upon by an enormous negro from Senegal with a *fez* as tall as a giant firecracker. Waiting single-handed on twenty men is a serious matter. And because the officers laughed when he served the soup in a tin basin used for washing dishes his feelings were hurt. It was explained that "Chocolat" in his own country was a prince, and that unless treated with tact he might get the idea that waiting on a table is not a royal prerogative. One of the officers was a genius at writing *impromptu* verses. During one course he would write them, and while Chocolat was collecting the plates would sing them. Then by the light of a candle on the back of a scrap of paper he would write another and sing that. He was rivalled in entertaining us by the officers who told anecdotes of war fronts from the Marne to Smyrna, who proposed toasts, and made speeches in response, especially by the officer who that day had received the *Croix de Guerre* and a wound.

I sat next to a young man who had been talking learnedly of dum-dum bullets and Parisian restaurants. They asked him to recite, and to my horror he rose. Until that moment he had been a serious young officer, talking *boulevard* French. In an instant he was transformed. He was a clown. To look at him was to laugh. He was an old *roué*, senile, pitiable, a *bourgeois*, an apache, a lover, and his voice was so beautiful that each sentence sang. He used words so difficult that to avoid them even Frenchmen will cross the street. He mastered them, played with them, caressed them, sipped of them as a connoisseur sips Madeira: he tossed them into the air like radiant bubbles, or flung them at us with the rattle of a *mitrailleuse*. When in triumph he sat down, I asked him, when not in uniform, who the devil he happened to be.

Again he was the bored young man. In a low tone, so as not to expose my ignorance to others, he said.

"I? I am Barrielles of the Theatre Odeon."

We were receiving so much that to make no return seemed ungracious, and we insisted that John T. McCutcheon should decorate the wall of the new mess-room with the caricatures that make the Chicago *Tribune* famous. Our hosts were delighted, but it was hardly fair to McCutcheon. Instead of his own choice of weapons he was asked to prove his genius on wet whitewash with a stick of charred wood. It was like asking McLaughlin to make good on a ploughed field. But in spite of the fact that the whitewash fell off in flakes, there grew upon the wall a tall, gaunt figure with gleaming eyes and teeth. Chocolat paid it the highest compliment. He gave a wild howl and fled into the night. Then in quick succession, while the Frenchmen applauded each swift stroke, appeared the faces of the song writer, the comedian, the wounded man, and the commanding officer. It was a real triumph, but the surprises of the evening were not at an end. McCutcheon had but just resumed his seat when the newly finished rear wall of the mess-hall crashed into the room. Where had been rocks and cement was a gaping void, and a view of a garden white with snow.

While we were rescuing the song writer from the *débris* McCutcheon regarded the fallen wall thoughtfully.

"They feared," he said, "I was going to decorate that wall also, and they sent Chocolat outside to push it in."

The next day we walked along the bank of the Vardar River to Gravec, about five miles north of Strumnitza station. Five miles farther was Demir-Kapu, the Gate of Iron, and between these two towns is a high and narrow pass famous for its wild and magnificent beauty. Fifteen miles beyond that was Krivolak, the most advanced French position. On the hills above Gravec were many guns, but in the town itself only a few infantrymen. It was a town entirely of mud; the houses, the roads, and the people were covered with it. Gravec is proud only of its church, on the walls of which in colours still rich are painted many devils with pitchforks driving the wicked ones into the flames.

One of the *poilus* put his finger on the mass of wicked ones.

"*Les Boches*," he explained.

Whether the devils were the French or the English he did not say, possibly because at the moment they were more driven against than driving.

Major Merse, the commanding officer, invited us to his headquarters. They were in a house of stone and mud, from which projected a wooden platform. When any one appeared upon it he had the look of being about to make a speech. The major asked us to take photographs of Gravec and send them to his wife. He wanted her to see in what sort of a place he was condemned to exist during the winter. He did not wish her to think of him as sitting in front of a *café* on the sidewalk, and the snap-shots would show her that Gravec has no cafés, no sidewalks and no streets.

But he was not condemned to spend the winter in Gravec.

Within the week great stores of ammunition and supplies began to pour into it from Krivolak, and the Gate of Iron became the ad-

After the retreat from Serbia.
English Tommies intrenched in the ten-mile plain outside Salonika. "Are they downhearted? No!"

vanced position, and Gravec suddenly found herself of importance as the French base.

To understand this withdrawal, find on the map Krivolak, and follow the railroad and River Vardar southeast to Gravec.

The cause of the retreat was the inability of the Serbians to hold Monastir and their withdrawal west, which left a gap in the former line of Serbians, French, and British. The enemy thus was south and west of Sarrail, and his left flank was exposed.

On December 3, finding the advanced position at Krivolak threatened by four divisions, 100,000 men, General Sarrail began the withdrawal, sending south by rail without loss all ammunition and stores. He destroyed the tunnel at Krivolak and all the bridges across the Vardar, and on his left at the Cerna River. The fighting was heavy at Prevedo and Biserence, but the French losses were small. He withdrew slowly, twenty miles in one week. The British also withdrew from their first line to their second line of defence.

Demir-Kapu, meaning the Gate of Iron, is the entrance to a valley celebrated for its wild and magnificent beauty. Starting at Demir-Kapu, it ends two kilometres north of Gravec. It rises on either side of the Vardar River and railroad line, and in places is less than a hundred yards wide. It is formed of sheer hills of rock, treeless and exposed.

But the fame of Gravec as the French base was short-lived. For the Serbians at Monastir and Gevgeli, though fighting bravely, were forced toward Albania, leaving the left flank of Sarrail still more exposed. And the Gate of Iron belied her ancient title.

With 100,000 Bulgars crowding down upon him General Sarrail wasted no lives, either French or English, but again withdrew. He was outnumbered, some say five to one. In any event, he was outnumbered as inevitably as three of a kind beat two pair. A good poker player does not waste chips backing two pair. Neither should a good general, when his chips are human lives. As it was, in the retreat seven hundred French were killed or wounded, and of the British, who were more directly in the path of the Bulgars, one thousand.

At Gevgeli the French delayed two days to allow the Serbian troops to get away, and then themselves withdrew. There now no longer were any Serbian soldiers in Serbia. So both armies fell back toward Salonika on a line between Kilindir and Doiran railroad-station, and all the places we visited a week before were occupied by the enemy. At Gravec a Bulgarian is pointing at the wicked ones who are being driven into the flames and saying: "The Allies," and at Strumnitza station in the mess-hall Bulgar officers are framing John McCutcheon's sketches.

And here at Salonika from sunrise to sunset the English are disembarking reinforcements, and the French building barracks of stone and brick. It looks as though the French were here to stay, and as though the retreating habit was broken.

The same team that, to put it politely, drew the enemy after them to the gates of Paris, have been drawing the same enemy after them to Salonika. That they will throw him back from Salonika, as they threw him back from Paris, is assured.

General Sarrail was one of those who commanded in front of Paris, and General de Castelnau, who also commanded at the battle of the Marne, and is now chief of staff of General Joffre, has just visited him here. General de Castelnau was sent to "go, look, see." He reports that the position now held by the Allies is impregnable.

The perimeter held by them is fifty miles in length and stretches from the Vardar River on the west to the Gulf of Orplanos on the east. There are three lines of defence. To assist the first two on the east are Lakes Beshik and Langaza, on the west the Vardar River. Should the enemy penetrate the first lines they will be confronted ten miles from Salonika by a natural barrier of hills, and ten miles of intrenchments and barb-wire. Should the enemy surmount these hills the Allies warships in the harbour can sweep him off them as a fire-hose rips the shingles off a roof.

The man who tells you he understands the situation in Salonika is of the same mental calibre as the one who understands a system for beating the game at Monte Carlo. But there are certain rumours as to the situation in the future that can be eliminated. First, Greece will not turn against the Allies. Second, the Allies will not withdraw from Salonika. They now are agreed it is better to resist an attack or stand a siege, even if they lose 200,000 men, than to withdraw from the Balkans without a fight.

The Briand government believes that had the Millerand government, which it overthrew, sent troops to aid the Serbian army in August this war would have been made shorter by six months. It now is trying to repair the mistake of the government it ousted. Among other reasons it has for remaining in the Balkans, is that the presence of 200,000 men at Salonika will hold Roumania from any aggressive movement on Russia.

To aid the Allies, Russia at Tannenberg made a sacrifice, and lost

200,000 men. The present French Government now feels bound in honour to help Russia by keeping the French-British armies at Salonika. As a visiting member of the government said to me:

"In this war there is no western line or eastern line. The line of the Allies is wherever a German attacks. France went to the Balkans to help Serbia. She went too late, which is not the fault of the present government. But there remains the task to keep the Germans from Egypt, to menace the railroad at Adrianople, and to prevent Roumania from an attack upon the flank of Russia. The Allies are in Salonika until this war is ended."

In Salonika you see every evidence that this is the purpose of the Allies; that both England and France are determined to hold fast.

Reinforcements of British troops are arriving daily, and the French are importing large numbers of ready-to-set-up wooden barracks, each capable of holding 250 men. Also along the water-front they are building storehouses of brick and stone. That does not suggest an immediate departure. At the French camp, which covers five square miles in the suburbs of Salonika when I visited it today, thousands of soldiers were actively engaged in laying stone roads, repairing bridges and erecting new ones. There is no question but that they intend to make this the base until the advance in the spring.

A battalion of Serbians 700 strong has arrived at the French camp. In size and physique they are splendid specimens of fighting men. They are now road building. Each day refugees of the Serbian army add to their number.

At four o'clock in the morning of the 14th of December, the Greek army evacuated Salonika and that strip of Greek territory stretching from it to Doiran.

From before sunrise an unbroken column of Greek regiments passed beneath the windows of our hotel. There were artillery, cavalry, pontoons, ambulances, and thousands of ponies and donkeys, carrying fodder, supplies, and tents. The sidewalks were invaded by long lines of infantry. The water-front along which the column passed was blocked with spectators.

As soon as the Greeks had departed sailors from the Allied warships were given shore leave, and the city took on the air of a holiday. Thus was a most embarrassing situation brought to an end and the world informed that the Allies had but just begun to fight. It was the clearing of the prize-ring.

The clearing also of the enemy's consulates ended another embarrassing situation. As suggested in a previous chapter, the consulates of the Central Powers were the hot-beds and clearing-houses for spies. The raid upon them by the French proved that this was true. The enforced departure of the German, Austrian, Bulgarian, and Turkish consuls added to the responsibilities of our own who has now to guard their interests. They will be efficiently served. John E. Kehl has been long in our consular service, and is most admirably fitted to meet the present crisis. He has been our representative at Salonika for four years, in which time his experience as consul during the Italian-Turkish War, the two Balkan wars, and the present war, have trained him to meet any situation that is likely to arrive.

What that situation may be, whether the Bulgar-Germans will attack Salonika, or the Allies will advance upon Sofia, and as an inevitable sequence draw after them the Greek army of 200,000 veterans, only the spring can tell.

If the Teutons mean to advance, having the shorter distance to go, they may launch their attack in April. The Allies, if Sofia is their objective, will wait for the snow to leave the hills and the roads to dry. That they would move before May is doubtful. Meanwhile, they are accumulating many men, and much ammunition and information. May they make good use of it.

CHAPTER 9

Verdun and St. Mihiel

Paris, January, 1916.

It is an old saying that *the busiest man always seems to have the most leisure.* It is another way of complimenting him on his genius for organization. When you visit a real man of affairs you seldom find him surrounded by secretaries, stenographers, and a battery of telephones. As a rule, there is nothing on his desk save a photograph of his wife and a rose in a glass of water. Outside the headquarters of the general there were no gendarmes, no sentries, no panting automobiles, no mud-flecked *chasseurs-à-cheval*. Unchallenged the car rolled up an empty avenue of trees and stopped beside an empty terrace of an apparently empty *château*. At one end of the terrace was a pond, and in it floated seven beautiful swans. They were the only living things in sight. I thought we had stumbled upon the country home of some gentleman of elegant leisure.

When he appeared the manner of the general assisted that impression. His courtesy was so undisturbed, his mind so tranquil, his conversation so entirely that of the polite host, you felt he was masquerading in the uniform of a general only because he knew it was becoming. He glowed with health and vigour. He had the appearance of having just come indoors after a satisfactory round on his private golf-links. Instead, he had been receiving reports from twenty-four different staff-officers. His manner suggested he had no more serious responsibility than feeding bread crumbs to the seven stately swans. Instead he was responsible for the lives of 170,000 men and fifty miles of trenches.

His duties were to feed the men three times a day with food, and all day and night with ammunition, to guard them against attacks from gases, burning oil, bullets, shells; and in counter-attack to send them

227

The ruined village of Gerbéviller, destroyed after their retreat by the Germans. Captain Gabriel Puaux, of the General-Headquarters Staff, and Mr. Davis.

forward with the bayonet across hurdles of barb-wire to distribute death. These were only a few of his responsibilities.

I knew somewhere in the *château* there must be the conning-tower from which the general directed his armies, and after luncheon asked to be allowed to visit it. It was filled with maps, in size enormous but rich in tiny details, nailed on frames, pinned to the walls, spread over vast drawing-boards. But to the visitor more marvellous than the maps showing the French lines were those in which were set forth the German positions, marked with the place occupied by each unit, giving the exact situation of the German trenches, the German batteries, giving the numerals of each regiment.

With these spread before him, the general has only to lift the hand telephone, and direct that from a spot on a map on one wall several tons of explosive shells shall drop on a spot on another map on the wall opposite. The general does not fight only at long distance from a map. Each morning he visits some part of the fifty miles of trenches. What later he sees on his map only jogs his memory. It is a sort of shorthand note. Where to you are waving lines, dots, and crosses, he beholds valleys, forests, miles of yellow trenches. A week ago, during a bombardment, a brother general advanced into the first trench. His chief of staff tugged at his cloak.

"My men like to see me here," said the general.

A shell killed him. But who can protest it was a life wasted? He made it possible for every *poilu* in a trench of five hundred miles to say: "Our generals do not send us where they will not go themselves."

We left the white swans smoothing their feathers, and through rain drove to a hill covered closely with small trees. The trees were small, because the soil from which they drew sustenance was only one to three feet deep. Beneath that was chalk. Through these woods was cut a runway for a toy railroad. It possessed the narrowest of narrow gauges, and its rolling-stock consisted of flat cars three feet wide, drawn by splendid Percherons. The live stock, the rolling-stock, the tracks, and the trees on either side of the tracks were entirely covered with white clay. Even the brakemen and the locomotive-engineer who walked in advance of the horses were completely painted with it. And before we got out of the woods, so were the passengers. This railroad feeds the trenches, carrying to them water and ammunition, and to the kitchens in the rear uncooked food.

The French marquis who escorted "*Mon Capitaine*" of the *Grand Quartier Général des Armées,* who was my "guide philosopher and friend," to the trenches either had built this railroad, or owned a controlling interest in it, for he always spoke of it proudly as "my express," "my special train," "my *petite vitesse*." He had lately been in America buying cavalry horses.

As for years he has owned one of the famous racing stables in France, his knowledge of them is exceptional.

When last I had seen him he was in silk, on one of his own thoroughbreds, and the crowd, or that part of it that had backed his horse, was applauding, and, while he waited for permission to dismount, he was smiling and laughing. Yesterday, when the plough horses pulled his express-train off the rails, he descended and pushed it back, and, in consequence, was splashed, not by the mud of the race-track but of the trenches. Nor in the misty, dripping, rain-soaked forest was there any one to applaud. But he was still laughing, even more happily.

The trenches were dug around what had been a chalk mine, and it was difficult to tell where the mining for profit had stopped and the excavations for defence began. When you can see only chalk at your feet, and chalk on either hand, and overhead the empty sky, this ignorance may be excused. In the *boyaux*, which began where the railroad stopped, that was our position. We walked through an endless grave with walls of clay, on top of which was a scant foot of earth. It looked like a layer of chocolate on the top of a cake.

In some places, underfoot was a corduroy path of sticks, like the false bottom of a rowboat; in others, we splashed through open sluices of clay and rain-water. You slid and skidded, and to hold yourself erect pressed with each hand against the wet walls of the endless grave.

We came out upon the "*hauts de Meuse.*" They are called also the "Shores of Lorraine," because to that province, as are the cliffs of Dover to the county of Kent, they form a natural barrier. We were in the quarry that had been cut into the top of the heights on the side that now faces other heights held by the enemy. Behind us rose a sheer wall of chalk as high as a five-story building. The face of it had been pounded by shells. It was as undismayed as the whitewashed wall of a schoolroom at which generations of small boys have flung impertinent spit-balls.

At the edge of the quarry the floor was dug deeper, leaving a wall between it and the enemy, and behind this wall were the posts of observation, the nests of the machine-guns, the raised step to which the men spring when repulsing an attack. Below and back of them were the shelters into which, during a bombardment, they disappear. They

"Through these woods ran a toy railroad."
This picture shows President Poincaré on the toy railroad en route to the trenches.

were roofed with great beams, on top of which were bags of cement piled three and four yards high.

Not on account of the sleet and fog, but in spite of them, the aspect of the place was grim and forbidding. You did not see, as at some of the other fronts, on the sign-boards that guide the men through the maze, jokes and nicknames. The mess-huts and sleeping-caves bore no such ironic titles as the Petit Café, the Anti-Boche, Chez Maxim. They were designated only by numerals, businesslike and brief. It was no place for humour. The monuments to the dead were too much in evidence. On every front the men rise and lie down with death, but on no other front had I found them living so close to the graves of their former comrades. Where a man had fallen, there had he been buried, and on every hand you saw between the chalk huts, at the mouths of the pits or raised high in a niche, a pile of stones, a cross, and a soldier's cap. Where one officer had fallen his men had built to his memory a mausoleum. It is also a shelter into which, when the shells come, they dive for safety. So that even in death he protects them.

I was invited into a post of observation, and told to make my entrance quickly. In order to exist, a post of observation must continue to look to the enemy only like part of the wall of earth that faces him. If through its apparently solid front there flashes, even for an instant, a ray of sunlight, he knows that the ray comes through a peep-hole, and that behind the peep-hole men with field-glasses are watching him. And with his shells he hammers the post of observation into a shambles. Accordingly, when you enter one, it is etiquette not to keep the door open any longer than is necessary to squeeze past it. As a rule, the door is a curtain of sacking, but hands and bodies coated with clay, by brushing against it, have made it quite opaque.

The post was as small as a chart-room, and the light came only through the peep-holes. You got a glimpse of a rack of rifles, of shadowy figures that made way for you, and of your captain speaking in a whisper. When you put your eyes to the peep-hole it was like looking at a photograph through a stereoscope. But, instead of seeing the lake of Geneva, the Houses of Parliament, or Niagara Falls, you looked across a rain-driven valley of mud, on the opposite side of which was a hill.

Here the reader kindly will imagine a page of printed matter devoted to that hill. It was an extremely interesting hill, but my captain, who also is my censor, decides that what I wrote was too interesting, especially to Germans. So the hill is "strafed." He says I can begin again vaguely with "Over there."

"Over there," said his voice in the darkness, "is St. Mihiel."

For more than a year you had read of St. Mihiel. *Communiqués*, maps, illustrations had made it famous and familiar. It was the town that gave a name to the German salient, to the point thrust in advance of what should be his front. You expected to see an isolated hill, a promontory, some position of such strategic value as would explain why for St. Mihiel the lives of thousands of Germans had been thrown upon the board. But except for the obstinacy of the German mind, or, upon the part of the Crown Prince the lack of it, I could find no explanation. Why the German wants to hold St. Mihiel, why he ever tried to hold it, why if it so pleases him he should not continue to hold it until his whole line is driven across the border, is difficult to understand. For him it is certainly an expensive position. It lengthens his lines of communication and increases his need of transport. It eats up men, eats up rations, eats up priceless ammunition, and it leads to nowhere, enfilades no position, threatens no one. It is like an ill-mannered boy sticking out his tongue. And as ineffective.

The physical aspect of St. Mihiel is a broad sweep of meadow-land cut in half by the Meuse flooding her banks; and the shattered houses of the Ferme Mont Meuse, which now form the point of the salient. At this place the opposing trenches are only a hundred yards apart, and all of this low ground is commanded by the French guns on the heights of Les Paroches. On the day of our visit they were being heavily bombarded. On each side of the salient are the French. Across the battle-ground of St. Mihiel I could see their trenches facing those in which we stood. For, at St. Mihiel, instead of having the line of the enemy only in front, the lines face the German, and surround him on both flanks. Speaking not as a military strategist but merely as a partisan, if any German commander wants that kind of a position I would certainly make him a present of it.

The colonel who commanded the trenches possessed an enthusiasm that was beautiful to see. He was as proud of his chalk quarry as an admiral of his first dreadnaught. He was as isolated as though cast upon a rock in mid-ocean. Behind him was the dripping forest, in front the mud valley filled with floating fogs. At his feet in the chalk floor the shells had gouged out holes as deep as rain-barrels. Other shells were liable at any moment to gouge out more holes. Three days before, when Prince Arthur of Connaught had come to tea, a shell had hit outside the colonel's private cave, and smashed all the teacups.

A FIRST-LINE TRENCH OUTSIDE OF VERDUN.
THE TRENCH ENFILADES THE VALLEY BEYOND, AND THE VALLEY
IS COVERED WITH BARBED-WIRE AND GUN-PITS.

It is extremely annoying when English royalty drops in sociably to distribute medals and sip a cup of tea to have German shells invite themselves to the party. It is a way German shells have. They push in everywhere. One invited itself to my party and got within ten feet of it. When I complained, the colonel suggested absently that it probably was not a German shell but a French mine that had gone off prematurely. He seemed to think being hit by a French mine rather than by a German shell made all the difference in the world. It nearly did.

At the moment the colonel was greatly interested in the fact that one of his men was not carrying a mask against gases. The colonel argued that the life of the man belonged to France, and that through laziness or indifference he had no right to risk losing it. Until this war the colonel had commanded in Africa the regiment into which criminals are drafted as a punishment. To keep them in hand requires both imagination and the direct methods of a *bucko* mate on a whaler. When the colonel was promoted to his present command he found the men did not place much confidence in the gas masks, so he filled a shelter with poisoned air, equipped a squad with protectors and ordered them to enter. They went without enthusiasm, but when they found they could move about with impunity the confidence of the entire command in the anti-gas masks was absolute.

The colonel was very vigilant against these gas attacks. He had equipped the only shelter I have seen devoted solely to the preparation of defences against them. We learned several new facts concerning this hideous form of warfare. One was that the Germans now launch the gas most frequently at night when the men cannot see it approach, and, in consequence, before they can snap the masks into place, they are suffocated, and in great agony die. They have learned much about the gas, but chiefly by bitter experience. Two hours after one of the attacks an officer seeking his field-glasses descended into his shelter. The gas that had flooded the trenches and then floated away still lurked below. And in a moment the officer was dead. The warning was instantly flashed along the trenches from the North Sea to Switzerland, and now after a gas raid, before any one enters a shelter, it is attacked by counter-irritants, and the poison driven from ambush.

I have never seen better discipline than obtained in that chalk quarry, or better spirit. There was not a single outside element to aid discipline or to inspire morale. It had all to come from within. It had all to spring from the men themselves and from the example set by their officers. The enemy fought against them, the elements fought against them, the place itself was as cheerful as a crutch. The clay climbed from their feet to their hips, was ground into their uniforms, clung to their hands and hair. The rain chilled them, the wind, cold, damp, and harsh, stabbed through their greatcoats. Their outlook was upon graves, their resting-places dark caverns, at which even a wolf would look with suspicion. And yet they were all smiling, eager, alert. In the whole command we saw not one sullen or wistful face.

It is an old saying: "So the colonel, so the regiment."

But the splendid spirit I saw on the heights of the Meuse is true not only of that colonel and of that regiment, but of the whole five hundred miles of trenches, and of all France.

February, 1916.

When I was in Verdun, the Germans, from a distance of twenty miles, had dropped three shells into Nancy and threatened to send more. That gave Nancy an interest which Verdun lacked. So I was intolerant of Verdun and anxious to hasten on to Nancy.

Today Nancy and her three shells are forgotten, and to all the world the place of greatest interest is Verdun. Verdun has been Roman, Austrian, and not until 1648 did she become a part of France. This is the fourth time she has been attacked—by the Prussians in 1792, again by the Germans in 1870, when, after a gallant defence of three weeks, she surrendered, and in October of 1914.

She then was more menaced than attacked. It was the Crown Prince and General von Strantz with seven army corps who threatened her. General Sarrail, now commanding the allied forces in Salonika, with three army corps, and reinforced by part of an army corps from Toul, directed the defence. The attack was made upon Fort Troyon, about twenty miles south of Verdun. The fort was destroyed, but the Germans were repulsed. Four days later, September 24, the real attack was made fifteen miles south of Troyon, on the village of St. Mihiel. The object of Von Strantz was to break through the Verdun-Toul line, to inclose Sarrail from the south and at Revigny link arms with the Crown Prince. They then would have had the army of Sarrail surrounded.

For several days it looked as though Von Strantz would succeed, but, though outnumbered, Sarrail's line held, and he forced Von Strantz to "dig in" at St. Mihiel. There he still is, like a dagger that has failed to reach the heart but remains implanted in the flesh.

Von Strantz having failed, a week later, on October 3, the Crown Prince attacked through the Forest of the Argonne between Varennes and Verdun. But this assault also was repulsed by Sarrail, who captured Varennes, and with his left joined up with the Fourth Army of General Langle. The line as then formed by that victory remained much as it is today. The present attack is directed neither to the north nor south of Verdun, but straight at the forts of the city. These forts form but a part of the defences. For twenty miles in front of Verdun have been spread trenches and barb-wire. In turn, these are covered by artillery positions in the woods and on every height. Even were a fort destroyed, to occupy it the enemy must pass over a terrain, every foot of which is under fire. As the defence of Verdun has been arranged, each of the forts is but a rallying-point—a base. The actual combat that will decide the struggle will be fought in the open.

Last month I was invited to one of the Verdun forts. It now lies in the very path of the drive, and to describe it would be improper. But the approaches to it are now what every German knows. They were more impressive even than the fort. The "glacis" of the fort stretched for a mile, and as we walked in the direction of the German trenches there was not a moment when from every side French guns could not have blown us into fragments. They were mounted on the spurs of the hills, sunk in pits, ambushed in the thick pine woods. Every step forward was made cautiously between trenches, or through mazes of barb-wire and iron hurdles with bayonet-like spikes. Even walking leisurely you had to watch your step. Pits opened suddenly at your feet, and strands of barbed-wire caught at your clothing. Whichever way you looked trenches flanked you. They were dug at every angle, and were not farther than fifty yards apart.

On one side, a half mile distant, was a hill heavily wooded. At regular intervals the trees had been cut down and uprooted and, like a wood-road, a cleared space showed. These were the nests of the "seventy-fives." They could sweep the approaches to the fort as a fire-hose flushes a gutter. That a human being should be ordered to advance against such pitfalls and obstructions, and under the fire from the trenches and batteries, seemed sheer murder. Not even a cat with nine lives could survive.

The German papers tell that before the drive upon Verdun was launched the German Emperor reproduced the attack in miniature. The whereabouts and approaches to the positions they were to take were explained to the men. Their officers were rehearsed in the part each was to play. But no rehearsal would teach a man to avoid the pitfalls that surround Verdun. The open places are as treacherous as

A valley in Argonne showing a forest destroyed by shells. Owing to the attack on the Verdun sector, it is again under fire.

quicksands, the forests that seem to him to offer shelter are a succession of traps. And if he captures one fort he but brings himself under the fire of two others.

From what I saw of the defences of Verdun from a "certain place" three miles outside the city to a "certain place" fifteen miles farther south, from what the general commanding the Verdun sector told me, and from what I know of the French, I believe the Crown Prince will find this second attack upon Verdun a hundred per cent more costly than the first, and equally unsuccessful.

CHAPTER 10

War in the Vosges

Paris, January, 1916.

When speaking of their five hundred miles of front, the French General Staff divide it into twelve sectors. The names of these do not appear on maps. They are family names and titles, not of certain places, but of districts with imaginary boundaries. These nicknames seem to thrive best in countries where the same race of people have lived for many centuries. With us, it is usually when we speak of mountains, as "in the Rockies," "in the Adirondacks," that under one name we merge rivers, valleys, and villages. To know the French names for the twelve official fronts may help in deciphering the communiqués. They are these:

Flanders, the first sector, stretches from the North Sea to beyond Ypres; the Artois sector surrounds Arras; the centre of Picardie is Amiens; Santerre follows the valley of the Oise; Soissonais is the sector that extends from Soissons on the Aisne to the Champagne sector, which begins with Rheims and extends southwest to include Chalons; Argonne is the forest of Argonne; the Hauts de Meuse, the district around Verdun; Woevre lies between the heights of the Meuse and the River Moselle; then come Lorraine, the Vosges, all hills and forests, and last, Alsace, the territory won back from the enemy.

Of these twelve fronts, I was on ten. The remaining two I missed through leaving France to visit the French fronts in Serbia and Salonika. According to which front you are on, the trench is of mud, clay, chalk, sand-bags, or cement; it is ambushed in gardens and orchards, it winds through flooded mud flats, is hidden behind the ruins of wrecked villages, and is paved and reinforced with the stones and bricks from the smashed houses.

Of all the trenches the most curious were those of the Vosges. They were the most curious because, to use the last word one associates with trenches, they are the most beautiful.

We started for the trenches of the Vosges from a certain place close to the German border. It was so close that in the inn a rifle-bullet from across the border had bored a hole in the *café* mirror.

The car climbed steadily. The swollen rivers flowed far below us, and then disappeared, and the slopes that fell away on one side of the road and rose on the other became smothered under giant pines. Above us they reached to the clouds, below us swept grandly across great valleys. There was no sign of human habitation, not even the hut of a charcoal-burner. Except for the road we might have been the first explorers of a primeval forest. We seemed as far removed from the France of cities, cultivated acres, stone bridges, and *châteaux* as Rip Van Winkle lost in the Catskills. The silence was the silence of the ocean.

We halted at what might have been a lumberman's camp. There were cabins of huge green logs with the moss still fresh and clinging, and smoke poured from mud chimneys. In the air was an enchanting odour of balsam and boiling coffee. It needed only a man in a Mackinaw coat with an axe to persuade us we had motored from a French village ten hundred years old into a perfectly new trading-post on the Saskatchewan.

But from the lumber camp the colonel appeared, and with him in the lead we started up a hill as sheer as a church roof. The freshly cut path reached upward in short, zigzag lengths. Its outer edge was shored with the trunks of the trees cut down to make way for it. They were fastened with stakes, and against rain and snow helped to hold it in place. The soil, as the path showed, was of a pink stone. It cuts easily, and is the stone from which cathedrals have been built. That suggests that to an ambitious young sapling it offers little nutriment, but the pines, at least, seem to thrive on it. For centuries they have thrived on it. They towered over us to the height of eight stories. The ground beneath was hidden by the most exquisite moss, and moss climbed far up the tree trunks and covered the branches. They looked, as though to guard them from the cold, they had been swathed in green velvet. Except for the pink path we were in a world of green—green moss, green ferns, green tree trunks, green shadows. The little light that reached from above was like that which filters through the glass sides of an aquarium.

It was very beautiful, but was it war? We might have been in the Adirondacks in the private camp of one of our men of millions. You expected to see the fire-warden's red poster warning you to stamp out the ashes, and to be careful where you threw your matches. Then the path dived into a trench with pink walls, and, overhead, arches of green branches rising higher and higher until they interlocked and shut out the sky. The trench led to a barrier of logs as round as a flour-barrel, the openings plugged with moss, and the whole hidden in fresh pine boughs. It reminded you of those open barricades used in boar hunting, and behind which the German Emperor awaits the onslaught of thoroughly terrified pigs.

Like a bird's nest it clung to the side of the hill, and, across a valley, looked at a sister hill a quarter of a mile away.

"On that hill," said the colonel, "on a level with us, are the Germans."

Had he told me that among the pine-trees across the valley Santa Claus manufactured his toys and stabled his reindeer I would have believed him. Had humpbacked dwarfs with beards peeped from behind the velvet tree trunks and doffed red nightcaps, had we discovered fairies dancing on the moss carpet, the surprised ones would have been the fairies.

In this enchanted forest to talk of Germans and war was ridiculous. We were speaking in ordinary tones, but in the stillness of the woods our voices carried, and from just below us a dog barked.

"Do you allow the men to bring dogs into the trenches?" I asked. "Don't they give away your position?"

"That is not one of our dogs," said the colonel. "That is a German sentry dog. He has heard us talking."

"But that dog is not across that valley," I objected. "He's on this hill. He's not two hundred yards below us."

"But, yes, certainly," said the colonel. Of the man on duty behind the log barrier he asked:

"How near are they?"

"Two hundred yards," said the soldier. He grinned and, leaning over the top log, pointed directly beneath us.

It was as though we were on the roof of a house looking over the edge at someone on the front steps. I stared down through the giant pine-trees towering like masts, mysterious, motionless, silent with the silence of centuries. Through the interlacing boughs I saw only shifting shadows or, where a shaft of sunlight fell upon the moss, a flash of vivid green. Unable to believe, I shook my head. Even the *boche* watchdog, now thoroughly annoyed, did not convince me. As though

War in the forest.
A cemetery for soldiers killed in the Vosges

reading my doubts, an officer beckoned, and we stepped outside the breastworks and into an intricate cat's-cradle of barbed-wire. It was lashed to heavy stakes and wound around the tree trunks, and, had the officer not led the way, it would have been impossible for me to get either in or out. At intervals, like clothes on a line, on the wires were strung empty tin cans, pans and pots, and glass bottles. To attempt to cross the entanglement would have made a noise like a peddler's cart bumping over cobbles.

We came to the edge of the barb-wire, and what looked like part of a tree trunk turned into a man-sized bird's nest. The sentry in the nest had his back to us, and was peering intently down through the branches of the tree tops. He remained so long motionless that I thought he was not aware of our approach. But he had heard us. Only it was no part of his orders to make abrupt movements. With infinite caution, with the most considerate slowness, he turned, scowled, and waved us back. It was the care with which he made even so slight a gesture that persuaded me the Germans were as close as the colonel had said. My curiosity concerning them was satisfied. The sentry did not need to wave me back. I was already on my way.

At the post of observation I saw a dog-kennel.

"There are watchdogs on our side, also?" I said.

"Yes," the officer assented doubtfully.

"The idea is that their hearing is better than that of the men, and in case of night attacks they will warn us. But during the day they get so excited barking at the *boche* dogs that when darkness comes, and we need them, they are worn-out and fall asleep."

We continued through the forest, and wherever we went found men at work repairing the path and pushing the barb-wire and trenches nearer the enemy. In some places they worked with great caution as, hidden by the ferns, they dragged behind them the coils of wire; sometimes they were able to work openly, and the forest resounded with the blows of axes and the crash of a falling tree. But an axe in a forest does not suggest war, and the scene was still one of peace and beauty.

For miles the men had lined the path with borders of moss six inches wide, and with strips of bark had decorated the huts and shelters. Across the tiny ravines they had thrown what in seed catalogues are called "rustic" bridges. As we walked in single file between these carefully laid borders of moss and past the shelters that suggested only a gamekeeper's lodge, we might have been on a walking tour in the

Alps. You expected at every turn to come upon a *châlet* like a Swiss clock, and a patient cow and a young woman in a velvet bodice who would offer you warm milk.

Instead, from overhead, there burst suddenly the barking of shrapnel, and through an opening in the tree-tops we saw a French biplane pursued by German shells. It was late in the afternoon, but the sun was still shining and, entirely out of her turn, the moon also was shining. In the blue sky she hung like a silver shield, and toward her, it seemed almost to her level, rose the biplane.

She also was all silver. She shone and glistened. Like a great bird, she flung out tilting wings. The sun kissed them and turned them into flashing mirrors. Behind her the German shells burst in white puffs of smoke, feathery, delicate, as innocent-looking as the tips of ostrich-plumes. The biplane ran before them and seemed to play with them as children race up the beach laughing at the pursuing waves. The biplane darted left, darted right, climbed unseen aerial trails, tobogganed down vast imaginary mountains, or, as a gull skims the crests of the waves, dived into a cloud and appeared again, her wings dripping, glistening and radiant. As she turned and winged her way back to France you felt no fear for her. She seemed beyond the power of man to harm, something supreme, super-human—a sister to the sun and moon, the princess royal of the air.

After you have been in the trenches it seems so selfish to be feasting and drinking that you have no appetite for dinner.

But after a visit to the defenders of the forests of the Vosges you cannot feel selfish. Visits to their trenches do not take away the appetite. They increase it. The air they breathe tastes like brut champagne, and gases cannot reach them. They sleep on pillows of pine boughs. They look out only on what in nature is most beautiful. And their surgeon told me there was not a single man on the sick-list. That does not mean there are no killed or wounded. For even in the enchanted forest there is no enchantment strong enough to ward off the death that approaches crawling on the velvet moss, or hurtling through the tree-tops.

War has no knowledge of sectors. It is just as hateful in the Vosges as in Flanders, only in the Vosges it masks its hideousness with what is beautiful. In Flanders death hides in a trench of mud like an open grave. In the forest of the Vosges it lurks in a nest of moss, fern, and clean, sweet-smelling pine.

CHAPTER 11

Hints For Those Who Want to Help

Paris, January, 1916.

At home people who read of some splendid act of courage or self-sacrifice on the part of the Allies, are often moved to exclaim: "I wish I could help! I wish I could *do* something!"

This is to tell them how easily, at what bargain prices, at what little cost to themselves that wish can be gratified.

In the United States, owing to the war, many have grown suddenly rich; those already wealthy are increasing their fortunes. Here in France the war has robbed every one; the rich are less rich, the poor more destitute. Every *franc* any one can spare is given to the government, to the Bank of France, to fight the enemy and to preserve the country.

The calls made upon the purses of the people never cease, and each appeal is so worthy that it cannot be denied. In consequence, for the war charities there is not so much money as there was. People are not less willing, but have less to give. So, in order to obtain money, those who ask must appeal to the imagination, must show why the cause for which they plead is the most pressing. They advertise just which men will benefit, and in what way, whether in blankets, gloves, tobacco, masks, or leaves of absence.

Those in charge of the relief organizations have learned that those who have money to give like to pick and choose. A tale of suffering that appeals to one, leaves another cold. One gives less for the wounded because he thinks those injured in battle are wards of the state. But for the children orphaned by the war he will give largely. So the petitioners dress their shop-windows.

To the charitably disposed, and over here that means every Frenchman, they offer bargains. They have "white sales," "fire sales." As, at our expositions, we have special days named after the different States, they have special days for the Belgians, Poles, and Serbians.

For these days they prepare long in advance. Their approach is heralded, advertised; all Paris, or it may be the whole of France, knows they are coming.

Christmas Day and the day after were devoted exclusively to the man in the trenches, to obtain money to bring him home on leave. Those days were *les journees du poilu*.

The services of the best black-and-white artists in France were commandeered. For advertising purposes they designed the most appealing posters. Unlike those issued by our suffragettes, calling attention to the importance of November 2, they gave some idea of what was wanted.

They did not show Burne-Jones young women blowing trumpets. They were not symbolical, or allegorical; they were homely, pathetic, humorous, human. They were aimed straight at the heart and pocketbook.

They showed the *poilu* returning home on leave, and on surprising his wife or his sweetheart with her hands helpless in the washtub, kissing her on the back of the neck. In the corner the dog danced on his hind legs, barking joyfully.

They showed the men in the trenches, and while one stood at the periscope the other opened their Christmas boxes; they showed father and son shoulder to shoulder marching through the snow, mud, and sleet; they showed the old couple at home with no fire in the grate, saying: "It is cold for us, but not so cold as for our son in the trench."

For every contribution to this Christmas fund those who gave received a decoration. According to the sum, these ran from paper badges on a pin to silver and gold medals.

The whole of France contributed to this fund. The proudest shops filled their windows with the paper badges, and so well was the fund organized that in every town and city petitioners in the streets waylaid every pedestrian.

Even in Modena, on the boundary-line of Italy, when I was returning to France, and sharing a lonely Christmas with the conductor of the wagon-lit, we were held up by train-robbers, who took our money and then pinned medals on us.

Until we reached Paris we did not know why. It was only later we learned that in the two days' campaign the *poilus* was benefited to the sum of many millions of *francs*.

A POSTER INVITING THE PROPRIETORS OF RESTAURANTS AND
HOTELS AND THEIR GUESTS TO WELCOME THE SOLDIERS WHO
HAVE PERMISSION TO VISIT PARIS, ESPECIALLY THOSE WHO
COME FROM THE DISTRICTS INVADED BY THE GERMANS.

In Paris and over all France, for everyone is suffering through the war, there is some individual or organization at work to relieve that suffering. Every one helps, and the spirit in which they help is most wonderful and most beautiful. No one is forgotten.

When the French artists were called to the front, the artists' models of the Place Pigalle and Montmartre were left destitute. They had not "put by." They were butterflies.

So some women of the industrious, busy-bee order formed a society to look after the artists' models. They gave them dolls to dress, and on the sale of dolls the human manikins now live.

Nor is anyone who wants to help allowed to feel that he or she is too poor; that for his *sou* or her handiwork there is no need. The *midinettes*, the "cash" girls of the great department stores and millinery shops, had no money to contribute, so some one thought of giving them a chance to help the soldiers with their needles.

It was purposed they should make cockades in the national colours. Every French girl is taught to sew; each is born with good taste. They were invited to show their good taste in the designing of cockades, which people would buy for a *franc*, which *franc* would be sent to some soldier.

The French did not go about this in a hole-in-a-corner way in a back street. They did not let the "cash" girl feel her artistic effort was only a blind to help her help others. They held a "salon" for the cockades.

And they held it in the same Palace of Art, where at the annual salon are hung the paintings of the great French artists. The cockades are exhibited in one hall, and next to them is an exhibition of the precious tapestries rescued from the Rheims cathedral.

In the hall beyond that is an exhibition of lace. To this, museums, duchesses, and queens have sent laces that for centuries have been family heirlooms. But the cockades of Mimi Pinson by the thousands and thousands are given just as much space, are arranged with the same taste and by the same artist who grouped and catalogued the queens' lace handkerchiefs.

And each little Mimi Pinson can go to the palace and point to the cockade she made with her own fingers, or point to the spot where it was, and know she has sent a *franc* to a soldier of France.

These days the streets of Paris are filled with soldiers, each of whom has given to France some part of his physical self. That his country may endure, that she may continue to enjoy and teach liberty, he has

ALL OVER FRANCE, ON CHRISTMAS DAY AND THE DAY AFTER, MONEY WAS COLLECTED TO SEND COMFORTS AND THINGS GOOD TO EAT TO THE MEN AT THE FRONT.

seen his arm or his leg, or both, blown off, or cut off. But when on the *boulevards* you meet him walking with crutches or with an empty sleeve pinned beneath his Cross of War, and he thinks your glance is one of pity, he resents it. He holds his head more stiffly erect. He seems to say: "I know how greatly you envy me!"

And who would dispute him? Long after the war is ended, so long as he lives, men and women of France will honour him, and in their eyes he will read their thanks. But there is one soldier who cannot read their thanks, who is spared the sight of their pity. He is the one who has made all but the supreme sacrifice. He is the one who is blind. He sits in perpetual darkness. You can remember certain nights that seemed to stretch to doomsday, when sleep was withheld and you tossed and lashed upon the pillow, praying for the dawn. Imagine a night of such torture dragged out over many years, with the dreadful knowledge that the dawn will never come. Imagine Paris with her bridges, palaces, parks, with the Seine, the Tuileries, the boulevards, the glittering shop-windows conveyed to you only through noise. Only through the shrieks of motor-horns and the shuffling of feet.

The men who have been blinded in battle have lost more than sight. They have been robbed of their independence. They feel they are a burden. It is not only the physical loss they suffer, but the thought that no longer are they of use, that they are a care, that in the scheme of things—even in their own little circles of family and friends—there is for them no place. It is not unfair to the *poilu* to say that the officer who is blinded suffers more than the private. As a rule, he is more highly strung, more widely educated; he has seen more; his experience of the world is broader; he has more to lose. Before the war he may have been a lawyer, doctor, man of many affairs. For him it is harder than, for example, the peasant to accept a future of unending blackness spent in plaiting straw or weaving rag carpets. Under such conditions life no longer tempts him. Instead, death tempts him, and the pistol seems very near at hand.

It was to save men of the officer class from despair and from suicide, to make them know that for them there still was a life of usefulness, work, and accomplishment, that there was organized in France the Committee for Men Blinded in Battle. The idea was to bring back to officers who had lost their sight, courage, hope, and a sense of independence, to give them work not merely mechanical but more in keeping with their education and intelligence. The President of France is patron of the society, and on its committees in Paris and New York are many distinguished names. The French Government has promised a house near Paris where the blind soldiers may be educated. When I saw them they were in temporary quarters in the Hôtel de Crillon, lent to them by the proprietor. They had been gathered from hospitals in different parts of France by Miss Winifred Holt, who for years has been working for the blind in her Lighthouse in New York. She is assisted in the work in Paris by Mrs. Peter Cooper Hewitt. The officers were brought to the Crillon by French ladies, whose duty it was to guide them through the streets. Some of them also were their instructors, and in order to teach them to read and write with their fingers had themselves learned the Braille alphabet. This requires weeks of very close and patient study. And no nurse's uniform goes with it. But the reward was great.

It was evident in the alert and eager interest of the men who, perhaps, only a week before had wished to "curse God, and die." But since then hope had returned to each of them, and he had found a door open, and a new life.

And he was facing it with the same or with even a greater courage than that with which he had led his men into the battle that blinded him. Some of the officers were modelling in clay, others were learning typewriting, one with a drawing-board was studying to be an architect, others were pressing their finger-tips over the raised letters of the Braille alphabet.

Opposite each officer, on the other side of the table, sat a woman he could not see. She might be young and beautiful, as many of them were. She might be white-haired and a great lady bearing an ancient title, from the *faubourg* across the bridges, but he heard only a voice.

The voice encouraged his progress, or corrected his mistakes, and a hand, detached and descending from nowhere, guided his hand, gently, as one guides the fingers of a child. The officer was again a child. In life for the second time he was beginning with A, B, and C. The officer was tall, handsome, and deeply sunburned. In his uniform of a *chasseur d'Afrique* he was a splendid figure. On his chest were the medals of the campaigns in Morocco and Algiers, and the crimson ribbon of the Legion of Honour. The officer placed his forefinger on a card covered with raised hieroglyphics.

"N," he announced.

"No," the voice answered him.

"M?" His tone did not carry conviction.

"You are guessing," accused the voice. The officer was greatly confused.

"No, no, *mademoiselle!*" he protested. "Truly, I thought it was an 'M.'"

He laughed guiltily. The laugh shook you. You saw all that he could never see: inside the room the great ladies and latest American countesses, eager to help, forgetful of self, full of wonderful, womanly sympathy; and outside, the Place de la Concorde, the gardens of the Tuileries, the trees of the Champs-Élysées, the sun setting behind the gilded dome of the Invalides. All these were lost to him, and yet as he sat in the darkness, because he could not tell an N from an M, he laughed, and laughed happily. From where did he draw his strength and courage? Was it the instinct for life that makes a drowning man fight against an ocean? Was it his training as an officer of the *Grande Armée*? Was it that spirit of the French that is the one thing no German knows, and no German can ever break? Or was it the sound of a woman's voice and the touch of a woman's hand? If the reader wants to contribute something to help teach a new profession to these gentlemen, who in the fight for civilization have contributed their eyesight, write to the secretary of the committee, Mrs. Peter Cooper Hewitt, Hôtel Ritz, Paris.

There are some other very good bargains. Are you a lover of art, and would you become a patron of art? If that is your wish, you can buy an original water-colour for fifty cents, and so help an art student who is fighting at the front, and assist in keeping alive his family in Paris. Is not that a good bargain?

As everybody knows, the École des Beaux-Arts in Paris is free to students from all the world. It is the *alma mater* of some of the best-known American artists and architects. On its rolls are the names of Sargent, St. Gaudens, Stanford White, Whitney Warren, Beckwith, Coffin, MacMonnies.

Certain schools and colleges are so fortunate as to inspire great devotion on the part of their students, as, in the story told of every college, of the student being led from the football field, who struggles in front of the grand stand and shouts: "Let me go back. I'd die for dear old ——"

But the affection of the students of the Beaux-Arts for their masters, their fellow students and the institution is very genuine.

They do not speak of the distinguished artists, architects, engravers, and sculptors who instruct them as "Doc," or "Prof." Instead they call him "master," and no matter how often they say it, they say it each

A POSTER ADVERTISING THE FUND TO BRING FROM THE TRENCHES "*PERMISSIONAIRES*," THOSE SOLDIERS WHO OBTAIN PERMISSION TO RETURN HOME FOR SIX DAYS.

time as though they meant it.

The American students, even when they return to Paris rich and famous, go at once to call upon the former master of their atelier, who, it may be, is not at all famous or rich, and pay their respects.

And, no matter if his school of art has passed, and the torch he carried is in the hands of younger Frenchmen, his former pupils still salute him as master, and with much the same awe as the village *curé* shows for the cardinal.

When the war came 3,000 of the French students of the Beaux-Arts, past and present, were sent to the front, and there was no one to look after their parents, families, or themselves, it seemed a chance for Americans to try to pay back some of the debt so many generations of American artists, architects, and sculptors owed to the art of France.

Whitney Warren, the American architect, is one of the few Americans who, in spite of the extreme unpopularity of our people, is still regarded by the French with genuine affection. And in every way possible he tries to show the French that it is not the American people who are neutral, but the American Government.

One of the ways he offers to Americans to prove their friendship for France is in helping the students of the Beaux-Arts. He has organized a committee of French and American students which works twelve hours a day in the palace of the Beaux-Arts itself, on the left bank of the Seine.

It is hard to understand how in such surroundings they work, not all day, but at all. The rooms were decorated in the time of the first Napoleon; the ceilings and walls are white and gold, and in them are inserted paintings and panels. The windows look into formal gardens and courts filled with marble statues and busts, bronze medallions and copies of *frescoes* brought from Athens and Rome. In this atmosphere the students bang typewriters, fold blankets, nail boxes, sort out woollen gloves, cigarettes, loaves of bread, and masks against asphyxiating gas. The mask they send to the front was invented by Francis Jacques, of Harvard, one of the committee, and has been approved by the French Government.

There is a department which sends out packages to the soldiers in the trenches, to those who are prisoners, and to the soldiers in the hospitals. There is a system of demand cards on which is a list of what the committee is able to supply. In the trenches the men mark the particular thing they want and return the card. The things most in demand seem to be corn-cob pipes and tobacco from America, sketch-books, and small boxes of water-colours.

The committee also edits and prints a monthly magazine. It is sent to those at the front, and gives them news of their fellow students, and is illustrated, it is not necessary to add, with remarkable talent and humour. It is printed by hand. The committee also supplies the students with post-cards on which the students paint pictures in water-colours and sign them. Every student and ex-student, even the masters paint these pictures. Some of them are very valuable. At two *francs* fifty centimes the autograph alone is a bargain. In many cases your fifty cents will not only make you a patron of art, but it may feed a very hungry family. Write to Ronald Simmons or Cyrus Thomas, École des Beaux-Arts, 17 Quai Malaquais.

There is another very good bargain, and extremely cheap. Would you like to lift a man bodily out of the trenches, and for six days not only remove him from the immediate proximity of asphyxiating gas, shells, and bullets, but land him, of all places to a French soldier the most desired, in Paris? Not only land him there, but for six days feed and lodge him, and give him a present to take away? It will cost you fifteen *francs*, or three dollars. If so, write to *Journal des Restaurateurs*, 24 Rue Richelieu, Paris.

In Paris, we hear that on Wall Street there are some very fine bargains. We hear that in gambling in war brides and ammunition everybody is making money. Very little of that money finds its way to France. Someday I may print a list of the names of those men in America who are making enormous fortunes out of this war, and who have not contributed to any charity or fund for the relief of the wounded or of their families. If you don't want your name on that list you might send money to the American Ambulance at Neuilly, or to any of the 6,300 hospitals in France, to the clearing-house, through H. H. Harjes, 31 Boulevard Haussman, or direct to the American Red Cross.

Or if you want to help the orphans of soldiers killed in battle write to August F. Jaccaci, Hôtel de Crillon; if you want to help the families of soldiers rendered homeless by this war, to the Secours National through Mrs. Whitney Warren, 16 West Forty-Seventh Street, New York; if you want to clothe a French soldier against the snows of the Vosges send him a Lafayette kit. In the clearing-house in Paris I have seen on file 20,000 letters from French soldiers asking for this kit. Some of them were addressed to the Marquis de Lafayette, but the clothes will get to the front sooner if you forward two dollars to the

Lafayette Kit Fund, Hotel Vanderbilt, New York. If you want to help the Belgian refugees, address Mrs. Herman Harjes, Hôtel de Crillon, Paris; if the Serbian refugees, address Monsieur Vesnitch, the Serbian minister to France.

If among these bargains you cannot find one to suit you, you should consult your doctor. Tell him there is something wrong with your heart.

CHAPTER 12

London, a Year Later

February, 1916.

A year ago you could leave the Continent and enter England by showing a passport and a steamer ticket. Today it is as hard to leave Paris, and no one ever *wants* to leave Paris, as to get out of jail; as difficult to invade England as for a rich man to enter the kingdom of heaven. To leave Paris for London you must obtain the permission of the police, the English consul-general, and the American consul-general. That gets you only to Havre. The Paris train arrives at Havre at nine o'clock at night, and while the would-be passengers for the Channel boat to Southampton are waiting to be examined, they are kept on the wharf in a goods-shed. An English sergeant hands each of them a ticket with a number, and when the number is called the passenger enters a room on the shed where French and English officials put him, or her, through a third degree. The examination is more or less severe, and sometimes the passenger is searched.

There is nothing on the wharf to eat or drink, and except trunks nothing on which to sit. If you prefer to be haughty and stand, there is no law against that. Should you leave the shed for a stroll, you would gain nothing, for, as it is war-time, at nine o'clock every restaurant and *café* in Havre closes, and the town is so dark you would probably stroll into the harbour.

So, like emigrants on our own Ellis Island, English and French army and navy officers, despatch bearers, American ambulance drivers, Red Cross nurses, and all the other picturesque travellers of these interesting times, shiver, yawn, and swear from nine o'clock until midnight. To make it harder, the big steamer that is to carry you across the Channel is drawn up to the wharf not forty feet way, all lights and warmth and cleanliness. At least ten men assured me they would return to Havre and across the street from the examination-shed start an all-night restaurant. After a very few minutes of standing around in the rain it was a plan to get rich quick that would have occurred to almost any one.

My number was forty-three. After seeing only five people in one hour pass through the examination-room, I approached a man of proud bearing, told him I was a detective, and that I had detected he was from Scotland Yard. He looked anxiously at his feet.

"How did you detect that?" he asked.

"Your boots are all right," I assured him. "It's the way you stand with your hands behind your back."

By shoving his hands into his pockets he disguised himself, and asked what I wanted. I wanted to be put through the torture-chamber ahead of all the remaining passengers. He asked why he should do that. I showed him the letter that, after weeks of experiment, I found of all my letters, was the one that produced the quickest results. It is addressed vaguely, "To His Majesty's Officers." I call it Exhibit A.

I explained that for purposes of getting me out of the goods-shed and on board the steamer he could play he was one of His Majesty's officers. The idea pleased him. He led me into the examination-room, where, behind a long table, like inspectors in a voting-booth on election day, sat French police officials, officers of the admiralty, army, consular, and secret services. Some were in uniform, some in plain clothes. From above, two arc-lights glared down upon them and on the table covered with papers.

In two languages they were examining a young Englishwoman who was pale, ill, and obviously frightened.

"What is your purpose in going to London?" asked the French official.

"To join my children."

To the French official it seemed a good answer. As much as to say: "Take the witness," he bowed to his English colleagues.

"If your children are in London," demanded one, "what are you doing in France?"

"I have been at Amiens, nursing my husband."

"Amiens is inside our lines. Who gave you permission to remain inside our lines?"

The woman fumbled with some papers.

"I have a letter," she stammered.

The officer scowled at the letter. Out of the corner of his mouth he said: "Permit from the 'W. O.' Husband, Captain in the Berkshires. Wounded at La Bassée."

He was already scratching his *visé* upon her passport. As he wrote, he said, cordially: "I hope your husband is all right again." The woman did not reply. So long was she in answering that they looked up at her. She was chilled with waiting in the cold rain. She had been on a strain, and her lips began to tremble. To hide that fact, and with no intention of being dramatic, she raised her hand, and over her face dropped a black veil.

The officer half rose.

"You should have told us at once, madam," he said. He jerked his head at the detective and toward the door, and the detective picked up her valise, and asked her please to follow. At the door she looked back, and the row of officials, like one man, bent forward.

One of them was engaged in studying my passport. It had been *viséed* by the representatives of all the civilized powers, and except the Germans and their fellow gunmen, most of the uncivilized. The officer was fascinated with it. Like a jig-saw puzzle, it appealed to him. He turned it wrong side up and sideways, and took so long about it that the others, hoping there was something wrong, in anticipation scowled at me. But the officer disappointed them.

"Very interestin'," he said. "You ought to frame it."

Now that I was free to leave the detention camp I perversely felt a desire to remain. Now that I was free, the sight of all the other passengers kicking each other's heels and being herded by Tommies gave me a feeling of infinite pleasure. I tried to express this by forcing money on the detective, but he absolutely refused it. So, instead, I offered to introduce him to a King's messenger. We went in search of the King's messenger. I was secretly alarmed lest he had lost himself. Since we had left the Balkans together he had lost nearly everything else. He had set out as fully equipped as the white knight, or a "temp. sec. lieutenant." But his route was marked with lost trunks, travelling-bags, hat-boxes, umbrellas, and receipts for reservations on steamships, railroad-trains, in wagon-lits, and dining-cars.

A King's messenger has always been to me a fascinating figure. In fiction he is resourceful, daring, ubiquitous. He shows his silver staff, with its running greyhound, which he inherits from the days of Henry VIII, and all men must bow before it. To speed him on his way, railroad-carriages are emptied, special trains are thrown together, steamers cast off only when he arrives. So when I found for days I

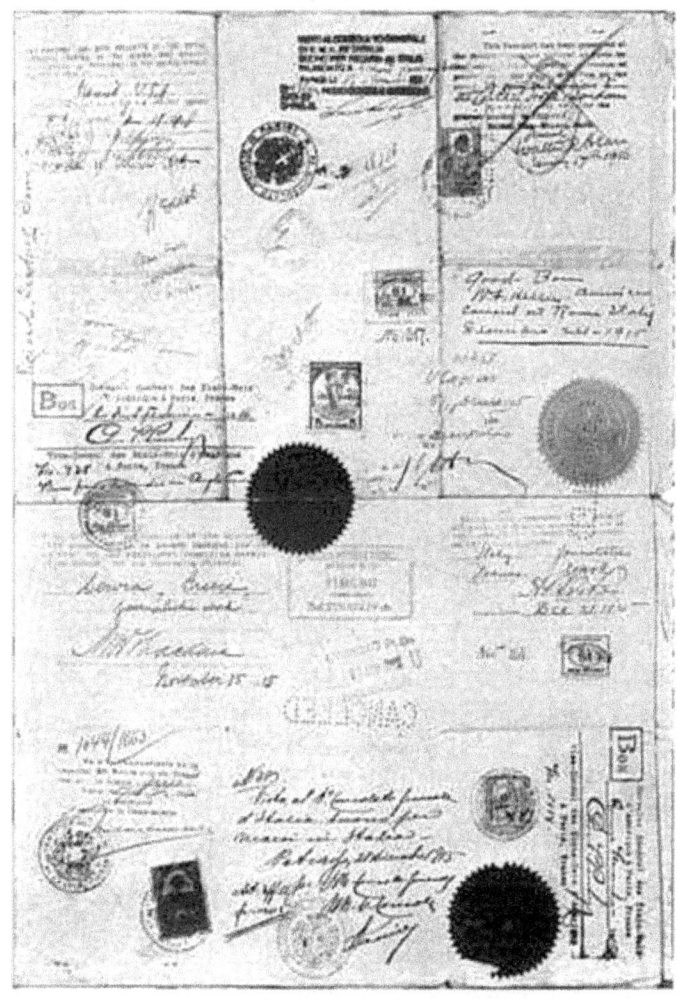

"Very interestin'. You ought to frame it."

was to travel in company with a King's messenger I foresaw a journey of infinite ease and comfort. It would be a royal progress. His ever-present, but invisible, staff of secret agents would protect me. I would share his special trains, his suites of deck cabins. But it was not like that. My King's messenger was not that kind of a King's messenger. Indeed, when he left the Levant, had it not been for the man from Cook's, he would never have found his way from the hotel to the right railroad-station. And that he now is safely in London is because at Patras we rescued him from a boatman who had placed him unresisting on a steamer for Australia.

I pointed him out to the detective. He recalled him as the gentleman who had blocked the exit gate at the railroad-station. I suggested that that was probably because he had lost his ticket.

"Lost his ticket! A King's messenger!" The detective was indignant with me. "Impossible, sir!"

I told him the story of the drunken bandsman returning from the picnic. "You can't have lost your ticket," said the guard.

"Can't I?" exclaimed the bandsman triumphantly. "I've lost the bass-drum!"

Scotland Yard reproved the K. M. with deference, but severely.

"You should have told us at once, sir," he said, "that you were carrying despatches. If you'd only shown your credentials, we'd had you safe on board two hours ago."

The King's messenger blushed guiltily. He looked as though he wanted to run.

"Don't tell me," I cried, "you've lost your credentials, too!"

"Don't be an ass!" cried the K. M. "I've mislaid them, that's all."

The detective glared at him as though he would enjoy leading him to the moat in the tower.

"You've been robbed!" he gasped.

"Have you looked," I asked, "in the unlikely places?"

"I always look there first," explained the K. M.

"Look again," commanded the detective.

Unhappily, the K. M. put his hand in his inside coat pocket and, with intense surprise, as though he had performed a conjuring trick, produced a paper that creaked and crinkled.

"That's it!" he cried.

"You come with me," commanded Scotland Yard, "before you lose it again."

Two nights later, between the acts at a theatre, I met a young old friend. Twenty years before we had made a trip through Central America and Venezuela. To my surprise, for I had known him in other wars, he was not in khaki, but in white waistcoat and lawn tie and tail-coat. He looked as though he had on his hand nothing more serious than money and time. I complained that we had not met since the war.

"It's a chance, our meeting tonight," he said, "for I start for Cairo in the morning. I left the Dardanelles last Wednesday and arrived here only today."

"Wednesday!" I exclaimed. "How could you do it?"

"Torpedo-boat from Moudros to Malta," he explained, "transport to Marseilles, troop train to Calais, and there our people shot me across the Channel on a hospital ship. Then I got a special to town."

"You *are* a swell!" I gasped. "What's your rank?"

"Captain."

That did not explain it.

"What's your job?"

"King's messenger."

It was not yet nine-thirty. The anti-treating law would not let me give him a drink, but I led him to where one was. For he had restored my faith. He had replaced on his pedestal my favourite character in fiction.

On returning to London for the fourth time since the war began, but after an absence of months, one finds her much nearer to the field of operations. A year ago her citizens enjoyed the confidence that comes from living on an island. Compared with Paris, where at Claye the enemy was within fifteen miles, and, at the Forest of Montmorency, within ten miles, London seemed as far removed from the front as Montreal. Since then, so many of her men have left for the front and not returned, so many German air-ships have visited her, and inhumanly assassinated her children and women, that she seems a part of it. A year ago an officer entering a restaurant was conscious of his uniform.

Today, anywhere in London, a man out of uniform, or not wearing a khaki armlet, is as conspicuous as a scarlet letter-box. A year ago the lamps had been so darkened that it was not easy to find the keyhole to your street door. Now you are in luck if you find the street. Nor does that mean you have lingered long at dinner. For after nine-thirty nowhere in London can you buy a drink, not at your hotel, not even at your club. At nine-thirty the waiter whisks your drink off the table. What happens to it after that, only the waiter knows.

A year ago the only women in London in uniform were the nurses. Now so many are in uniform that to one visitor they presented the most surprising change the war has brought to that city. Those who live in London, to whom the change has come gradually, are probably hardly aware how significant it is. Few people, certainly few men, guessed that so many positions that before the war were open only to men, could be filled quite as acceptably by women. Only the comic papers guessed it. All that they ever mocked at, all the suffragettes and "equal rights" women ever hoped for seems to have come true. Even women policemen. True, they do not take the place of the real, immortal London bobby, neither do the "special constables," but if a young girl is out late at night with her young man in khaki, she is held up by a policewoman and sent home. And her young man in khaki dare not resist.

In Paris, when the place of a man who had been mobilized was taken by his wife, sister, or daughter, no one was surprised. Frenchwomen have for years worked in partnership with men to a degree unknown in England. They helped as bookkeepers, shopkeepers; in the restaurant they always handled the money; in the theatres the ushers and box openers were women; the government tobacco-shops were run by women. That Frenchwomen were capable, efficient, hard working was as trite a saying as that the Japanese are a wonderful little people. So when the men went to the front and the women carried on their work, they were only proving a proverb.

But in England careers for women, outside those of governess, typist, barmaid, or show girl, which entailed marrying a marquis, were as few as votes. The war has changed that. It gave woman her chance, and she jumped at it. "When Johnny Comes Marching Home Again" he will find he must look for a man's job, and that men's jobs no longer are sinecures. In his absence women have found out, and, what is more important, the employers have found out that to open a carriage door and hold an umbrella over a customer is not necessarily a man's job. The man will have to look for a position his sister cannot fill, and, judging from the present aspect of London, those positions are rapidly disappearing.

That in the ornamental jobs, those that are relics of feudalism and snobbery, women should supplant men is not surprising. To wear gold lace and touch your hat and whistle for a taxicab, if the whistle is a mechanical one, is no difficult task. It never was absolutely necessary that a butler and two men should divide the labour of serving one cup of coffee, one lump of sugar, and one cigarette. A healthy young woman might manage all three tasks and not faint. So the innovation of female butlers and footmen is not important. But many of the jobs now held in London by women are those which require strength, skill, and endurance. Pulling on the steel rope of an elevator and closing the steel gates for eight hours a day require strength and endurance; and yet in all the big department stores the lifts are worked by girls. Women also drive the vans, and dragging on the brake of a brewery-wagon and curbing two draft-horses is a very different matter from steering one of the cars that made peace hateful. Not that there are no women chauffeurs. They are everywhere. You see them driving lorries, business cars, private cars, taxicabs, ambulances.

In men's caps and uniforms of green, gray, brown, or black, and covered to the waist with a robe, you mistake them for boys. The other day I saw a motor-truck clearing a way for itself down Piccadilly. It was filled with over two dozen Tommies, and driven recklessly by a girl in khaki of not more than eighteen years. How many indoor positions have been taken over by women one can only guess; but if they are in proportion to the out-of-door jobs now filled by women and girls, it would seem as though half the work in London was carried forward by what we once were pleased to call the weaker sex. To the visitor there appear to be regiments of them. They look very business-like and smart in their uniforms, and whatever their work is they are intent upon it.

As a rule, when a woman attempts a man's work she is conscious. She is more concerned with the fact that she is holding down a man's job than with the job. Whether she is a lady lawyer, lady doctor, or lady journalist, she always is surprised to find herself where she is. The girls and women you see in uniform by the thousands in London seem to have overcome that weakness. They are performing a man's work, and their interest is centred in the work, not in the fact that a woman has made a success of it. If, after this, women in England want the vote, and the men won't give it to them, the men will have a hard time explaining why.

During my few days in England, I found that what is going forward in Paris for blind French officers is being carried on in London at St. Dunstan's, Regent's Park, for blind Tommies. At this school the classes are much larger than are those in Paris, the pupils more numerous, and they live and sleep on the premises. The premises are very beautiful. They consist of seventeen acres of gardens, lawns, trees, a lake, and a

"They have women policemen now."

stream on which you can row and swim, situated in Regent's Park and almost in the heart of London. In the days when London was farther away the villa of St. Dunstan's belonged to the eccentric Marquis of Hertford, the wicked Lord Steyne of Thackeray's *Vanity Fair*. It was a country estate. Now the city has closed in around it, but it is still a country estate, with ceilings by the Brothers Adam, portraits by Romney, sideboards by Sheraton, and on the lawn sheep. To keep sheep in London is as expensive as to keep race-horses, and to own a country estate in London can be afforded only by Americans.

The estate next to St. Dunstan's is owned by an American lady. I used to play lawn-tennis there with her husband. Had it not been for the horns of the taxicabs we might have been a hundred miles from the nearest railroad. Instead, we were so close to Baker Street that one false step would have landed us in Mme. Tussaud's. When the war broke out the husband ceased hammering tennis-balls, and hammered German ships of war. He sank several—and is now waiting impatiently outside of Wilhelmshaven for more.

St. Dunstan's also is owned by an American, Otto Kahn, the banker. In peace times, in the winter months, Mr. Kahn makes it possible for the people of New York to listen to good music at the Metropolitan Opera House. When war came, at his country place in London he made it next to possible for the blind to see. He gave the key of the estate to C. Arthur Pearson. He also gave him permission in altering St. Dunstan's to meet the needs of the blind to go as far as he liked.

When I first knew Arthur Pearson he and Lord Northcliffe were making rival collections of newspapers and magazines. They collected them as other people collect postal cards and cigar-bands. Pearson was then, as he is now, a man of the most remarkable executive ability, of keen intelligence, of untiring nervous energy. That was ten years ago. He knew then that he was going blind. And when the darkness came he accepted the burden; not only his own, but he took upon his shoulders the burden of all the blind in England. He organized the National Institute for those who could not see. He gave them of his energy, which has not diminished; he gave them of his fortune, which, happily for them, has not diminished; he gave them his time, his intelligence.

If you ask what the time of a blind man is worth, go to St. Dunstan's and you will find out. You will see a home and school for blind men, run by a blind man. The same efficiency, knowledge of detail, intolerance of idleness, the same generous appreciation of the work of others, that he put into running *The Express* and *Standard*, he now exerts at St. Dunstan's. It has Pearson written all over it just as a mile away there is a building covered with the name of Selfridge, and a cathedral with the name of Christopher Wren. When I visited him in his room at St. Dunstan's he was standing with his back to the open fire dictating to a stenographer. He called to me cheerily, caught my hand, and showed me where I was to sit. All the time he was looking straight at me and firing questions:

"When did you leave Salonika? How many troops have we landed? Our positions are very strong, aren't they?"

He told the stenographer she need not wait, and of an appointment he had which she was not to forget. Before she reached the door he remembered two more things she was not to forget. The telephone rang, and, still talking, he walked briskly around a sofa, avoided a table and an armchair, and without fumbling picked up the instrument. What he heard was apparently very good news. He laughed delightedly, saying: "That's fine! That's splendid!"

A secretary opened the door and tried to tell him what he had just learned, but was cut short.

"I know," said Pearson. "So-and-so has just phoned me. It's fine, isn't it?"

He took a small pad from his pocket, made a note on it, and laid the memorandum beside the stenographer's machine. Then he wound his way back to the fireplace and offered a case of cigarettes. He held them within a few inches of my hand. Since I last had seen him he had shaved his moustache and looked ten years younger and, as he exercises every morning, very fit. He might have been an officer of the navy out of uniform. I had been in the room five minutes, and only once, when he wrote on the pad and I saw that as he wrote he did not look at the pad, would I have guessed that he was blind.

"What we teach them here," he said, firing the words as though from a machine-gun, "is that blindness is not an 'affliction.' We won't allow that word. We teach them to be independent. Sisters and the mothers spoil them! Afraid they'll bump their shins. Won't let them move about. Always leading them. That's bad, very bad. Makes them think they're helpless, no good, invalids for life. We teach 'em to strike out for themselves. That's the way to put heart into them. Make them understand they're of use, that they can help themselves, help others, learn a trade, be self-supporting. We trained them to row. Some of them never had had oars in their hands except on the pond at

Hempstead Heath on a bank holiday. We trained a crew that swept the river."

It was fine to see the light in his face. His enthusiasm gave you a thrill. He might have been Guy Nickalls telling how the crew he coached won at New London.

"They were the best crews, too. University crews. Of course, our coxswain could see, but the crew were blind. We've not only taught them to row, we've taught them to support themselves, taught them trades. All men who come here have lost their eyesight in battle in this war, but already we have taught some of them a trade and set them up in business. And while the war lasts business will be good for them. And it must be nursed and made to grow. So we have an 'after-care' committee. To care for them after they have left us. To buy raw material, to keep their work up to the mark, to dispose of it. We need money for those men. For the men who have started life again for themselves. Do you think there are people in America who would like to help those men?"

I asked, in case there were such people, to whom should they write.

"To me," he said, "St. Dunstan's, Regent's Park."[1]

I found the seventeen acres of St. Dunstan's so arranged that no blind man could possibly lose his way. In the house, over the carpets, were stretched strips of matting. So long as a man kept his feet on matting he knew he was on the right path to the door. Outside the doors hand-rails guided him to the workshops, schoolrooms, exercising-grounds, and kitchen-gardens. Just before he reached any of these places a brass knob on the hand-rail warned him to go slow. Were he walking on the great stone terrace and his foot scraped against a board he knew he was within a yard of a flight of steps. Wherever you went you found men at work, learning a trade, or, having learned one, intent in the joy of creating something.

To help them there are nearly sixty ladies, who have mastered the Braille system and come daily to teach it. There are many other volunteers, who take the men on walks around Regent's Park and who talk and read to them. Everywhere was activity. Everywhere someone

---

1. In New York, the Permanent Blind Relief War Fund for Soldiers and Sailors of Great Britain, France, and Belgium is working in close association with Mr. Pearson. With him on the committee, are Robert Bacon, Elihu Root, Myron T. Herrick, Whitney Warren, Lady Arthur Paget, and George Alexander Kessler. The address of the fund is 590 Fifth Avenue.

was helping someone: the blind teaching the blind; those who had been a week at St. Dunstan's doing the honours to those just arrived. The place spoke only of hard work, mutual help, and cheerfulness. When first you arrived you thought you had over the others a certain advantage, but when you saw the work the blind men were turning out, which they could not see, and which you knew with both your eyes you never could have turned out, you felt apologetic.

There were cabinets, for instance, measured to the twentieth of an inch, and men who were studying to be masseurs who, only by touch, could distinguish all the bones in the body. There was Miss Woods, a blind stenographer. I dictated a sentence to her, and as fast as I spoke she took it down on a machine in the Braille alphabet. It appeared in raised figures on a strip of paper like those that carry stock quotations. Then, reading the sentence with her fingers, she pounded it on an ordinary typewriter. Her work was faultless.

What impressed you was the number of the workers who, over their task, sang or whistled. None of them paid any attention to what the others were whistling. Each acted as though he were shut off in a world of his own. The spirits of the Tommies were unquenchable.

Thorpe Five was one of those privates who are worth more to a company than the sergeant-major. He was a comedian. He looked like John Bunny, and when he laughed he shook all over, and you had to laugh with him, even though you were conscious that Thorpe Five had no eyes and no hands. But was he conscious of that? Apparently not. Was he down-hearted? No! Someone snatched his cigarette; and with the stumps of his arms he promptly beat two innocent comrades over the head. When the lady guide interfered and admitted it was she who had robbed him, Thorpe Five roared in delight.

"I bashed 'em!" he cried. "Her took it, but I bashed the two of 'em!"

A private of the Munsters was weaving a net, and, as though he were quite alone, singing, in a fine baritone, "Tipperary." If you want to hear real close harmony, you must listen to Southern darkeys; and if you want to get the sweetness and melancholy out of an Irish chant, an Irishman must sing it. I thought I had heard "Tipperary" before several times, and that it was a march. I found I had not heard it before, and that it is not a march, but a lament and a love-song. The soldier did not know we were listening, and while his fingers wove the meshes of the net, his voice rose in tones of the most moving sweetness. He did not know that he was facing a window, he did not know that he was staring straight out upon the city of London. But we knew, and when in his rare baritone and rare brogue he whispered rather than sang the lines:

Goodbye, Piccadilly—
Farewell, Leicester Square,
It's a long, long way to Tipperary

—all of his unseen audience hastily fled.

There was also Private Watts, who was mending shoes. When the week before Lord Kitchener visited St. Dunstan's, Watts had joked with him. I congratulated him on his courage.

"What was your joke?" I inquired.

"He asked me when I was a prisoner with the Germans how they fed me, and I said: 'Oh, they gave me five beefsteaks a day.'"

"That was a good joke," I said. "Did Kitchener think so?"

The man had been laughing, pleased and proud. Now the blank eyes turned wistfully to my companion.

"Did his lordship smile?" he asked.

Those blind French officers at the Crillon in Paris and these English Tommies are teaching a great lesson. They are teaching men who are whining over the loss of money, health, or a job, to be ashamed. It is not we who are helping them, but they who are helping us. They are showing us how to face disaster and setting an example of real courage. Those who do not profit by it are more blind than they.

Letters From the Front
Edited by Charles Belmont Davis

On June 15 1914 Richard sailed on the *Utah* for New York, arriving there on the 22nd. For a few weeks after his return he remained at Mount Kisco completing his articles on the Mexican situation but at the outbreak of the Great War he at once started for Europe, sailing with his wife on August 4, the day war was declared between England and Germany.

On *Lusitania*—August 8, 1914.

Dear Chas:

We got off in a great rush, as the Cunard people received orders to sail so soon after the Government had told them to cancel all passengers, that no one expected to leave by her, and had secured passage on the *Lorraine* and *St. Paul*.

They gave me a "regal" suite which at other times costs $1,000 and it is so darned regal that I hate to leave it. I get sleepy walking from one end of it to the other; and we have open fires in each of the three rooms. Generally when one goes to war it is in a transport or a troop train and the person of the least importance is the correspondent. So, this way of going to war I like. We now are a cruiser and are slowly being painted grey, and as soon as they got word England was at war all lights were put out and to find your way you light matches.

You can imagine the effect of this Ritz Carlton idea of a ship wrapped in darkness. Gerald Morgan is on board, he is also accredited to *The Tribune*, and Frederick Palmer. I do not expect to be allowed to see anything but will try to join a French army. I will leave Bessie near London with Louise at some quiet place like Oxford or a village on the Thames. We can "take" wireless, but not send it, so as no one is sending and as we don't care to expose our position, we get no news. We are running far North and it is bitterly cold. I think Peary will sue us for infringing his copyrights.

I will try to get in touch with Nora. I am worried lest she cannot get at her money. As British subjects no other thing should upset them. Address me American Embassy, London. I send such love to you both. God bless you.

Dick.

Richard arrived in Liverpool August 13, and made arrangements for his wife to remain in London. Unable to obtain credentials from the English authorities, he started for Brussels and arrived there in time to see the entry of the German troops, which he afterward described so graphically. Indeed this article is considered by many to be one of the finest pieces of descriptive writing the Great War has produced.

For several days after Brussels had come under the control of the Germans Richard remained there and then decided to go to Paris as the siege of the French capital at the time seemed imminent. He and his friend Gerald Morgan, who was acting as the correspondent of the *London Daily Telegraph*, decided to drive to Hal and from there to continue on foot until they had reached the English or French armies where they knew they would be among friends. At Hal they were stopped by the German officials and Morgan wisely returned to Brussels. However, Richard having decided to continue on his way, was promptly seized by the Germans and held as an English spy. For a few days he had a most exciting series of adventures with the German military authorities and his life was frequently in danger. It was finally due to my brother's own strategy and the prompt action of our Ambassador to Belgium, Brand Whitlock, that he was returned to Brussels and received his official release.

On August 27, Richard left Brussels for Paris on a train carrying English prisoners and German wounded, and en route saw much of the burning and destruction of Louvain.

Brussels, August 17, 1914.

Dearest:

Write me soon and often! All is well here so long as I know you are all right, so do not fail to tell me all, and keep me in touch. If *I* do not write much it is because letters do not get through always, and are read. But you know I love you, and you know twice each day I pray for you and wish for you all the time. I feel as though I had been gone a month. Gerald Morgan and I got in last night; this is a splendid new hotel; for $2.50 I get a room and bath like yours on the "royal suite," only bigger. This morning the minister did everything he could for us. There are about twenty Americans who want credentials. They say they will take no Americans, but to our minister they said they would make exception in favour of three, so I guess the three will be John McCutcheon, Palmer and myself. John and I, if anyone gets a pass, are sure.

With the passes we had, Gerald and I started out in a yellow motor, covered with flags of the Allies, and saw a great deal. How I wished you were with me, you would so have loved it. The country is absolutely beautiful. We were stopped every quarter mile to show our passes and we got a working idea of how it will be. Tonight I dined with Mr. Whitlock, the minister, and John McCutcheon came in and Irving Cobb. John and I will get together and go out. All you need is a motor car and you can go pretty much everywhere, *except* near where there is fighting. So what I am to do to earn my wages I don't know. I am now going to bed and I send my darlin' all love. Today I sent you a wire. If it got to you let me know. Take such good care of yourself. Remember me to Louise, and, *write me*. All love, *dear, dear* one. My wife and my sweetheart.

        Your husband,
            Richard.

The following is the last letter that got through.

                            Brussels, August 21, 1914.

Dearest One:

I cannot say much, as I doubt if this will be opened by you. The German army came in and there was no fighting and I am very well. I am only distressed at not being able to get letters from you, and not being able to send them. I will write a long one, and hold it until I am sure of some way by which it can reach you.

    You know what I would say.

Mrs. Davis had waited in London to meet Richard on his return from the war, but a misunderstanding as to the date of his return, coupled with her strong sense of duty to his interests at home, gave occasion for the letter which follows:

London, August 31, 1914.

Dearest One:

Not since the Herald Square days have I had such a blow as when I drove up to 10 Clarges, and found you gone! *It was nobody's fault! you were so right to go*; and *I could not come.* I am so distressed lest it was my cable saying I could not get back that decided you to go before the fifth. But Ashford says it was not. He tells me the cable came at *three* in the morning and that you had arranged to be called at six-thirty in order to leave for Scotland. So, for sending that cable I need not blame myself too much. I sent you so many messages I do not know which got through. But I think it must have been one saying I could not return in time to see you before the fifth, *then*, no trains were running. The very next day the Germans started a troop train, and I took it.

The reason I could not come by automobile was because I had a falling out with the "mad dogs" and they would not give me a pass. So Evans, with whom I was to motor to Holland, got through Friday afternoon and sent the cable. As soon as I reached Holland, I cabled I was coming and kept on telegraphing every step of the journey, which lasted three days.

I telegraphed last from Folkestone; even telling you what to have for my supper. As you directed, Ashford opened the cables, and when I drove up, he was at the door in tears. He had made a light in your rooms and, of course, as I looked up I thought you still were in them. When they told me I was a day late, I cried, too. It was the bitterest disappointment I ever knew. I had taken the very first train out of Brussels, the one with the wounded, and for three days had been having one hell of a time.

But I kept thinking of seeing you, and hearing your dear voice. So the trip did not matter. I was only thinking of *seeing you*, and thanking God I was shut of the dirty Germans. We had nothing to eat, and we slept on the floor of the train, the Germans kept us locked in, and, all through even Holland, we were under arrest. But nothing mattered, because I was so happy at thought of meeting you. As I said neither of us was at fault. You just *had* to go, and I could *not come.* But, you can feel how I felt to learn you were at sea.

I was so glad I could use your old rooms. I went to the table where you used to write and was so glad I could at least be as near to you as that. No other place in London could have held me that night. Not Buckingham Palace. I found little things you had left. I loved even the funny pictures on the wall because we had talked of them together. It was *rotten, rotten* luck. But only the Germans and their hellish war were to blame. I drove straight to the cable office, and tried to wireless you, knowing you would feel glad to know I was well, and safe and sound. But the cable people could not send my message. You were then out of reach of wireless, on the Irish coast.

And for nine days there was no way to tell you I had come back as fast as trains and boats and the dirty Germans would let me. Oh, my dear, dear one, *how I love* you. If only I could have seen you for just five minutes. As it was, I thought for five days more we would be together. What I shall do now, I don't know. I must go back with either the French or the English until my contract expires, and then, I can join you. Tomorrow I am trying to see Asquith and Churchill to get with the army. And I will at once return across the channel. But, do not worry! I will never again let a German come within *one mile* of me! After this, between me and the Germans, there will be some hundreds of thousands of English or French.

So after this reaches you I will soon be on my way *home*. Don't worry. Get James back and Amelia and everyone else who can make you comfortable, and trust in the good Lord. I have your cross and St. Rita around my neck, and in spite of what the *Kaiser* says, God is looking after other people than Germans. Certainly he has taken good care of me. And he will guard you, and our "blessed" one. And in a little time, dear, *dear* heart, I will be back, and I will become a grocer. God love you and keep you, as he does. And you will never know *how I love you!* Goodnight, dearest, sweetheart and wife! I am writing this at your table, and, thanking God you are going to the farm, and to peace and happiness. *I send you all the love in all the world.*

Richard.

London, September 3rd.

My Dearest One:
It was a full moon again tonight and I think you were on deck and saw it, because by now, you have passed the four days at

sea and should be in the St. Lawrence. So I knew you saw the moon, too, and I sent you a kiss, *via* it. It was just over St. James Palace but also it was just over you.

Today has been a day of worries. Wheeler cabled that the papers wanted me to be "neutral" and not write against the Germans. As I am not interested in the German vote, or in advertising of German breweries (such a hard word to *say*) I thought, considering the *exclusive* stories I had sent them, instead of kicking, they ought to be sending me a few bouquets. Especially, as I got cables from Gouvey, Whigham, *Scribner's* and others congratulating me on the anti-German stories. So I cabled Wheeler to tell papers of his syndicate, dictation from them as to what I should write was "unexpected," that they could go to name-of-place censored and that if he wished I would release him from his contract tonight. Considering that without credentials I was with French, Belgian and German armies and saw entry of Germans into Brussels and sacking of Louvain and got arrested as a spy, they were a bit ungrateful. I am now wondering *what* I would have seen *had I had* credentials.

I saw Anthony Hope at the club last night. He had to go back to the country, so I dined alone on English oysters. Fancy anyone being *neutral* in this war! Germany dropping bombs in Paris and Antwerp on women and churches and scattering mines in the channel where they blow up fishermen and burning the cathedrals! A man who now would be neutral would be a coward. Good night, *near, dear, dear* one. It has been several weeks since I had sleep, so if I rave and wander in my letters forgive me. You know how I am thinking of you. God bless you. God keep you for me.

  Your husband who loves you *so*!

London, September 7th.

Dearest:

I just got your cable saying you were at the farm, and well! *how happy it made me!* I cabled you to Quebec, and to Mt. Kisco, and when two days passed and I heard nothing, today I was scared, so I cabled Gouvey to look after you, and also to Wheeler. I went to the Brompton Oratory today, which is the second most important church here (the cardinal lives at Westminster) and burned the *biggest candle* they had for you and the "blessing." A big woman all in black was kneeling in the little chapel and when I could not get the candle to stand up, she beckoned to one of the priests, and he ran and fixed it. Then she went on praying.

And *who* do you think she was? Queen Amelie of Portugal, you see her pictures in the *Tattler* and *Sphere* opening bazaars. So she must be very good or she would not be saying her prayers all alone with the poor people and seeing that my Bessie's candle was burning. I have been waiting here hoping to get some sort of credentials from Kitchener. But though Winston Churchill has urged him, and tomorrow is going to urge him again, they give me no hope. So I'll just go over "on my own" and I bet I'll see more than anyone else. I have fine papers, anyhow. I am now writing for the morning *Chronicle* over here. Today I finished the *Scribner* article, so *that* is off my mind. And now that you are home, I have no "worries." I wish I had got your cable earlier. I would have had *oysters* and champagne in *bath tubs*. Give my love to all the flowers, and to Shea and Paedrig, and Tom, and Louise, and Gouvey and the lake. And take *such* good care of yourself, and love me, and be happy for I do so love you dear one. *I do so love you.*

   Your Husband.

                September 15th.

Dearest:

Tonight I got your cable in answer to mine asking if you were well. All things considered twenty-four hours was not so long for them to get the answer to me. You *bet* I will be careful. I don't want to get nearer to a German than twenty miles. At the battlefield I collected five German spiked helmets but at the Paris gate they took *all* of them from me. I *was* mad! I wanted to keep them in my "gym," and pound them with Indian clubs. I wrote all day yesterday, so today I did not work. There is nothing more here to do. And as soon as my contract is up October 1st, I will make towards *you!*

Seeing the big battle was great luck. So far I have seen more than anyone. I have had no credentials; and yet have been with *all* the armies. Now I am just beating time, until I can get home. The fighting is too far away even if I could go to it. But I can't without being arrested. And I am fed up on being arrested. Today all the little children came out of doors. They have been locked up for fear of airships. It was fine to see them playing in the Champs Elysees and making forts out of pebbles, and rolling hoops.

God loves you, dear one, and I trust in Him. But I am awful sick for a sight of you. What a lot we will have to tell each other. One thing I never have to tell you, but it makes me happy when I can. It is this: *I love you!* And every minute I think of you.

With all my love.
Your
Richard.

Paris, September 15th, 1914.

Dear Chas.:

I got this morning your letter of August 25th. In it you say kind things about my account of the Germans entering Brussels. Nothing so much pleases me as to get praise from you or to know my work pleases you. Since the Germans were pushed in every one here is breathing again. But for me it was bad as now the armies are too far to reach by taxicab, and if you are caught anywhere outside the city you are arrested and as a punishment sent to Tours. Eight correspondents, among them two *Times* men and John Reed and Bobby Dunn, were sent to Tours Sunday.

I had another piece of luck that day with Gerald Morgan. I taxicabed out to Soissons and saw a wonderful battle. So, now I can go home in peace. Had I been forced to return without seeing any fighting I never would have lived it down. I am in my old rooms of years ago. I got the whole imperial suite for eight francs a day. It used to be 49 *francs* a day. Of course, Paris that closes tight at nine is hardly Paris, but the beauty of the city never so much impressed me. There is no fool running about to take your mind off the gardens and buildings. What *most* makes me know I am in Paris, though, are the packages of segars lying on the dressing table.

Give my love to Dai, and tell her I hope soon to see you. The war correspondent is dead. My only chance was to get with the English who will take one American and asked Bryan to choose, he passed it to the Press Association and they chose Palmer. But I don't believe the official correspondents will be allowed to see much. I saw the Germans enter Brussels, the burning of Louvain and the Battle of Soissons and had a very serious run in with the Germans and nearly got shot. But now

if you go out, every man is after you, and even the *gendarmes* try to arrest you. It is sickening. For never, of course, was there such a chance to describe things that everyone wants to read about. Again my love to Dai and you. I will see you soon.
Richard.

In October Richard returned to the United States and settled down to complete his first book on the war. During this period and indeed until the hour of his death my brother devoted the greater part of his time to the cause of the Allies. He had always believed that the United States should have entered the war when the Germans first outraged Belgium, and to this effect he wrote many letters to the newspapers. In addition to this he was most active in various of the charities devoted to the causes of the Allies, wrote a number of appeals, and contributed money out of all proportion to his means. The following appeal he wrote for the Secours National:

You are invited to help women, children and old people in Paris and in France, wherever the war has brought desolation and distress. To France you owe a debt. It is not alone the debt you incurred when your great grandfathers fought for liberty, and to help them, France sent soldiers, ships and two great generals, Rochambeau and La Fayette. You owe France for that, but since then you have incurred other debts.

Though you may never have visited France, her art, literature, her discoveries in Science, her sense of what is beautiful, whether in a bonnet, a *boulevard* or a triumphal arch, have visited you. For them you are the happier; and for them also, to France you are in debt.

If you have visited Paris, then your debt is increased a hundred fold. For to whatever part of France you journeyed, there you found courtesy, kindness, your visit became a holiday, you departed with a sense of renunciation; you were determined to return. And when after the war, you do revisit France, if your debt is unpaid, can you without embarrassment sink into debt still deeper? What you sought Paris gave you freely. Was it to study art or to learn history, for the history of France is the history of the world; was it to dine under the trees or to rob the Rue de la Paix of a new model; was it for weeks to motor on the white roads or at a cafe table watch the world pass? Whatever you sought, you found. Now, as in 1776 we fought, today

France fights for freedom, and in behalf of all the world, against militarism that is 'made in Germany.'

Her men are in the trenches; her women are working in the fields, sweeping the Paris *boulevards*, lighting the street lamps. They are undaunted, independent, magnificently capable. They ask no charity. But from those districts the war has wrecked, there are hundreds of thousands of women and little children without work, shelter or food. To them throughout the war zone the Secours National gives instant relief. In one day in Paris alone it provides 80,000 free meals. Six cents pays for one of these meals. One dollar from you will for a week keep a woman or child alive.

The story is that one man said, 'In this war the women and children suffer most. I'm awfully sorry for them!' and the other man said, 'Yes I'm five dollars sorry. How sorry are you?'

"If ever you intend paying that debt you owe to France do not wait until the war is ended. Now, while you still owe it, do not again impose yourself upon her hospitality, her courtesy, her friendship.

But, pay the debt now.

And then, when next in Paris you sit at your favourite table and your favourite waiter hands you the menu, will you not the more enjoy your dinner if you know that while he was fighting on the Aisne, it was your privilege to help a little in keeping his wife and child alive.

The winter of 1914-15 Richard and his wife spent in New York, and on January 4, 1915, their baby, Hope, was born. No event in my brother's life had ever brought him such infinite happiness, and during the short fifteen months that remained to him she was seldom, if ever, from his thoughts, and no father ever planned more carefully for a child's future than Richard did for his little daughter.

On April 11 my brother and his wife took Hope to Crossroads for the first time. In his diary of this time he writes:

> Only home in the world is the one I own. Everything belongs. It is so comfortable and the lake and the streams in the woods where you can get your feet wet. The thrill of thinking a stump is a trespasser! You can't do that on ten acres.

A cause in which Richard was enormously interested at this time was that of the preparedness of his own country, and for it he worked unremittingly. In August, 1915, he went to Plattsburg, where he took a month of military training.

On October 19, 1915, Richard sailed on the *Chicago* for France and his second visit to the Great War. He arrived at Paris on October 30, and shortly afterward visited the Western front at Amiens and Artois. He also interviewed Poincare, and through him the French President sent a message to the American people. At this time my brother had received permission from the authorities to visit all of the twelve sectors of the French front under particularly advantageous conditions, and was naturally most anxious to do so. However, through a misunderstanding between the syndicate he represented and certain of the newspapers using its service, he found it advisable, even although against his own judgment, to go to Greece, and to postpone his visit to the sectors of the French front he had not already seen. On November 13 he left Paris bound for Salonica.

On Way to France, Oct. 18, 1915.

Dearest One:

You are much more brave than I am. Anyway, you are much better behaved. For all the time you were talking I was crying, not with my eyes only, but with *all* of me. I am so sad. I love you so, and I will miss you so. I want you to keep saying to yourself all the time, "This is the most serious effort he ever made, because the chances of seeing anything are so *small*, and because never had he such a chance to *help*. But, all the time, every minute he thinks of me. He wants me. He misses my voice, my eyes, my presence at his side when he walks or sleeps. He never loved me so greatly, or at leaving me was so unhappy as he is now."

Goodbye, dear heart. My God-given one! Would it not be wonderful, if tonight when I am up among the boats on the top deck that girl in the Pierrot suit, and in her arms Hope, came, and I took them and held them both? You will walk with her at five, and I will walk and think of you and love you and long for you.

God keep you, dearest of wives, and mothers.
Richard.

October 24.

My Dear Daughter:

So many weeks have passed since I saw you that by now you

are able to read this without your mother looking over your shoulder and helping you with the big words. I have six sets of pictures of you. Every day I take them down and change them. Those your dear mother put in glass frames I do not change. Also, I have all the sweet fruits and chocolates and red bananas. How good of you to think of just the things your father likes. Some of them I gave to a little boy and girl. I play with them because soon my daughter will be as big. They have no mother like you, *of course*; they have no mother like *yours*—for except my mother there never was a mother like yours; so loving, so tender, so unselfish and thoughtful.

If she is reading this, kiss her for me. These little children have a little father. He dresses them and bathes them himself. He is afraid of the cold; and sits in the sun; and coughs and shivers. His children and I play hide-and-seek, and, as you will know some day, for that game there is no such place as a steamer, with boats and ventilators and masts and alleyways. Some day we will play that game hiding behind the rocks and trees and rose bushes. Every day I watch the sun set, and know that you and your pretty mother are watching it, too. And all day I think of you both.

Be very good. Do not bump yourself. Do not eat matches. Do not play with scissors or cats. Do not forget your dad. Sleep when your mother wishes it. Love us both. Try to know how we love you. *That* you will never learn. Goodnight and God keep you, and bless you.

  Your Dad.

            Paris, November 1.

Dearest One:

Today is "moving" day, and I feel like —— censored word, at the thought of your having the moving to direct and manage by yourself. I can picture Barney and Burke loading, and unloading, and coal and wood being stored, and provisions and ice, and finally Hope brought down to take her third—no—fourth motor ride. And God will see she makes it all safely, and that in her new house you are comfortable.

Last night I dreamed about Hope and you, a long dream, and it made me so happy. Something happened today that you will like to hear. When the war came the French students at the Beaux Arts had to go to fight. The wives and children had nothing

R. H. D. AND CAPTAIN GABRIEL PUAUX OF THE
GENERAL HEADQUARTERS STAFF AT THE RUINED
VILLAGE OF GERBEVILLE.

to live on. So, the American students, about a dozen of them, organized a relief league. The Beaux Arts is in a most wonderful palace built by Cardinal Richelieu and decorated later by Napoleon. In this they were gathering socks, asphyxiating masks, warm clothes. They were hand painting postcards for fifty cents apiece. The "masters" as they call their teachers, also were painting them. I gave them some money which was received politely, but, as it would not go far, without much enthusiasm. As I was going, I said, "I'll be back tomorrow to get some facts and I'll write a story about what you're doing."

This is the part that is embarrassing to write, but you will understand. They gave a cheer and a yell just as though I had said, "Peace is declared" or "I will give you Carnegie's fortune." And they danced around, and shook hands, and Whitney Warren, who is at the head of it, all but cried. Later, he told me the letter I had written for his wife's fund for orphans by the war had brought in $5000, that was why they were so pleased. So we, you and I, will try to look at it that way, and try to believe that from this separation, which is cruel for us, others may get some benefit. Tomorrow, I am to be received at the Elysée by the President, and I am going to try to make him say something that will draw money from America for the French hospitals. If he will only ask, I know our people will give. In a day or two, I think I will be allowed to see something, but, that you will know best by reading *The Times*.

Your loving husband is lonely for you, and so it will be always.
 Richard.

November 17th.

Dear Sweetheart:

My last letter was such a complaining one that I am ashamed. But, not leaving me to decide what was best for the papers, made me mad. Since I wrote, I ought to be madder, for I have been to the trenches outside of Rheims in Champagne; and, had they not devilled the spirit out of me with cables, I believe I could have written such a lot of stories of France that no one else has had the opportunity to write. Believe me no one has yet told the story of the trench war. Anyway, in spite of all the photographs and articles, to me it was all new. I was allowed to go alone, and given *carte blanche* to see whatever I wished. I saw everything, but it would not be possible to write of it yet.

It was wonderful.

I was in the three lines, reaching the *first* line by moonlight. No one spoke above a whisper. The Germans were only 300 to 400 yards distant. But worst of all were the rats. They ran over my feet and I was a darned sight more afraid of them than the Germans. I saw the Cathedral, and the only hotel open (from which I sent you and Hope a postal) was the same one in which we stopped a year ago. I had sent the hotel my book in which I said complimentary things, and I got a great welcome. They even gave me a room with a fire in it, and so I was warm for the first time since I left the Crossroads. And this morning it *snowed*. On my way back to Paris, I stopped to tell the General what I had seen and to thank him. He said, "Oh, that is nothing. When you return, I will take you out myself, and I will show you something worthwhile." I am going to carry a rat-trap, and two terriers on a leash.

Tonight, when I got back, there was a letter from you, but no writing, but there was a photo of her, and me holding her. How is it possible that any living thing is so beautiful as my child? How fat, and wonderful, and dear, and lovable, and how terribly I want to hold her as I am holding her in the picture, and how much better as I really don't need my left arm to hold such a mite), if I had you close to me in it. I miss you so, and love you so! I told Wheeler before I left as I was not going to waste time travelling I would not go to Servia. So, as soon as I arrived, I was fretted with cables to go. I cabled to stop giving me advice, that I had a much better chance in France than anyone could have anywhere else. Maybe, before I arrive, the Greeks will have joined the Germans, in which case, *I won't leave the ship*. I'll come straight back on her to the Allies.

Richard.

November 20th.

This is the way Hope's cat looks, "My whiskers!" she says, "I never knew I was to be let in for anything like this!" When I told her about the big rats in the trenches she wanted to go with me next time, but, today when I told her that the Crown Prince of Servia made his servants eat live mice (he is no longer Crown Prince), she looked just as she does in the picture. "Then, what do *I* eat in Servia?" she said, and I told her both of us would live on goat's milk.

287

Hope Davis

You will be glad when I tell you I have been, warm. We came pretty far south in two days, and, the damp chill of Paris is gone. On the train a funny thing happened. An English officer and I got talking and he was press censor at Salonica where I am going after Athens. I asked him to look over the many letters I had and tell me if any of them would be likely to get me in bad, being addressed to pro-Germans, for example. He said, "Well, *this* chap is all right anyway. I'll vouch for him, because this letter is addressed to me."

We leave, the Basses, the English officer and I, in a small tub of a boat for Patras, and train to Athens. I will try to go at once to Servia. Harjes, who are the Paris house of J. P. Morgan, gave me a "mission" to try and organize for the Servians the same form of relief as has been arranged for the Belgians. He gave me permission if I saw the need for help was imminent (and it will be) to cable him for whatever I thought the Serbs most needed. So, it is a chance to do much. To get out news will be impossible. However, here I am and tomorrow I'll be good and seasick.

I have your charm around my neck, and all the pictures, and the luck-bringing cat, and the scapular, and the love you give me to keep me well and bring us soon together. That is the one thing I want. God bless you both,

Hope's dad and your husband.

Richard Harding Davis and Hope Davis

Athens, November 26th.

Dear Heart:

I am off tonight for Salonica. I am not very cheerful for I miss you very, very terribly, and the further I go, the worse I feel. But now I am nearly as far as I can get, and when you receive this I will—thank God—be turned back to Paris, and London, and *home*! I thought so often of you this morning when I took a holiday and climbed the Acropolis. On the top of it I picked a dandelion for you. It was growing between the blocks of marble that have been there since 400 years before our Lord: before St. Paul preached to the Athenians. I was all alone on the rock, and could see over the Ægean Sea, Corinth, Mount Olympus, where the Gods used to sit, and the Sphinx lay in wait for travellers with her famous riddle. It takes two days and one night to go to Salonica, and the boats are so awful no one undresses but sleeps in his clothes on top of the bed.

Goodbye, sweetheart, and give *such* a kiss to my precious daughter. How beautiful she is. Even the waiter who brought me a card stopped to exclaim about her picture. So, of course, being not at all proud I showed him her in my arms. I want you both so and I love you both *so*. And, I wanted you so this morning as I always do when there is a beautiful landscape, or flowers, or palms. I know how you love them. The dandelion is very modest and I hope the censor won't lose it out, for she has a long way to go and carries a burden of love. I wish I was bringing them in the door of the Scribner cottage at this very minute.

Richard.

Volo, November 27.

I got here today, after the darnedest voyage of two days in a small steamer. We ran through a snow storm and there was no way to warm the boat. So, I *died*. You know how cold affects me—well—this was the coldest cold I ever died of. I poured alcohol in me, and it was like drinking iced tea. Now, I am on shore in a cafe near a stove. We continue on to Salonica at midnight. There are 24 men and one woman, Mrs. Bass, on board. I am much too homesick to write more than to say I love you, and I miss you and Hope so, that I don't look at the photos. Did you get the cable I sent Thanksgiving—from Athens, it read: "Am giving thanks for Hope and you." I hope the censor let that get by him.

The boat I was on was a refrigerator ship; it was also peculiar in that the captain dealt baccarat all day with the passengers. It was a sort of floating gambling house. This is certainly a strange land. Snow and roses and oranges, all at once. I must stop. I'm froze. Give the kiss I want to give to *her*, and know, oh! how I love and love and love her mother—*never so much as now.*

Salonica November 30th, 1915.

Dear Old Man:

I got here tonight and found it the most picturesque spot I ever visited. I am glad I came. It was impossible to get a room but I found John McCutcheon and two other men occupying a grand suite and they have had a cot put in for me. Tomorrow I hope to get a room. The place is filled with every nation except Germans and even they are here out of uniforms. We had a strange time coming. The trip from Athens should have taken two nights and a day but we took four. The captain of the boat anchored and played baccarat whenever he thought there were enough passengers not seasick to make it worth his while. He played from eleven in the morning until four in the morning. I don't know now who ran the ship.

It is so cold when you bathe, the steam runs off you. I never have suffered so. But, it looked as though everyone else was singing "It's going to be a hard, hard winter" from the way they, dress. Tomorrow I am going to buy fur pants. You can't believe what a picture it is. Servians, French, Greeks, Scots in kilts, London motor cars, Turks, wounded and bandaged Tommies and millions of them fighting for food, for drink, for a place at the "movies," and more "rumours" than there are words in the directory. Tomorrow, I present my letters and hope to get to the "front." I only hope the front doesn't come to us. But, it ought to be a place for great stories. All love to you old man, and bless you both. How I look forward to our first lunch in your wonderful home! And to sit in front of your fire, and hear all the news. All love to you both.

Richard.

December 6, 1915.

Dearest One:

I have been away so could not write. They took us to the French and English "front" and away from Greece; we were in Bulgaria and Servia. It was at a place where the three boundaries met. We saw remarkable mountain ranges and deep snow, and some fine artillery. But throwing shells into that bleak, white jumble of snow and rocks—there was fifty miles of it—was like throwing a baseball at the Rocky Mountains. Still, it was seeing something. Now, I have a room, and a very wonderful one. I had to bribe everyone in the hotel to get it; and I have something to write and, no more moving about I hope, for at least a week. I am able to see the ships at anchor for miles, and the landing stage for all the warships is just under my window. As near as McCoy Rock from the terrace. It is like a moving picture all the time.

I bought myself an oil stove and a can of Standard oil, and, instead of trying to warm the hotel with my body, I let George do it. But it is a very small stove, and to really get the good of it, I have to sit with it between my legs. Still, it is such a relief to be alone, and not to pack all the time. McCutcheon and Bass, Hare and Shepherd are fine, but I felt like the devil, imposing on them, and working four in a room is no joke. We dine together each night. Except them, I see no one, but have been writing. Also, I have been collecting facts about Servian relief. Harjes, Morgan's representative in Paris, gave me *carte blanche* to call on him for money or supplies; but I waited until today to cable, so as to be sure where help was most needed. It is still cold, but that *awful* cold spell was quite unprecedented and is not likely to come again. I *never* suffered so from cold, and, as you know, I suffer considerable.

All the English officers who had hunted in cold places, said neither had they ever felt such cold. Seven hundred Tommies were frost bitten and toes and fingers fell off. I do not say anything about how awful it is not to hear. But, if I had had your letters forwarded to this dump of the Levant, I never would have got them. Now, I have to wait for them until I get to Paris, but there I will surely get them. Cables, of course, can reach me, but no cables mean to me that you are all right. Nor do I want to "talk" about Christmas.

You know how I feel about that, and about missing the first one *she* has had. But it will be the *last* one we will know apart. Never again!

I want you in my arms and to hear you laugh and see your eyes. I am in need of you to make a fuss over me. McCutcheon and Co. don't care whether I have cold hands or not. You do. Your ointment and gloves saved my fingers from falling off like the soldiers' did. And your "housewife" I use to put on buttons, and, your scapular and medal keep me well. But your love is what really lifts me up and consoles me. When I think how you and I care for each other, then, I am scared, for it is very beautiful. And we must not ever be away from each other again.

God keep you my beloved, and both my blessings. I cannot bear it—when I think of all I am missing of her, and, all that she is doing. God guard you both. My darling and dear wife and mother of Hope.

    Your husband,
        Richard.

Salonica, December 18th.

Dearest Wife and Sweetheart:

I am very blue tonight, and never was so homesick. Yesterday just to feel I was in touch with you I sent a cable through the fog, it said, "Well, homesick, all love to you both." I did not ask if you and Hope were well, because I *know* the good Lord will not let any harm come to you. I am certainly caught by the heels this time. And it will be the last time. As you know, I meant only to go to France where no time would be wasted in travel, and I would be able to get back soon. But the blockade held up the ship and on the other one the captain stayed at anchor, and, then when I got here, the Allies retreated, and I had to stay on to cover what is to come next. What that is, or whether nothing happens, you will know by the time this reaches you. So, here I am.

For *ten* days until this morning we have never seen the sun. In sixty years nothing like it has happened. The Salonicans said the English transports brought the fog with them. Anyway, I got it. My room is right on the harbour. I never thought I would *love* an oil stove. I always thought they were ill-smelling, air-destroying. But this one saved my life. I wrote with it between my knees, I dry my laundry on it, and use the tin pan on top of it to take the dampness out of the bed. The fog kept everything like a sponge. Coal is thirty dollars a ton. To get wood for firewood the boatmen row miles out, and wait below the transports to get the boxes they throw overboard.

I go around asking *everybody* if this place is not now a dead duck for news. But they all give me no encouragement. They say it is the news centre of the world. I hope it chokes. I try to comfort myself by thinking you are happy, because you have Hope, and I have nobody, except John McCutcheon and Bass and Jimmie Hare, and they are as blue as I am, and no one can get any money. I cabled today to Wheeler for some *via* the State Department. I went to the Servian camp for the little orphans whose fathers have been killed, and they all knelt and kissed my hands. It was awful. I thought of Hope, and hugged a few and carried them around in my arms and felt much better.

Today for the first time, I quit work and went to see an American film at the cinema to cheer me. But when I saw the streetcars, and "ready to wear" clothes, and the policemen I got suicidal. I went back and told the others and they all rushed off to see "home" things, and are there now. This is a yell of a letter, but it's the only kind I can write. My stories and cables are rotten, too. I have seen nothing—just travelled and waited for something to happen.

Goodnight, dearest one. I love you so. You will never know how much I love you. Kiss my darling for me, and, think only of the good days when we will be together again. Such good days.

    Goodnight again—all love.

        Richard.

        Harbour Salonica, December 19th.

I am a happy man tonight! And that is the first time I have been able to say so since I left you. The backbone of the trip is broken! and my face is turned West—toward you and Hope. John McCutcheon gave me a farewell dinner tonight of which I got one half, as the police made me go on board at nine, although we do not sail until five in the morning. So there was time for only one toast, as I was making for the door. Was it to your husband? It was not. It was to Hope Davis, two weeks yet of being one year old, and being toasted by the war correspondents in Salonica. They knew it would please me. And I went away very choken and happy.

Such a boat as this is! I have a sofa in the dining-room, and at present it is jammed with refugees and all smoking and not an air port open. What a relief it will be to once more get among clean people. We must help the Servians, and God knows they need help. But, if they would help each other, or themselves, I would like them better. I am now on deck under the cargo light and, on the top floor of the Olympus Hotel, can see John's dinner growing gayer and gayer. It is like the man who went on a honeymoon alone. I am so happy tonight. You seem so near now that I am coming West.

How terribly I have missed you, and wanted you, and longed for your voice and *laugh*, and to have you open the door of my writing room, and say, "A lady is coming to call on you," and then enter the dearest wife and dearest baby in the world!

God bless you, and all my love.
Richard.

Rome,
Christmas Eve, 1915.

My Dearest, Dearest, Dearest:

I planned to get to Paris late Christmas night. I cabled Frazier at the Embassy, to have all my letters at the Hotel de l'Empire. I *meant* to spend the night reading of you and Hope. I made a record trip from Salonica. By leaving the second steamer at Messina and taking an eighteen-hour trip across Italy I saved ten hours. But when I got here I found the French Consul had taken a holiday, *and was out buying christmas presents!* So, I could not get permission to enter France. With some Red Cross Americans, I raged around the French Consulate, but it was no use. So I am here, and cannot leave *until midnight Christmas*. When I found I could not get away, I told Cook's to give me their rapid-fire guide, and I set out to *see Rome*.

The manager of Cook's was the same man who, 19 years ago, sold me tickets to the Greek war in Florence, when the American Consulate was in the same building with Cook's, and Charley was Consul. So he gave me a great guide. We began at ten this morning and we stopped at six. They say it takes five years to see Rome, but when I let the rapid-fire guide escape, he said he had to compliment me; we climbed more stairways and hills than there are in all New York and Westchester County; and there is just one idea in my mind, and that is that you and I must see this sacred place together.

On all this trip I have wanted *you*, but *never* so as today. And I particularly inquired about the milk. It is said to be excellent.

So we will come here, and you, with all your love of what is fine and beautiful, will be very happy, and Hope will learn Italian, and to know what is best in art, and statues and churches. I have seen 2900 churches, and all of them built by Michael Angelo and decorated by Raphael; and it was so wonderful I cried. I bought candles and prayers, and I am afraid Christian Science had a dull day. Tomorrow we start at nine, and go to high mass at St. Peter's, and then into the country to the catacombs, where the early Christians hid from the Romans. It is not what you would call an English Christmas, but it is so beautiful and wonderful that you *both are very near.*

I sent you a cable, the second one, because it is not sure they are forwarded, and I hung up a stocking for Hope. One of the peasant women made in Salonica. I am bringing it with me. And the cat is on my window—still looking out on the Romans. The green leaf I got in the forum, where Mark Antony made his speech over Caesar's body. It is the plant that gave Pericles the idea of the Corinthian column. You remember. It was growing under a tile someone had laid over it—and the yellow flower was on my table at dinner, so I send it, that we may know on Christmas Eve we dined together.

Goodnight, now, and God bless you. I am off to bed now, in a bed with sheets. The first in six days. How I *love* you, and *love* you. Such good wishes I send you, and such love to you both. May the good Lord bless you as he has blessed me—with the best of women, with the best of daughters. I am a proud husband and a proud father; and soon I will be a *happy* husband and a *happy* father.

Goodnight, dear heart.
Richard.

Paris, December 28th, 1915.

Dear Old Man:

Hurrah for the Dictator! He has been a great good friend to me. I will know today about whether I can go back to the French front. If not I will try the Belgians and then London, and home. I spent Christmas day in Rome in the catacombs. I could not wear my heart upon my sleeve for duchesses to peck at. It is just as you say, Dad and Mother made the day so dear and beautiful. I did not know how glad I would be to be back here for while the trip East led to no news value, to me personally it was interesting. But I am terribly tired after the last nine days, sleeping on sofas, decks, a different deck each night and writing all the time and such poor stuff. But, oh! when I saw Paris I knew how glad I was! *What* a beautiful place, what a kind courteous people. We will all be here some day.

Tell Dai she must be my interpreter. All love to her, and you, and good luck to the syndicate. *Your* syndicate. I have not heard from mine for six weeks. They have not sent me a single clipping of anything, so I don't know whether anything got through or not, and I have nothing to show these people here that might encourage them to send me out again. They certainly have made it hard hoeing. Tell Guvey his letter about the toys was a great success here, and copied into several papers.

Goodbye, and God bless you, and good luck to you.

Dick.

Paris, December 31st, 1915.

Dear Old Man:

To wish you and Dai a Happy New Year. It will mean a lot to us when we can get together, and take it together, good and bad. I am awfully pleased over the novel coming out by the Harper's and, in landing so much for me out of *The Dictator*. You have started the New Year for me splendidly. I expect I will be back around the first of February. I am now trying to "get back," but, I need more time. I can only put the trip down to the wrong side of the ledger. Personally, I got a lot out of it, but I am not sent over here to improve my knowledge of Europe, but to furnish news and stories and that has not happened.

I am constantly running against folks who knew you in Florence, and I regret to say most of them are in business at the Chatham bar. What a story they make; the M———'s and the like, who know Paris only from the cocktail side. One of our attaches told me today he had been lunching for the last 18 months at the grill room of the Chatham, where the "mixed grill" was as good as in New York. He had no knowledge of any other place to eat. The Hotel de l'Empire is a terrible tragedy. They are so poor, that I believe it is my eight *francs* a day keeps them going; nothing else is in sight. But, it is the exception.

Never did a people take a war as the French take this worst of all wars. They really are the most splendid of people. I only wish I could have had one of them for a grandfather or grandmother.

Bessie writes that Hope is growing wonderfully and beautifully, and I am sick for a sight of her, and for you. Goodnight and God bless you and the happiest of New Years to you both.
Your loving brother,
Dick.

These postcards are "originals" painted by students of the Beaux-Arts to keep alive, and to keep those students in the trenches. They are for Dai.

Paris, December 31, 1915.

Dearest One:

The old year, the dear, old year that brought us Hope, is very near the end. I am not going to watch him go. I have drunk to the New Year and to my wife and daughter, and before there is "a new step on the floor, and a new face at the door," I will be asleep. Of all my many years, the old year, that is so soon to pass away, has been the *best*, for it has brought you to me with a closer tie, has added to the love I have for every breath you breathe, for your laugh and your smile, and deep concern, that comes if you think your worthless husband is worried, or cross, or dismayed. Each year I love you more; for I know you more, and to know more of the lovely soul you are, is to love more. Just now we are in a hard place. I am sure you cannot comprehend how her father, her "Dad" and your husband can keep away. Neither do I understand.

But, for both your sakes, I want, before I own up that this adventure has been a failure, to try and pull something out of the wreck. If the government says I *can*, then I still may be able to do something. If it says, "*no*," then it's *Home, boys, Home, and that's where I want to be. It's home, boys, home, in the old countree. 'Neath the ash, and the oak, and the spreading maple tree, it's home, boys, home, to mine own countree!* This is Hope and you. So know, that in getting to you I have not thrown away a minute. I have been a slave-driver, to others as well as to myself. But you cannot get favours with a whip; and, the French war office has other matters to occupy it, that it considers of more importance than an impatient war correspondent. So long as you understand, it will not matter. Nothing hurts, except that you may not understand. The moment I see you, and you see me, you will understand.

So, goodnight, and God bless you, you, my two blessings. Here is to our own year of 1915, your year and Hope's year, and, because I have you both, my year. I send you all the love in all the world.

    Richard.

January 5, 1916.

My Dearest One:

What Pictures! What Happiness! What a proud Richard! On top of my writing yesterday that I had had no sketches of yours, and no kodaks of Hope, eight came tonight, and oh! I am so proud, so homesick. What a wonderful nurse and mother you are! Was ever there anything so lovable? And that she should be ours, to hold and to love, and to make happy. These last eight days in Paris, in and out, have made me so homesick for those I love, that you will never know what the delays meant. I felt just the way poor women feel who kidnap babies. In the parks I know the nurse-maids are afraid of me. I stick my head under the hoods of the baby carriages, and stop and stand watching them at play. And tonight when all these beautiful pictures came, I was the happiest father anywhere.

The delay was no one's fault, not mine anyway, nor can I blame anyone. These people are splendid. They are willing to do anything for one, but it takes time. When they are fighting for their lives and have not seen their own babies in a year, that you want to see yours is only natural and to oblige you they can't see why they should upset the whole war. But now it looks less as though I would have to call it a failure. And Hope may be proud of me, and you may be proud of me, and I will have enough ammunition to draw on for many articles and letters, and another book.

It has been a cruel time; and when I tell you how I worked to get it over, and to be back with you, you will understand many things. The most important of all will be how I love you. Only wait until I can lay eyes on you, you will just take one look and know that it couldn't be helped, that the delay was the work of others, that, all I wanted was my Bessie and my Hope.

How heavy she will be, if she is anything like the picture of her on the coverlet, she is a prize baby. And if she is anything like as beautiful as in the baby carriage she is an angel straight from God. I want to sit in the green chair and have you on one knee and her majesty on the other, and have her climb over me, and pull my hair and bang my nose, and in time to know how I love you both.

Goodnight, dear heart, I wish you had had yourself in the picture. I have three in the summer time with you holding her and that is the way I like to see you, that is the way I think of you. I love you, and I love her for making you so happy, and I love her for her sake, and because she is *ours*: and has tied us tighter and closer even than it has ever been. I love you so that I can't write about it, and I am going to do nothing all spring but just sit around, and be in everybody's way, watching you together.

How jealous I am of you, and homesick for you. Of course, she knows "mamma" is *you*; and to look at you when they ask, "Where's mother?" Who else could be her mother *but the dearest woman in the world*, and the one who loves her so, and in so wonderful a way. She is beautiful beyond all things human I know. If ever a woman deserved a beautiful daughter, *you do,* for you are the best of mothers, and you know how "to care greatly."

Goodnight, my precious, dear one, and God keep you, as He will, and help me to keep you both happy. What you give me you never will know.

    Richard.

The Last Days

After a short visit to London, Richard returned to New York in February, 1916. During his absence his wife and Hope had occupied the Scribner cottage at Mount Kisco, about two miles from Crossroads.

        Mount Kisco—February 28, 1916.

Dear Old Man:

No word yet of the book, except the advts. I enclose. I will send you the notices as soon as they begin to appear. I am so happy over the dedication, and, very proud. So, Hope will be when she knows. As I have not read the novel it all will come as a splendid and pleasant surprise. I am looking forward to sitting down to it with all the pleasure in the world.

You chose the right moment to elope. Never was weather so cold, cruel and bitter. Hope is the only one who goes out of doors.

I start the fires in the Big House tomorrow and the plumbers and paper hangers, painters enter the day after.

The attack on Verdun makes me sick. I was there six weeks ago in one of the forts but of course could not then nor can I now write of it. I don't believe the drive ever can get through. For two reasons, and the unmilitary one is that I believe in a just God. Give my love to Dai, and for you always
     Dick.
P. S. I am happy you are both so happy, but those postcards with the palms were cruelty to animals.

On the 21st of March, 1916, Richard and his wife and daughter moved from the Scribner cottage to Crossroads, and a few days later he was attacked by the illness that ended in his death on April 11. He had dined with his wife and afterward had worked on an article on preparedness, written some letters and telegrams concerning the same subject and, while repeating one of the latter over the telephone, was stricken. Within a week of his fifty-third year, just one year from the day he had first brought his baby daughter to her real home, doing the best and finest work of his career in the cause of the Allies and preparedness, quite unconscious that the end was near, he left us.

MRS. R. H. DAVIS AND HOPE DAVIS

ALSO FROM LEONAUR
AVAILABLE IN SOFTCOVER OR HARDCOVER WITH DUST JACKET

IRON TIMES WITH THE GUARDS *by An O. E. (G. P. A. Fildes)*—The Experiences of an Officer of the Coldstream Guards on the Western Front During the First World War.

THE GREAT WAR IN THE MIDDLE EAST: 1 *by W. T. Massey*—The Desert Campaigns & How Jerusalem Was Won---two classic accounts in one volume.

THE GREAT WAR IN THE MIDDLE EAST: 2 *by W. T. Massey*—Allenby's Final Triumph.

SMITH-DORRIEN *by Horace Smith-Dorrien*—Isandlwhana to the Great War.

1914 *by Sir John French*—The Early Campaigns of the Great War by the British Commander.

GRENADIER *by E. R. M. Fryer*—The Recollections of an Officer of the Grenadier Guards throughout the Great War on the Western Front.

BATTLE, CAPTURE & ESCAPE *by George Pearson*—The Experiences of a Canadian Light Infantryman During the Great War.

DIGGERS AT WAR *by R. Hugh Knyvett & G. P. Cuttriss*—"Over There" With the Australians by R. Hugh Knyvett and Over the Top With the Third Australian Division by G. P. Cuttriss. Accounts of Australians During the Great War in the Middle East, at Gallipoli and on the Western Front.

HEAVY FIGHTING BEFORE US *by George Brenton Laurie*—The Letters of an Officer of the Royal Irish Rifles on the Western Front During the Great War.

THE CAMELIERS *by Oliver Hogue*—A Classic Account of the Australians of the Imperial Camel Corps During the First World War in the Middle East.

RED DUST *by Donald Black*—A Classic Account of Australian Light Horsemen in Palestine During the First World War.

THE LEAN, BROWN MEN *by Angus Buchanan*—Experiences in East Africa During the Great War with the 25th Royal Fusiliers—the Legion of Frontiersmen.

THE NIGERIAN REGIMENT IN EAST AFRICA *by W. D. Downes*—On Campaign During the Great War 1916-1918.

THE 'DIE-HARDS' IN SIBERIA *by John Ward*—With the Middlesex Regiment Against the Bolsheviks 1918-19.

AVAILABLE ONLINE AT **www.leonaur.com**
AND FROM ALL GOOD BOOK STORES

ALSO FROM LEONAUR
AVAILABLE IN SOFTCOVER OR HARDCOVER WITH DUST JACKET

FARAWAY CAMPAIGN by F. James—Experiences of an Indian Army Cavalry Officer in Persia & Russia During the Great War.

REVOLT IN THE DESERT by T. E. Lawrence—An account of the experiences of one remarkable British officer's war from his own perspective.

MACHINE-GUN SQUADRON by A. M. G.—The 20th Machine Gunners from British Yeomanry Regiments in the Middle East Campaign of the First World War.

A GUNNER'S CRUSADE by Antony Bluett—The Campaign in the Desert, Palestine & Syria as Experienced by the Honourable Artillery Company During the Great War.

DESPATCH RIDER by W. H. L. Watson—The Experiences of a British Army Motorcycle Despatch Rider During the Opening Battles of the Great War in Europe.

TIGERS ALONG THE TIGRIS by E. J. Thompson—The Leicestershire Regiment in Mesopotamia During the First World War.

HEARTS & DRAGONS by Charles R. M. F. Crutwell—The 4th Royal Berkshire Regiment in France and Italy During the Great War, 1914-1918.

INFANTRY BRIGADE: 1914 by John Ward—The Diary of a Commander of the 15th Infantry Brigade, 5th Division, British Army, During the Retreat from Mons.

DOING OUR 'BIT' by Ian Hay—Two Classic Accounts of the Men of Kitchener's 'New Army' During the Great War including *The First 100,000* & *All In It*.

AN EYE IN THE STORM by Arthur Ruhl—An American War Correspondent's Experiences of the First World War from the Western Front to Gallipoli-and Beyond.

STAND & FALL by Joe Cassells—With the Middlesex Regiment Against the Bolsheviks 1918-19.

RIFLEMAN MACGILL'S WAR by Patrick MacGill—A Soldier of the London Irish During the Great War in Europe including *The Amateur Army*, *The Red Horizon* & *The Great Push*.

WITH THE GUNS by C. A. Rose & Hugh Dalton—Two First Hand Accounts of British Gunners at War in Europe During World War 1- Three Years in France with the Guns and With the British Guns in Italy.

THE BUSH WAR DOCTOR by Robert V. Dolbey—The Experiences of a British Army Doctor During the East African Campaign of the First World War.

AVAILABLE ONLINE AT **www.leonaur.com**
AND FROM ALL GOOD BOOK STORES

ALSO FROM LEONAUR
AVAILABLE IN SOFTCOVER OR HARDCOVER WITH DUST JACKET

THE 9TH—THE KING'S (LIVERPOOL REGIMENT) IN THE GREAT WAR 1914 - 1918 *by Enos H. G. Roberts*—Mersey to mud—war and Liverpool men.

THE GAMBARDIER *by Mark Severn*—The experiences of a battery of Heavy artillery on the Western Front during the First World War.

FROM MESSINES TO THIRD YPRES *by Thomas Floyd*—A personal account of the First World War on the Western front by a 2/5th Lancashire Fusilier.

THE IRISH GUARDS IN THE GREAT WAR - VOLUME 1 *by Rudyard Kipling*—Edited and Compiled from Their Diaries and Papers—The First Battalion.

THE IRISH GUARDS IN THE GREAT WAR - VOLUME 1 *by Rudyard Kipling*—Edited and Compiled from Their Diaries and Papers—The Second Battalion.

ARMOURED CARS IN EDEN *by K. Roosevelt*—An American President's son serving in Rolls Royce armoured cars with the British in Mesopatamia & with the American Artillery in France during the First World War.

CHASSEUR OF 1914 *by Marcel Dupont*—Experiences of the twilight of the French Light Cavalry by a young officer during the early battles of the great war in Europe.

TROOP HORSE & TRENCH *by R.A. Lloyd*—The experiences of a British Lifeguardsman of the household cavalry fighting on the western front during the First World War 1914-18.

THE EAST AFRICAN MOUNTED RIFLES *by C.J. Wilson*—Experiences of the campaign in the East African bush during the First World War.

THE LONG PATROL *by George Berrie*—A Novel of Light Horsemen from Gallipoli to the Palestine campaign of the First World War.

THE FIGHTING CAMELIERS *by Frank Reid*—The exploits of the Imperial Camel Corps in the desert and Palestine campaigns of the First World War.

STEEL CHARIOTS IN THE DESERT *by S. C. Rolls*—The first world war experiences of a Rolls Royce armoured car driver with the Duke of Westminster in Libya and in Arabia with T.E. Lawrence.

WITH THE IMPERIAL CAMEL CORPS IN THE GREAT WAR *by Geoffrey Inchbald*—The story of a serving officer with the British 2nd battalion against the Senussi and during the Palestine campaign.

AVAILABLE ONLINE AT **www.leonaur.com**
AND FROM ALL GOOD BOOK STORES

www.ingramcontent.com/pod-product-compliance
Lightning Source LLC
Chambersburg PA
CBHW031617160426
43196CB00006B/170